Scandals and Party Moots

Polish Studies in Culture, Nations and Politics

Edited by Joanna Kurczewska and Yasuko Shibata

Vol. 2

PETER LANG

Frankfurt am Main · Berlin · Bern · Bruxelles · New York · Oxford · Warszawa · Wien

Adriana Mica

Scandals and Party Moots

Mass Protests during
the Ceauşescu Regime in Romania

PETER LANG
Internationaler Verlag der Wissenschaften

Bibliographic Information published by the Deutsche Nationalbibliothek
The Deutsche Nationalbibliothek lists this publication in the
Deutsche Nationalbibliografie; detailed bibliographic data is
available in the internet at http://dnb.d-nb.de.

Cover Design:
© Olaf Gloeckler, Atelier Platen, Friedberg

The publication was financially supported
by the University of Gdańsk.

ISSN 2192-1822
ISBN 978-3-631-62182-0

© Peter Lang GmbH
Internationaler Verlag der Wissenschaften
Frankfurt am Main 2012
All rights reserved.

www.peterlang.de

Contents

Acknowledgements

This study of scandals began as a PhD dissertation at the Graduate School for Social Research, Polish Academy of Sciences, under the supervision of my professor, the first expert in scandals I had the honour to meet, Jacek Kurczewski from the University of Warsaw. The intellectual context and fellowship offered by this institution encouraged and facilitated the defending of the thesis at the Institute of Applied Social Sciences, University of Warsaw in 2009.

Following this successful defense, I had some time to complete my reflections and prepare the final manuscript presented herein. At this stage, I profited from, and also tried to address the critical, yet highly valuable insights I was offered by my PhD reviewers: Wojciech Pawlik from the University of Warsaw, and Janine Wedel from George Mason University. The last step – the publication of the study per se – was undertaken with the support of the University of Gdańsk, where I am currently working.

The research and fieldwork of the book has greatly benefited from the openness, counselling and advice of the following institutions: the Romanian Institute for Recent History, the Romanian Institute for the Investigation of Communist Crimes and the Memory of the Romanian Exile, the Open Society Archives at Central European University, and the "November 15, 1987" Association – Braşov. I would like to recognize the empirical help and guidance in the field received from historian Nicolae Videnie and the president of the above-named association, Florin Postolachi.

Introduction

Leaders of any communist state have to keep a watchful eye on certain *scandal hot-spots*. As Kamiński (1992: 179) points out, such events exert pressure on the state, causing it to respond and reform. Scandals may erupt as a result of social, economic or political demands voiced through rebellious manifestations of society, political activism of the diaspora or in programs on foreign radio stations. Considering that during the communist era in Romania – for several reasons – collective confrontation with the regime was a rare phenomenon, such outbursts were perceived as real scandals. This statement pertains to society at large, to the diaspora and, eventually, to the "broader outside world".

An analysis of mass protests from this *scandal perspective* might be useful for several reasons. It assumes an exploration of the strategies employed not only by strikers or protesters, but also those embraced by the institutions under attack. The case studies contained herein show that in the aftermath of such events, the communist state employed a tactic of large-scale scapegoating in order "to face its face". The book further analyses the anatomy of the process, the internal resistance it faced, and the circulating counts of indictment. The matter is all the more interesting, as there is empirical data indicating that the process of scapegoating folded upon the hierarchical layers within the party nomenklatura as well.

According to Rychard (1993: 12), in Poland, "spontaneous changes" were more common than "planned reforms". The author identifies two types of spontaneous changes: "violent changes characteristic of social riots and revolts", and "'everyday' changes accompanying various adaptation processes by way of which people try to modify the centralized system" (Rychard, 1993: 12). Adopting Rychard's terminology, the Ceaușescu regime might be described as a period when we were dealing more with planned reforms and various adaptation processes, than with spontaneous changes via "social riots and reforms". It is worth noting that until late 1970s, the scandalousness of Ceaușescu's actions in the international arena contributed to the visibility of the reforms (from above) that were implemented in Romania. I am referring here to the instances when the norm offender is represented by the Romanian powers-that-be, while the Soviet leaders could be regarded as being the norm audience.

Scandals over the first type of spontaneous changes in Romania constitute the focus of this book. In my interpretation, the late-communist and present perceptions of the extremely repressive character of Ceaușescu's rule in the 1970s and 1980s are linked to the high level of scandalization provoked by the dynamics of strikes and revolts as well as by the low number of these. Contributing to this narrative is also the so-called "dramatic climax" (see Kurczewski,

2009b) of the 1989 revolution – i.e. the execution of Ceauşescu. After 1989, what also worked in favor of this interpretation was the lack of comparative studies between Romania and other former socialist countries.

This discoursive consciousness regarding the high level of repression during the Ceauşescu regime and the "normality" of a low number of mass protests contesting his rule should be further analyzed in the context of its reception of the development of mass movements in other former socialist countries. As such, by comparison, the evolution of the *Solidarity* trade union movement in Poland is framed as – by all means – spectacular, yet also an evolution pertaining to a certain level of "normality" and linked to this country's history of social protest.

Therefore, what we are witnessing is that, within the mainstream Romanian historical discourse, the absence or occurrence of political protest (i.e. of "spontaneous changes") is retrospectively used to account for the respective repressive or less repressive character of the communist regime in question. Thus, the vicious circle goes as follows: the low number of protests contributed to the intensity of scandals over mass protests, and the scandalousness of these acts further contributed to the depiction of the regime as highly repressive. Whereas, the mode in which social change during communism occurred via "planned reforms" has not been researched, or the modality in which the scandalousnesness of several moves of the regime on the international political arena has contributed to the visibility and legitimacy of these moves.

The next element which stands out with respect to the scandals over mass protests during the Ceauşescu regime is the complete ritualization of their dynamics. At first sight, the scandal rituals in late communism appear even to be more integrated than those emerging in post-communism – see, for example, the evolution of disclosure scandals in Mica (2008b; 2009b), and the discussion about the context and impact of these scandals on the reinforcing of the significance of certain values in society in Kurczewski's (1995) work. In this latter case, the frustration of rituals of admittance and attribution of fault also bear upon the (perceived) role of scandal in society. Scandal rituals in Ceauşescu's era, as will be shown, unfold according to Turner's (1975) model of *social drama* and Braithwaite's (1992) theory of *reintegrative shaming* – thus manifesting a great dramaturgical potential. This element leads us to rituals of acknowledgement of guilt and self-criticism.

The importance of public apology in recent Romanian history stems from the fact that self-criticism has been widely employed in the communist context as "late" as the 1980s. The presence of self-criticism might be taken as the anthropological core of the mechanisms of communist regime self-preservation. When it comes to the early post-communist period, the phenomena of public apology are moderated at best, while we witness a proliferation of discourses of public criticism and distribution of guilt/fault. Regarding the late communist period, we notice that what Garfinkel (1956) has termed as *status degradation ceremonies* have become institutionalized. These degradation ceremonies were meetings of degradation and stigmatization, which quite often also included a component of public apology by the offender.

The investigation of these meetings with the tools of legal anthropology and ethnomethodology indicate that they have evolved in the genre of *moots* (see the parallel with Gibbs' (1963) hearings in the *Kpelle moots*, for example), and – as stated – they have employed processes that recall Braithwaite's reintegrative shaming. Thus, they were composed of rituals of *distribution of fault* and rituals of *admittance of guilt/fault* respectively. Such moots have been employed in several scenarios – ranging from illegal immigration to participation in mass protests; as well as at different levels – from the factory level to that of the party. They have played an *investigative* and *reconciliatory* role alike.

To a certain degree it can be claimed that the prevalent discourse in the field of Romanian transitional justice delays the treatment of these public appologies and acts of admittance of guilt/fault as real sociological phenomena. They are either poked fun at or (at best) reported in a way that points to their contrafactual character. The sociological analysis is rendered superfluous by the assumption that they had been staged.

At this point in the discussion, I would risk the hypothesis that, as in the case of the low number of mass protests, the proliferation of such rituals of public apology during the Ceauşescu era is considered "normal", and for this reason their analysis is impeded from emerging. Thus, I had decided to investigate the shaming practices in the dynamics of the *party moots on mass protests* which followed the outburst of such like scandals, and to leave other elements in the dynamics of communist scandals aside.

Besides investigating the ritualization of party moots on mass protests, the book is concerned with two phenomena connected to scandals during the Ceauşescu regime: *convergence* and *contamination*. The former is a notion borrowed from literature on moral panic (Hall and Jefferson, 1991; Hall et al., 1994), whereas the latter follows the work of Adut (2005; 2008) on scandals. The purpose of the book is twofold. Firstly it seeks to document the emergence of these phenomena in connection with the so-called *scandals over mass protests*. Secondly, it poses an inquiry into the types of mechanisms backing contamination and convergence. An analysis of published accounts on the cases in question, and proceedings of party meetings held subsequent to scandals over mass protests, leads to the formulation of the following hypothesis: the dynamics of convergence and contamination are dependent on the outcome of three interrelated phenomena: *attribution of fault, admittance of one's guilt/fault* and *moot bullying.*

I analyze four case studies: the Jiu Valley strike (1977), the Braşov revolt (1987), the Timişoara events (15-21 December 1989), and the miners' march on Bucharest (June, 1990). As stated, I am primarily interested in the dynamic of the *moots* [luări in discuţie] – a deliberative assembly for the administration of justice or for the informal settlement of disputes – held after scandals resulting from mass protests. The topic is covered in part IV – *The Ritualization of Party Moots during the Ceauşescu Regime* (Jiu Valley 1977 and Braşov 1987) and partly in part V – *Scripts of Other Cases of Convergence in Reply to Scandals over Mass Protests* (Timişoara 1989 and Bucharest 1990).

Case study 1: The Strike – Jiu Valley: In early August 1977, about 35,000 miners from Jiu Valley went on strike after the promulgation of a law reducing the retirement age. The delegates sent to the Valley were taken hostage by the miners who called for Ceauşescu to come in person. The first secretary arrived on the third day of the strike.

Case study 2: The Revolt – Braşov: On 15 November 1987, in Braşov, local elections for the Popular Councils were supposed to take place. Workers from the *Steagul Roşu* [the Red Flag] truck factory used this opportunity to manifest their discontent over pay cuts and food shortages. A riot erupted in the city center, resulting in the party headquarters and the town hall being devastated.

Case study 3: The Beginning of the Revolution – Timişoara: On 15 December 1989, in Timişoara, the protest of parishioners against the eviction of the Hungarian Reformed pastor, Tőkés László, evolved into an anti-communist demonstration which soon engaged the whole city. Eventually, on 21 December 1989 the anti-communist Romanian Revolution began in Bucharest as well.

Case study 4: The June Miners' March – Bucharest: All three marches of the miners in 1990 (*mineriads* [mineriade])[1] were preceded by large, public manifestations of protest against the neo-communist character of the provisional government (the Front) and President Ion Iliescu. By far, the most controversial of the mineriads took place in June. Miners from Jiu Valley arrived in Bucharest in order to put an end to a demonstration, which had been going on for 52 days on the University Square. Besides the headquarters of the parties, miners attacked the university, the Institute of Architecture and the offices of certain anti-government newspapers and NGOs.

Two of the most notorious mass protests during the Ceauşescu regime – the 1977 Jiu Valley strike and the 1987 Braşov revolt – can be regarded as having

---

1   Four relatively violent instances of civil unrest took place in the early years of post-communist Romania. They are often referred to as mineriads.

been *governed by scandal*. They are analyzed in the second, third and fourth chapters of this book. I also try to present the dynamics of convergence and contamination by analyzing the proceedings of the party moots, which were held after the outburst and appeasement of the mass protests.

The 1989 and 1990 episodes are brought about only in the last chapter. They concern the Timişoara events of 15-21 December 1989 and the June 1990 miners' march on Bucharest – i.e. the so-called *third mineriad* [a treia mineriadă]. As far as the former is concerned, unlike in Jiu Valley 1977 and Braşov 1987, the Timişoara party moots on mass protests took place during – not after – the events in the city. Another element of disparity is also the fact that the 17 December moots involved the highest echelons of power in the Communist Party at that time. The case of the miners' march on Bucharest (June 1990) is relevant solely for the discussion of the phenomenon of convergence. This is an event which took place in early post-communist Romania. Still, I believe that it strengthens the conclusions of my previous analysis.

In examining the events of Jiu Valley in 1977, I used collections of published interviews and documents (documents drafted by the Ministry of Internal Affairs – County Inspectorate Hunedoara), as well as the interviews I conducted during my fieldwork in 2005 and 2006. For the Braşov events in 1987, I rely mainly on the interviews I conducted in 2006 and the proceedings of party meetings in Braşov. With regard to the case of Timişoara in 1989, I work with stenographic transcripts of the meeting of the Political Executive Committee of the Central Committee of the Romanian Communist Party – December 17, 1989; the teleconference of Ceauşescu with two communist officials in Timişoara – December 17, 1989 and with Ceauşescu's address to the nation – December 20, 1989. Finally, in the case of the June 1990 miners' march, I analyze the conclusions of the *Parliamentary Committee of Enquiry into the events that took place from 13-15 June 1990* (Romanian Parliament, 1991) and President Iliescu's book, *Revoluţie şi reformă* [Revolution and Reform] (1994).

There are three issues which the present book seeks to address:

1. The introduction of a so-called *scandal-perspective* on several events which occurred during the Ceauşescu regime in Romania. As the study aims to document, in scandals which benefited the Romanian communist regime – both internally and internationally – it usually played the role of the *norm offender*; the role of *norm audience* was given to the Soviet Union. *The reaction of Ceauşescu to the Warsaw Pact invasion of Czechoslovakia in 1968, the sports scandal in Prague, 1977* and *the sports scandal in Los Angeles, 1984* are cases in point. The typology of scandals detrimental to the regime is varied. Thus, besides the so-called *sports scandals*, one can also

list: *scandals over mass protests, diplomatic scandals, scandals over defection of intelligence officials,* etc.

2. An analysis of the mechanisms of appeasing the scandals over mass protests. One of these mechanisms, for example, is framing them in terms of scandals over "acts of hooliganism". This strategy – to borrow from literature on moral panic – might be termed as *convergence.*

3'. An analysis of the mechanisms governing the dynamics of convergence in the unfolding of scandals over mass protests. I seek to evidence that convergence took place concurrently with a phenomenon which, in the literature on scandals, is designated as *contamination.* As will be documented in the first chapter, contamination is an externality of scandal. More explicitly, the scandal determined the sequences of investigation and – eventually – the castigation of party leaders and activists. Thus, the first-order transgression – that being of the protesters – also exposed serious deficiencies within the local party circles, which further resulted in a campaign of castigation.

3". The book puts forth a hypothesis, that – at least at the level of local party members and functionaries – the dynamics of convergence and contamination are determined by the unfolding and outcome of three phenomena: the attribution of fault, the admittance of guilt/fault and – to a certain extent – the *moot bullying* (a term which I introduce). Each of these three mechanisms worked together in order to guarantee that the dramaturgical nature of scandal will not be disturbed – i.e. that the rituals of reintegrative shaming (in this case) of the offenders will come full circle.

The book has five chapters. The bulk of the theoretical considerations are concentrated in the first chapter, which discusses scandals, general elements of moral panic, the general process of ritualization of scandal and related reintegrative shaming practices. Additionally, the fourth chapter provides compact theoretical sections discussing notions such as moots, the Kpelle moots, and bullying and/or mobbing. The second, third and fourth chapters are mainly empirical. The former two present the case studies of the Jiu Valley strike and the Braşov revolt for review and discuss them in terms of scandal and the ritualization of party moots that were held subsequent to the outburst of these events. The fifth chapter continues this analysis and additionally addresses cases of ideological convergence with the "hooliganism" which took place in 1989 and in 1990.

The theoretical section of the book reviews theories of scandal and employs a definition of the term as put forward by Adut (2004; 2005). It speaks in terms of publicizing a norm transgression to a norm audience. Further, notions such as: *norm audience* (Adut, 2005), *kibitzer audience* (see Gladys Engel Lang and Kurt

Lang in Thompson, 2008), *externalities (contamination, provocation)* (Adut, 2005) and the formula, *"scandal as a factor of evolution"* (Nałkowski, 1952: 19-25; Kurczewski, 2003: 163-164) are introduced. The theoretical fragment further analyses the notion of *moral panic* as well as several closely connected terms: deviance exploitation, signification spirals, types of convergence between the object of moral panic and other social problems (real convergence, some convergence and no convergence). Moral panic has been introduced in the discussion in order to make more obvious the particularity of scandal as a process of norm entrepreneurship, and to conceptually highlight mechanisms typical of moral panic, yet which are highly probable to surface during the development of scandal in a communist setting. Next, following Turner (1975), Sims (2009) and Kurczewski (2003), I focus on scandal as social drama and try to develop a theoretical framework that would account for shaming practices occurring during the fourth phase of the social drama – *reintegration*. This leads me to the notion of reintegrative shaming practices which have been also, coincidentally, developed in the field of restorative justice in relation to Braithwaite's (1992) theoretical framework. After a brief introduction into this field and critical approaches to Braithwaite's program, I bring the reintegrative shaming practices back on the agenda of scandal, and concentrate on those aspects which are relevant with respect to scandal theory.

Regarding the more specific question of scandals in Romanian communism, the book promotes two refinements The first concerns the applicability of the term when studying certain events which occurred during the communist regime, the second elaborates upon and exemplifies a typology of Romanian communist scandals, in which communist authorities play the role of a norm audience, kibitzer audience and norm offender in the cases of *first-order* and *second-order transgressions*, respectively.

My research is primarily concerned with the representative character of the mechanism of convergence, contamination, provocation and scandal as a factor of evolution in the case studies under review. My interest in drawing a picture of the scandal dynamics during the communist regime is only minor. The specific case studies are illustrative for the interplay of the mechanisms of scandal. What could be stated is that, indeed, scandals over mass protests have been a precarious occurrence, and it is to the understanding of this occurrence, that this book is intended to contribute.

Regarding the would-be statistics of scandals during the communist regime in Romania, I am afraid that the intentions of the present study did not envisage drawing a thorough sketch of these. On the basis of the case studies under review, I would advance the hypothesis that the presence of sports scandals and scandals over the defection of intelligence officials constitute a prominent characteristic of this profile. There is indeed a need to elaborate a typology of incipient affairs and scandals which were either less publicized, or have even been forgotten in the present times. I also identified the necessity of an inventory of state campaigns and mock-trials that the communist state tried to present as real scandals at the time. As stated in the book however, the collection of such statistics is conditioned by access to resources, such as the communist and former state security archives, which unfortunately is restricted for public use. My conviction is however, that the advancement of a so-called scandal perspective preserves the researcher from employing an over-ideologized or politically biased perspective when analyzing the phenomena which occurred during the communist regime. In this sense, a similar approach might facilitate a less evasive feedback from former members of the Communist Party and officers of the communist State Security. On a side note, the survey of memoirs and accounts written by former officers of State Security indicate that these favor a discourse drafted in terms of scandal and that they are inclined towards revealing such scandalous events.

I have conducted seven interviews for my Jiu Valley case study. I.V. acted as defendant in the trials of the miners. P.P. was the attorney for the miners during the exoneration process of those sentenced in 1977. One interviewee – V.A. – at the time of the strike was the chief engineer of the Aninoasa mine. I.D. is a former journalist of the local newspaper in Petroşani who was charged with writing speeches for two miners for Ceauşescu's arrival in Jiu Valley in 1977. His testimony is relevant for offering detailed insights into the preparations of the party activists and journalists for the visit of Ceauşescu. The moment is significant considering that the newspaper, *Scânteia,* camouflaged the direct negotiations with the miners which were forced upon Ceauşescu as a voluntary "work visit" of the President. G.C., V.B. and I.A. are local historians and journalists, and they had not been involved in the strike. The first two interviewers provided excellent information about the process of scapegoating that followed the miners' strike. I.A.'s contribution is of special importance, in that he discusses extensively the moments of military deployment in the Jiu Valley's coal mine between 1977 and 1989.

For the case study of Braşov, the interviewees selected were participants in the strike. On the basis of these testimonies, I have reconstructed and further analysed the consequences of participating in the events for the protesters. The interviews were unstructured and were conducted in order to supplement the information about the interviewees existent in the already published materials I used. All the interviews were recorded and later transcribed.

In both cases, Jiu Valley 1977 and Braşov 1987, I should underline that my empirical research supplements the collection of documents and interviews that are already published. For example, in case of Jiu Valley 1997, the collections of interviews and documents edited by Barbu and Chirvasă (1997), Barbu and Boboc (2005), and Boboc and Barbu (2007) contain the testimonies of several protesters and party members (both at the local and national level). Furthermore, they also reproduce excerpts from the reports found in the archives of the former communist State Security Department and the miners' criminal sentences.

In the case of the 1987 revolt I analyze the dynamics of attribution of fault and the phenomenon of admittance of guilt/fault during party meetings that were held at the level of the *Steagul Roşu* factory. After introducing the hearings in the Kpelle moots (Gibbs, 1963), I argue that the 1987 party meetings – although of an obviously different kind – could be also regarded as moots. Hence, I designate the plenaries as *party moots on mass protests* and I scrutinize the development of a specific kind of bullying during these party meetings, i.e. the so-called *moot bullying*. Eventually, I present evidence indicating that in the aftermath of the 1977 Jiu Valley miners' strike, moots also took place regarding the miners about to be tried for acts of disorder during and shortly after the strike. What is striking in the case of the 1987 Braşov revolt is that these party moots are concordant with a reintegrative shaming logic (as far as both the party members and the protesters are concerned), while in the case of the Jiu Valley strike the dimension of stigmatizing shaming (regarding at least the protestors) is more predominant.

The main research technique applied is content analysis of stenographic transcripts and reports. The aim was to reveal the dynamics of moots held afterwards or concomitant with scandals over mass protests and the employment of the mechanisms of convergence in the immediate post-communist period. The focus on the externality of contamination revealed that in cases of mass protests, the Romanian communist authorities displayed a tendency to misrepresent or transmute the transgression into another type of transgression. However, the scandal as such remains – though its subject changes, it is usually convergent with the original one. Furthermore, the scandal determined the sequences of investigation and – eventually – the castigation of party leaders and activists. In other words, the first-order transgression – that of the protesters – also exposed serious deficiencies within local party circles which further resulted in a campaign of castigation. The analysis also shows that establishing the responsible group for the events dictates the dynamics of the second-order transgression (i.e. the castigation of party leaders and activists). Equally important, the logic of the allocation of responsibility is supposedly holed up in a normative code that indicates the distribution of responsibility among the collective and the activists, which, if followed, should prevent the outburst and development of such scandalous events. The analysis of the investigations allowed an indirect reading of the violation of these norms, as they are deduced from the types of responsibility which have been allocated to different collective and individual actors in the aftermath of the events. Hence, the advancement of contamination is directly linked to a normative structure. The question however, arises as to what extent this is a case of an initial normative structure governing the allocation of responsibility, or one of a normative structure brought about by the allocation of responsibility.

In the final part of the book, I introduce two new case studies: the Timişoara events of 1989 and the June 1990 miners' march on Bucharest. From the historical point of view, the two events are separated by the Romanian 1989 anti-communist revolution. The subchapter on the Timişoara events is concerned with two phenomena. The first analyzes mechanisms of persuasion, attribution of fault and admittance of one's guilt/fault which took place during the December 17, 1989 meeting of the Political Executive Committee that discussed the lack of resolution of the police, army and state security units regarding the protesters in Timişoara. Thereafter, it documents how Ceauşescu initially planned convergence between hooliganism and a coup d'état of foreign powers. This framing was shortly (within hours) replaced with an ideological convergence between hooliganism and an anti-socialist coup d'état of foreign powers. Eventually, on December 20, 1989 Romanian TV delivered a story of ideological convergence between hooliganism – fascism – terrorism and anti-national coup d'état of foreign powers. The subchapter on the June 1990 miners' march on Bucharest begins with a review of the main theoretical accounts of the 1990, 1991 and 1999 miners' marches. The empirical analysis focuses on the tactics of ideological convergences in relation with the June 14-15, 1990 episode.

PART I
SCANDAL[*]

The following chapter is in line with and builds upon Adut's (2005; 2008) definition of scandal in terms of "the disruptive publicity of transgression". The discussion is constructed in such a way as to both advance a perspective of scandal and to accomplish a theoretical review of the existing literature in the field. Thereafter, I bring in another process of norm entrepreneurship and social control: the moral panic. The comparative dimension notwithstanding, the input of this section pertains to conceptually clarifying and locating the mechanisms of moral panic, which – as will be shown by the empirical material – are sometimes borrowed and incorporated into the logic of scandal. The third and fourth parts of the chapter consider the general phenomenon of the ritualization of scandal, and the particular aspect of shaming practices. Regarding this latter topic, I focus on that type of shaming which might be termed reintegrative. I choose to theoretically elaborate upon this type for the reason that the discussion anticipates the analysis of rituals of attribution of fault and admittance of guilt/fault put forward when presenting the empirical material pertaining to the scandals over mass protests during the Ceauşescu regime – see part III – *The Reply to Scandals over Mass Protests during the Ceauşescu Regime*, and part IV – *The Ritualization of Party Moots during the Ceauşescu Regime*.

1. Mechanisms of Scandal

"Scandal is a polysemic word" (Adut, 2005: 217). To give just a glimpse of the range of possible definitions I refer to the Explicative Dictionary of the Romanian Language (***), which provides two main meanings of the word – one in terms of *cause* and one in terms of *effect*. Moreover, in Romanian a notion exists of "making/producing scandal", in the sense that somebody "raises hell's delight". The three dictionary definitions are:
1. making/producing scandal;
2. scandal (collective uproar) as an effect;
3. scandal (political, financial etc. misconduct) as a cause.

Furthermore, the notion *to scandalize* designates the act of being indignant with somebody or something, but also – offending the moral sense of one person (Explicative Dictionary of the Romanian Language, ***; Merriam-Webster Online, ***).

Then again, following Girard (1988: 132-133), all the above could be rendered under the heading "modern sense" of scandal and scandalize – a

---

*   For an earlier version of this section's treatment see Mica (2011b).

sense which "only recaptures a glimmer of the evangelical meaning". In the latter – evangelical – connotation, based on the principle of the *mimeticism* of human relationships, scandal is the model/obstacle of desires for one another. More explicitly, scandal (*skandalon* being "mimetic stumbling-block"[2]) is triggered by mimetic desire and generates mimetic rivalry. Thereupon, the notion *to be scandalized* signifies being subjected to this mimetic desire and – inevitably – mimetic rivalry[3]. Furthermore, *to scandalize somebody* could also mean to be an obstacle in somebody's path (Girard, 1988: 157)[4]. In this understanding of the term, "theory of scandal" ("the theory of *skandalon*") stands for "theory of mimetic desire" (Girard, 1988: 159). This approach is distinct from theories of scandal that serve as guidelines for the theoretical apparatus of the book.

The approach to the mass protests developed within the limits of this sub-chapter brings us to Sherman's, *Scandal and Reform. Controlling Police Corruption* (1978), which talks about corrupt police departments. In the present study, the communist regime is analogous with a corrupt police department only in the sense that both are labelled as deviant organizations, and that in both cases scandal occurs against the background of this deviation. In a communist state, strikes challenge the regime's discourse – about itself and its relationship with society.

---

2   "Derived from *skadzein*, which means to limp, *skandalon* designates the obstacle that both attracts and repels at the same time" (Girard, 1988: 132).

3   "Desire clearly understands that, in desiring what another desires, it makes a rival and an obstacle of this model. It would be wise to give up, but if desire were wise it would not be desire. Finding only obstacles in its path, it incorporates them in its vision of the desirable and brings them into the foreground; it can no longer desire without them and cultivates them avidly. Thus it becomes full of hatred for the obstacle, and allows itself to be scandalized [...]. By becoming a part of the vicious circle of scandal, men forge the destiny they deserve. Desire is a noose that each one ties around his own neck; it is tightened at each tug of the scandalized" (Girard, 1988: 133).

4   "The faith of the disciples is clothed in triumphant messianism. It is nonetheless real for all this. Peter has shown us this, but a part of him is still weighing the adventure he is about to experience in terms of worldly success. What is the sense of a commitment that only ends in failure, suffering, or death? On this occasion Peter is severely reprimanded: 'Get behind me, Satan! You are an obstacle in my path'; [*you scandalize me*] (Matt. 16: 23). When it is proved to Peter that he is wrong, he immediately changes direction and begins to run in the opposite direction at the same speed as before. At the second announcement of the Passion, only a few hours before the arrest, Peter does not react in the least as he did the first time. '*You will all lose faith in me this night*' [*be scandalized*]" (Girard, 1988: 157).

I find the work of Sherman to be important, because it points to bases and possible perspectives on the strategies of reform employed by a nest of corruption subsequent to an outburst of scandal. The book defines scandal as a form of social control and analyzes the vigor of the effects of little scandals, big scandals and scandal events in revealing the corrupt character of an organization and restoring it to the right track.

Accordingly, at the outburst of a scandal, the bulk of strategies employed by the deviant organization is aimed at showing that the deviance uncovered by the scandal is an *unfortunate* fact, which – while true – can be assigned only to *some* of its members and is not characteristic of the entire organization. In other words, the instinct of self-preservation commands the organization to elude its overall deviant characteristic by blaming it on the individual deviances of its members. Thus – if these strategies are successful – the individual deviation saves the organizational one.

In Adut's (2005) review of scandal theories, Sherman's is included in the cluster of "constructivist" perspectives, which stress the social construction of reactions to transgressions. The other group is comprised of "objectivist" theories, which treat scandal as "the epiphenomena of real transgressions" and assume – to a certain extent – the moralizing tone of victims or denouncers of deviance (Adut, 2005: 216; Adut, 2008: 8-11). Wedel's *Shadow Elite. How the World's New Power Brokers Undermine Democracy, Government, and the Free Market* (2009) might be termed as such an objectivist approach to scandal. The author points to the so-called "flexians'" resistance to shaming and public expression of disapproval. Accordingly, the re-emergence of actors in key positions of power points to occurrences of scandal with no sanctions.

In his study, *A Theory of Scandal: Victorians, Homosexuality, and the Fall of Oscar Wilde*, Adut (2005) advances a definition of scandal in terms of "the disruptive publicity of transgression". Such a concept is indented to better serve the purposes of an analysis of the dynamics of scandal and reactions to transgression. Furthermore, notions such as: *offender/transgressor, norm audience, externalities (contamination, provocation)* are also introduced in the analysis (see Adut, 2004; Adut, 2005). In his follow-up book, *On Scandal: Moral Disturbances in Society, Politics, and Art*, Adut (2008) reformulates (to a certain extent) the theoretical apparatus. Scandal is discussed in relation to: the *transgression*, the *publicizer*, the *public* and the above mentioned *externalities*.

In the following section, I will synthesize the hitherto contribution of this author. Furthermore, I will extend the theoretical apparatus as to include the notion *kibitzer audience* and the formula *"scandal as a factor of evolution"* (see Nałkowski, 1952; Kurczewski, 2003). The transgression, the publicizer and the public are "the three basic elements of scandal" (Adut, 2008: 12). The externalities (contamination and provocation) and scandal as a factor of evolution are the effects (both short term and systemic).

Special attention has to be given to the specific formula of the disruptive publicity of transgression, as it is different from the fact that a transgression was known to have existed (Adut, 2005: 215-216). More explicitly, simply *knowing* about a transgression does not necessarily provoke the norm audience to react; it is the *publicity* that applies the pressure. Furthermore, publicization (as Adut phrases it) of a transgression – because of its never fully predictable externalities – might prove more costly for members of the norm audience than *camouflaging* it. The fact that there is a need for the publicity of a transgression in order to instigate a reaction to the occurrence of transgression was also pointed out by Malinowski (1989). His fieldwork in the Trobriand Islands revealed that "'group-reaction' and the 'supernatural sanction'" are not "active principles" in the dynamic of scandal (Malinowski, 1989: 80). The first revelation concerning this matter came to Malinowski when he witnessed a burial of a young man "of sixteen or so". The young man fell from a coco-nut palm and killed himself. However, it soon came to Malinowski's knowledge that the boy committed suicide after being apostrophized in public by the lover of the cousin he was having a romantic involvement with. Yet, the tribe – although well aware that the couple's relationship broke the rules of exogamy – did not penalize the transgression, as nobody "blew the whistle".

> If the affair is carried on *sub rosa* with a certain amount of decorum, and if no one in particular stirs up problem – "public opinion" will gossip, but not demand any harsh punishment. If, on the contrary, scandal breaks out – everyone turns against the guilty pair and by ostracism and insults one or the other may be driven to suicide (Malinowski, 1989: 80).

The other noteworthy aspect is the double signification of the suicide. On the one hand, it authenticates the accusations; on the other, it reduces to a lower standing the person(s) who induced shame in the norm offender and who drove him to desperation. To a large extent, this might be termed as a phenomenon of the "control of shame" (Elster, 1999: 157)[5].

---

5   "Under normal conditions, hypocrisy is part of what makes the world go around, not so much by forcing us to express emotions we don't have as by keeping us from expressing those we have. In everyday life under non-patological conditions, veils are more important than masks. There are even norms regulating the emotions that are appropriate to express as sanctions for norms violation. Although society would be a horrible place if norms of politeness and minimal helpfulness were not respected and enforced, it would not be much better if norm violators were consistently terrorized. These meta-norms are also sustained by emotions. The target of moralizing [...] may feel anger rather than shame. Third parties may express disapproval of moralizers who express their

> Two motives must be registered in the psychology of suicide: first, there is always some sin, crime or passionate outburst to expiate, whether a breach of exogamous rules, or adultery, or an unjust injury done, or an attempt to escape one's obligations; secondly, there is a protest against those who have brought this trespass to light, insulted the culprit in public, forced him into an unbearable situation (Malinowski, 1989: 97).

Furthermore, although not a mechanism of administering justice, suicide "affords the accused and oppressed one [...] a means of escape and rehabilitation" (Malinowski, 1989). Therefore, the rituals of shaming offer closing to all parties involved.

Following Thompson, one should distinguish between *first-* and *second-order transgressions*. This inspired Ekström and Johansson (2006: 4-17) to introduce the concept of *first-* and *second-order talk scandals*[6]. Briefly stated, second-order transgression implies the following: the scandal arises from one norm transgression, but during its development, another transgression takes place. In the case of the *talk scandals*, these second-order transgressions refer to some scandalous statements that were made in the media subsequent to the outburst of the first-order transgression, statements which affected some scandalous dimensions in their own right (Ekström and Johansson, 2006: 15). This might refer not only to a person's behavior during a scandal, but also to a revelation of other potentially scandalous items. Further, Thompson, Ekström and Johansson claim it to often be the case that these second-order transgressions cause more reputational harm than the intrigue of the original scandal (see also Thompson, 2010).

The *publicizer* is the one publicizing the transgression. This might be the author of the transgression (in cases when the transgression is committed or recognized in public). Or, it might be the one publicizing the real, apparent or alleged transgression of someone else. It is noteworthy that it is not the novelty or probity of the information that determines the outburst and impact of the scandal, but the presence of negative and sustained interest (Adut, 2008: 14-15).

The *public* "is a collectivity that has reasons to be interested in the event" (Adut, 2008: 16). Adut has initially discussed the public as *norm audience*. Although the 2008 formulation also gravitates around this framing, I believe that

---

disapproval too strongly. In Tahiti, there is both control by shame (*ha'ama*) and control of shame [...]" (Elster, 1999: 157).

6   Accordingly, the definition of "talk scandals" goes as follows: "they represent a new step in the mediatization of scandals because they are not only communicated and dramatized in the media, but also in most cases originate in the media. There are not necessarily original actions outside the media; the disclosure of backstage actions outside the media is no longer a general characteristic of political scandals" [*sic*] (Ekström and Johansson, 2006: 2, 3).

the usage of the word *public* allows for a more comprehensive approach, and that it gathers several types of audiences, of which the norm audience is just one. From the array of possible alternatives, I will explore the notions of *norm audience* and *kibitzer audience*. These concepts are also those that will help classify the scandals during communism in Romania – see section II.1 – *The Dynamics of Scandal during the Ceauşescu Regime*.

The term *norm audience* is adopted from Robert Ellickson's work on the evolution of social norms. Hence, the willingness of the norm audience to overtly react to specific normative infractions is an essential part in the development of scandal:

> scandal, as a social occurrence, assumes the publicization of an apparent transgression to a "norm audience", to use Ellickson's term [...] The norm audience is a public united by some level of identification with the norm that has apparently been violated, and it is in some capacity attentive and negatively responsive to the publicized transgression (Adut, 2005: 217-218).

In terms of its effects, scandal is regarded as a technique of norm entrepreneurship and status enhancement (Adut, 2004)[7]. Furthermore, society could be regarded as being comprised of several norm audiences, for all of which engagement in scandal is more or less contagious. An illustrative discussion was given by Waisbord (2004) who analyzed the relationship between scandals, media and citizenship in Argentina. The author argues that specific weapon-related scandals and the broader category of "gate scandals" seem to appeal rather to political circles and news-rooms[8], while, the violation of civil rights and official responsibility and duplicity in the murders of ordinary citizens

---

7   Adut (2004: 571-572) broadens the meaning of *norm entrepreneurship* as to cover not only the advancement of new norms but also the solidification of the under-enforced ones.

8   The author makes a distinction between the category of scandals which involve official crimes and governmental corruption – the so called *gates* – on the one hand, and scandals which involve ordinary citizens and deal with human rights violations on the other (Waisbord, 2004).
     "This taxonomy suggests several characteristics of Argentine scandals. The first category includes the typical scandals involving official crimes and misdemeanours – scandals that carry the suffix *gate*, such as Swiftgate, Yomagate, Milkgate, PAMIgate, and so on. Human rights scandals, instead, have not been dubbed gates. There was no 'Catamarcagate', 'Carrascogate', 'Cabezasgate', or 'AMIAgate', although officials were implicated in wrongdoing (murder, cover-up, mishandling of investigations) in all these scandals. *Gate* seems to be used to denominate only those scandals that fit the Watergate mold, that is, *purely affaires d'etat* that involve government corruption and deceit but neither involve ordinary citizens nor deal with human rights violations" (Waisbord, 2004: 1075).

attract the participation and very active engagement of the public (Waisbord, 2004: 1096-1097). In the words of Waisbord (2004: 1090, 1094, 1096), with reference to gate scandals, the ordinary citizens of contemporary Argentina act like "citizens-as-audiences", whereas in the case of human rights scandals they act like "audiences-as-citizens"[9]. The contrast between the two publics is that the former is rather nonchalant, whereas the latter – more engaged. Reportedly, the differentiated engagement in scandal is symptomatic for the broader context of the Argentinean dynamics of scandal – i.e. a political context of "scandal fatigue" – "a permanent sense of déjà vu among overstimulated and bored audiences inattentive to new images of suffering" (Waisbord, 2004: 1091). In other words, the great viscosity of political scandal dynamics in Argentina effected – in the long run – a certain kind of apathy and indifference in ordinary citizens. While the author himself does not phrase it in these terms, it can be inferred that the Argentinean society became somehow alienated from gate scandals. Hence, these are left to function more as a mechanism of power politics, and less as a mechanism of social integration.

This leads Waisbord to conclude that scandal is differently linked to the media and citizenship, and implicitly, that the intensity of the reaction of the public to normative transgressions is, to a large degree, influenced by the potential threat that the specific violation poses to their lives and to their community. Accordingly, this should also explain why corruption scandals are less instigating for ordinary citizens, than – for example – human rights scandals.

We could further theoretically extend the above case study of the norm audience by introducing the work of Jiménez (2004) on the emergence and development of political scandals in Spain. Paraphrasing Arnold Heidenheimer's analysis of corruption, Jiménez also operates with a triple spectrum of illicitness. These are: the black, the gray and the white zone of illicit behavior (Jiménez, 2004: 1108). The black zone consists of behavior about which there is a societal consensus that it is illicit and that it should be condemned and punished; the gray zone comprises practices which are subject to conflicting opinions as to whether they should be punished or not; finally – the white zone includes those activities which are tolerable for the reason that their punishment would do more harm than good to the society.

In any case, the battle for public opinion will oscillate between being focused either on the level of facts (who did what, if he or she did it or did not do it, etc.) in the black zone or on the level of interpretations and meanings about those same facts in the gray zone (Jiménez, 2004: 1109).

---

9   "Scandals need to be analyzed on two levels: as occasions for citizenship (audiences-as-citizens) and as media events (citizens-as-audiences)" (Waisbord, 2004: 1090).

Closely related to Adut's norm audience is what might be termed the *kibitzer audience*. Thompson (2008: 573) – following the work of Gladys Engel Lang and Kurt Lang – describes the audience of non-professionals as a kind of kibitzer audience. The non-professionals are potential witnesses of the events taking place in the political field, and sometimes even targeted receptors of political messages. Their illustration as an audience points to the fact that although they are not directly involved in the political rivalries, the non-professionals do have and publicly formulate opinions on the subject of the ongoing political games – opinions, which happen to further influence the dynamics and outcome of these episodes.

Kibitzer refers to a *commentator* of an ongoing game. The word is commonly used in chess, bridge, poker and Go subcultures. Seemingly, it has roots both in Yiddish and German (Yiddish *kibitsen*, German *kiebitzen*)[10]. The usage of the term is not necessarily pejorative, as the kibitzer might provide useful comments and analysis. And seemingly, no matter how disturbing they might be, kibitzers' comments are part of the fun. The importance of kibitzers in bridge was revealed during the *Great Kibitzers' Strike of 1926*. Reportedly, Smith – a kibitzer – felt insulted when a player concealed a queen of spades behind another card. The incident led to the formation of a national kibitzer union and negotiations which went on for several months. The following excerpt is from an article dealing with the 1926 strike and it reveals how the absence of kibitzers "depressed" the players.

> There was, of course, consternation within the clubs. With no kibitzer to say, "You should have played it the other way around" or "Only a fathead would have led the king of diamonds", post-mortem discussions were routine and without color. Without kibitzers, the players became careless and listless; games simply dragged along, sometimes without comment of any sort. The players began to lose weight, had no appetites. In many cases, games were actually canceled. Jymes, or Hymes, or whatever his name was, eventually offered a public apology to Smith for concealing the spade queen, but by then it was too late. Sympathy strikes were springing up all over the country, a national kibitzers' union was formed, and card players were presented with an ultimatum in the form of a set of rules (Kaufman, 1955: 104).

Nowadays, the notion also indicates a computer chess program's *tutor mode* that signals bad moves and offers hints during the game.

---

10   "Of course anyone with a Jewish grandma knows that kibitzer is Yiddish for a busybody, a meddler who offers unsolicited advice. But mostly it's used only in the chess world today and hasn't really crossed over into mainstream English. A Google News search turns up just 25 hits. Sad for such a great word. At least it's more than 'zugzwang'" (Mig, 2006).

The difference between the kibitzer and norm audience in scandal is that the former is more of a *consumer* of the scandal, while the norm audience *plays a very important part in its development*. In other words, there might be cases of scandal without a kibitzer audience while it would be quite difficult to imagine one without a norm audience.

When I use the term kibitzer audience, I make reference to a kind of audience which is not in the first line of the battle, but rather plays the role of an observer, or a witness. As its designation as kibitzer speaks for itself, the kibitzer audience weights the behavior of the nucleus of the norm audience in a scandal and, in certain cases, it can express approval or disapproval with respect to its actions and manners. A similar attitude can be also taken up towards the norm offender.

To a certain extent, the kibitzer audience enjoys a position similar to that of the audience in the dynamics of what Goffman (1990: 205-207) has described as "creating a scene". In Goffman's reading, a scene perturbs a habitual performance team and in actuality it is *quite the opposite* of a performance team.

> A "performance" may be defined as all the activity of a given participant on a given occasion which serves to influence in any way any of the other participants [...]
> I will use the term "performance team" or, in short, "team" to refer to any set of individuals who cooperate in staging a single routine (Goffman, 1990: 26, 85).

Hence, "the scene" might be termed as the disruptive publicity of a transgression, while the norm audience and the norm offender as "the performers". Goffman (1990: 206) gave several scenarios of what could be qualified as a "scene". In the main, "creating a scene" denotes a disruption in the dramaturgical cooperation set up by two or several team-mates in front of an audience. It could also stand for a confrontation between the audience and the performer(s) as such, where the audience overtly challenges the performers.

> This is what happens when an individual screws up his social courage and decides to "have it out" with another or "really tell him off" (Goffman, 1990: 205).

Returning to the former definition of the "scene"/"creating a scene", in this case the performance of teamwork in front of the audience is replaced with one of dissension. Hence, this would be a classic case of the performance given by a norm audience – or by a norm offender for that matter – which is witnessed and commented upon by a kibitzer audience. This is noteworthy because of the lack of understanding – the scandal is not a performance team of two team-mates, but rather a solo performance.

Thus, the norm audience (one of the team-mates) witnesses and reacts to the transgression of the norm offender (the public disruption of dramaturgical cooperation). The kibitzer audience witnesses the performance of the norm

audience or of the norm offender after the disruption of dramaturgical cooperation. Hence, the kibitzer audience might be the audience of the performance
before the disruption, but it might as well be a *new* audience. A similar reading
of scandal in terms of scene could be also set up in cases when the scene is
defined as an overt confrontation between the performers and the audience. In
this case, the performer assumes the role of the norm audience, while the
audience becomes the norm offender. Hence, the audience of the scene stands
for what I refer to as kibitzer audience.

Adut's emphasis of the importance of "the public" in the definition of scandal
as "transgression" together with Goffman's distinction between "the front" and "the
backstage" gives yet another reason to consider scandal in terms of "scene".

What distinguishes the kibitzer of a game (chess, bridge, etc.) from the kibitzer audience of a scandal is that the latter has much more resources to
influence the dynamics of the witnessed process. Further, the scandal kibitzer is
not only able to comment and influence the events, but can also – eventually –
take part in them. More explicitly, public disapproval of the norm audience's
behavior by kibitzers might lead to what Thompson (in Adut, 2004: 555)
designates as second-order transgressions. In such a case, the first-order kibitzer
audience becomes a second-order norm audience. By the same token, one could
imagine cases when the reaction of the norm audience to first-order transgressions evolves in anticipation of the reaction of the would-be kibitzer audience. If
this pertains, then it seems reasonable to argue that the response of the kibitzer
audience to the first-order transgression can be regarded as an externality in its
own right.

What the above implies is that the norm audiences are not habituated, but
that there is a whole process of winning them over, or of keeping them out of a
scandal. These processes have been analyzed by Adut (2005; 2008) who
employed the term *externalities*, which I discuss below.

Briefly stated, the *externalities* can be best synthesized as the side-effects
and repercussions of the publicity of a certain transgression to third parties
(Adut, 2005: 215). According to Adut, it is the conduct of these externalities that
clinches the matter of transforming an alleged transgression into a scandal. And,
by the same token, it is the anticipation of these externalities that might keep
certain transgressions from being publicized. Once again – not being made
public does not mean something is not spoken or gossiped about. Although a
phenomenon of social control in its own, gossip and slandering employ different
methods than scandal (Braithwaite, 1992: 109).

When discussing the case of Oscar Wilde, Adut (2005; 2008) argues that a
certain superstition towards these sequels kept the British high society from
publicizing the flashy transgressions of the famous author – transgressions

which, reportedly, were well and widely known. Thus, it can be inferred that in similar cases it takes either somebody who has nothing to lose, or is highly motivated, in order to publicize the transgression. It is also highly recommended for the person to enjoy a high status in the society or to at least have such a patron backing the endeavor.

As it is linked to the issue of shame, the concept of *contamination* plays an important role in the explorations of this work.

> The contaminations of third parties are frequently moral in nature. Scandals discredit or disgrace by undermining the reputation and social standing of the ones they afflict. But it is crucial to stress that the logic of contamination derives largely from that of shame. Hence, contamination does not ipso facto imply moral deficiency and may often contradict rationality. When publicized, the sins of the father will often defile the son. What is more, the scandalous publicity of a transgression can also contaminate audiences along with its denouncers (Adut, 2005: 221).

Contamination suggests the potential of the reputational harm that the development of any scandal poses. The engine of scandal consumes images, puts labels and often stigmatizes not only the transgressing party, but also the persons in their proximity. According to the logic of contamination, these persons might be: the trespasser's family, friends, or the organization to which he belongs. More explicitly, the higher the status and the social visibility of the social and/or official rank of the disclosed offender, the greater the contamination – and proportions of the scandal – can be expected.

The mechanism of contamination appears as a result of the fact that scandals operate "according to a collectivistic logic and entail the exercise of popular justice" (Adut, 2005: 220). And thus, the scandal brings under the close scrutiny of the public eye not only the behavior as such, but also the micro-mechanisms of social control that seemingly have been too permissive with the transgressive behavior in question. It should not be forgotten that the dramaturgical nature of scandal requires the news of the normative transgression to come as a great surprise to everyone involved. Furthermore, the revelation and the disappointment can be so great that it quickly transforms into distrust. The dissemination of distrust to a certain institution might even lead to its bankruptcy or – in extreme cases – to the bankruptcy of other similar institutions.

The concept of contamination should be viewed in correlation with that of *pollution* – as this was discussed by Douglas (1992). Adut (2005: 216) talks about the third parties lured into the scandal in terms of "polluted or provoked third parties". The concept of contamination (as an externality of scandal when following Adut) and that of pollution effected by transgressions (as discussed by Douglas in terms of transmitting danger by contact) certainly converge. Yet, Douglas' (1992: 33) discussion of pollution beliefs in terms of agents triggering moral indignation indicates that contamination (as a mechanism discernible in the dynamics of scandal) is different from that of pollution (as a mechanism of transmitting danger). This fact gives us two hypotheses for consideration. One would be to advance an analysis of the mechanism of contamination in scandal in terms of "moral pollution"; and second, following Malinowski's (1989: 80) work, to regard the pollution rules as "active principles" triggering moral indignation – i.e. contamination in scandal. As stated above, Malinowski's fieldwork in the Trobriand Islands revealed that the publicity of a transgression, and not the "'group-reaction' and 'supernatural sanction'" are the "active principles" in the dynamics of scandal.

Especially vulnerable to scandal are organizations characterized by a high degree of exclusivity – like the army, military organizations, churches etc. Here "the logic of scandal combines guilt by suspicion and guilt by association" (Adut, 2008: 25). This leads to the tendency to advance norm work solely through internal disciplining. The intensity of contamination is determined by the high status of the norm offender and by the "taboo properties" of the transgression. The more the organization is characterized by closure and impermeability, the more likely the contamination to spread and engulf the institution as a whole (Adut, 2008: 28).

The logic of contamination requires a balance between the status of the transgressor and the gravity of the transgression. This is especially visible in cases of scandals emerging from catastrophes or other devastating events. Usually, officials at the top are called on to give an account or to take the blame. The same pertains to situations of ambiguity or events which occur as cumulative effects. The blame has to be individualized.

In Adut's (2005: 221) study, *provocation* is listed as the second type of externality. Compared to contamination, it rather stimulates pro-scandal enterprises. It is usually the case of specific transgressions such as public heresy, art scandals and civil disobedience. In this case the transgression is deliberate and ostentatious, and it is committed with the purpose of overtly provoking and annoying the norm audience. It is aimed at showing that the norm as such can – and should be – transgressed. So, the ideal externality would be to persuade others in following the transgression of the norm. Provocation aims at an affirmative action of normative outlawry at the expense of the norm audience.

The externalities of scandal (be they contamination or provocation) pertain to choices of social affiliation in a context which – as indicated by Turner's (1975: 35) analysis of social drama – lays great stress on "loyalty and obligation" as well as "interest". According to Turner (1975: 37), "Social dramas [...] are units of aharmonic and disharmonic process, arising in conflict situations". The author distinguishes "four main phases of public action": *breach, crisis, redressive action* and *reintegration* or *schism*. The classification and conceptualization of these phases have been successfully integrated in recent studies of scandals – either by insisting on their dramaturgical nature (see Bell's (2006) discussion of the Clinton-Lewinsky scandal), or rather by discussing single instances (see Sims, 2009).

Eventually, the last theoretical term to be taken into account is *scandal as a factor of evolution*. This notion will prove its usefulness in the forthcoming analysis of certain scandals that took place in communist Romania. As will be shown, many brought about consistent changes at the level of the national public policies. The formula, "scandal as a factor of evolution", is the title of a brief column written at the time of the Dreyfus affair by Nałkowski (see 1952: 19-25) – a Polish geographer and social scientist. More recently, it was used by Kurczewski (2003) in his study of the perceived level of corruption among the Polish political elite.

> The scandals, their failures and successes determine the line of admissible conduct. This line is undergoing evolution – not necessarily a unilinear one – though, in general, it seems that the civilizing process – to refer to Norbert Elias' theory – in this area continues (Kurczewski, 2003: 163-164).

2. Scandal and Mechanisms of Moral Panic

The foregoing section dealt with mechanisms of scandal which are specific to this social phenomenon. Yet, as will be shown in the following chapters of the book, a particular trait of scandal in communism was the reinterpretation of the transgression. This leads us to the mechanism that in the literature on moral panic is depicted as convergence. In the following analysis, I will theoretically locate the moral panic and try to draw a conceptual distinction between it and the scandal. Observably, although we are talking about two distinct processes, these borrow mechanisms from each other and their dynamics are interconnected.

Moral panic can be regarded as a *chronic scandal*. It is a process in which the recurrent transgression of the norm – although publicized – does not become normalized. There is solidarity regarding the perception of the deviance as sensational or threatening in a certain way. Then again, the consensus in rejecting the deviance can be contrasted with the consensus regarding the opportunity for the deviant behavior. McRobbie and Thornton (1995), among other authors, pointed to the fact that there are dynamics of moral panic at the level of the society, dynamics which require an updating of the theory and a new model of moral panic. As in the case of scandal – where we are dealing with different types, such as political, sexual, environmental, procedural scandals, etc. – in the case of moral panic we can draw up a certain typology. Moral panic can be observed in relation to youth, class, gender, ethnicity, race, generation etc. Regarding generation for example, Comaroff and Comaroff (1999) present a case study of moral panic about the piracy of body parts which overlaps to a certain extent with moral panic about the trafficking of women from countries of the former Soviet Bloc, which became prevalent in Central and Eastern Europe after 1989. Another application of the term moral panic to social phenomena occurring in Eastern Europe is Mica's (2010) study of dog population management in Romania and Moldavia.

In light of the ambiguity of the term moral panic – which can be defined as pointing both to organization and to fear/exaggeration – with the passage of time some of these moral panics came to be viewed as exaggerations, while some of them are still regarded as a desirable social response. According to Johansson (2000), moral panic over youth is rather part of the first category, while moral panic over anti-democratic and anti-modernist movements can be viewed as part of the second one.

I will try to show that sometimes Romanian authorities reacted to mass protests in terms of "hooliganism". Literature on moral panic uses the term of *ideological convergence* in order to describe a process of signification that misrepresents what it is supposed to describe. Mass protests initiated also second-order transgressions, which revealed crises at the local and national level of the party. The reactions to these second-order transgressions – while possibly viewed as part of a dynamic – still seem unfit to be regarded as pointing to a *folk devil*. The party members were rather supposed to be subjected to vigilance, and – in the aftermath of the scandal – to scapegoating.

I will try to show that the events of 1977, 1987, 1989 and 1990 involved elements of convergence between mass protests and "acts of hooliganism". Further – that there are reasons to presume the subsistence of ideological convergence. As stated, the notion of convergence is borrowed from literature on moral panic. I will argue that certain mechanisms which occur during the unfolding of moral panic prove to be quite useful when dealing with political scandals over mass protests in communist Romania.

It is hard to document the actual effect of these convergences on society. This notwithstanding, I seek to evidence that the ideological exploitation of elements of moral panic over hooliganism took place in 1977 and 1987, and that these episodes inspired eventually the mobilization of the law enforcement and the army in 1989, and in 1990 – the socio-professional category of the miners. On the other hand, there is also the ideological exploitation – or better stated *counter*-ideological exploitation – of the notions *hooligans* and *hoodlums* [golani], which took place during the 1990 demonstrations in Bucharest, which did not further develop partly because of the authorities' monopoly over the television. While all this pertains, there is still the possibility of analyzing how the media reacted to the events that took place in 1989 and especially in 1990 and examine whether they constructed a folk-devil of "hooligans" and "hoodlums" [*golani*] to justify government-applied measures. Such content analysis might indicate that the mainstream media did present matters in such a light, to the benefit of the powers-that-be. While the book does not attempt to probe whether 1990 was a case of moral panic or not, it argues that the reaction of the communist authorities to scandals over mass protests adopted mechanisms of convergence of the kind usually prescribed to moral panic.

Perhaps, this state of affairs was inherited from the long years of communism which developed dissimulation practices. For the purposes of illustration, one might consider a somehow analogous example: the convergence between *Romanian emigration* and *iron-guardists*. The latter is a folk-devil usually correlated with the Romanian diaspora in the West. According to Pelin (2007), in order to diminish the impact of Radio Free Europe, Romanian authorities and the State Security apparatus advanced a far-fetched cliché that cataloged the diaspora as iron-guardists.

> Against its own findings, the *Securitate* in its current practice, with stubbornness worthy of a better cause, embittered to present the journalists from Munich as iron-guardists, and their activity as expression of an iron-guard mentality. It paid a high price for this flagrant hypocrisy (Pelin, 2007: 25) [*author's translation, author's emphasis*].

In the following section I will present the standard definition of moral panic, as drawn up by the founder of the concept – Cohen (see 1993) – in his study of media and social reactions to the Mods and Rockers phenomenon in the United Kingdom, in the 1960s (for ulterior elaborations see Goode and Ben-Yehuda, 1994). Later I will introduce Hier's (2002) formulation of moral panic through a "moral economy of harm" in the context of the full-scale process of moral regulation. It is my conviction that this latter conceptualization will allow for a more comprehensive connection of moral panic to the notion of scandal, as it is defined in the foregoing analysis. It should be also stated that my purpose is not to draw an exhaustive literature review of moral panic. The present discussion concentrates solely on the conceptual delineation of moral panic mechanisms, and not on bringing further refinements in this particular field.

The following is an often-cited definition of the phenomenon by Cohen, who is credited with coining this sociological term[11].

---

11   It seems, however, that the actual copyright belongs to Jock Young who used the term in 1971 (Welch, Price and Yankey, 2002: 3).

> Societies appear to be subject, every now and then, to periods of moral panic. A condition, episode, person or group of persons emerges to become defined as a threat to societal values and interests; its nature is presented in a stylized and stereo-typical fashion by the mass media; the moral barricades are manned by editors, bishops, politicians and other right-thinking people; socially accredited experts pronounce their diagnoses and solutions; ways are coping are evolved or (more often) resorted to; the condition then disappears, submerges or deteriorates and becomes more visible. Sometimes the object of the panic is quite novel and other times it is something which has been in existence long enough, but suddenly appears in the limelight. Sometimes the panic passes over and is forgotten, except in folklore and collective memory; at other times it has more serious and long lasting repercussions and might produce such changes as those in legal and social policy or even in the way the society conceives itself [...] The Teddy Boys, the Mods and Rockers, the Hells Angels, the Skinheads and the Hippies have all been phenomena of this kind. There have been parallel reactions to the drug problem, student militancy, political demonstrations, football hooliganism, vandalism of various kinds and crime and violence in general (Cohen, 1993: 9).

As stated earlier, Cohen drew an emphatic picture of official societal reactions to the phenomenon of Mods and Rockers in the United Kingdom. In his study, moral panic is analyzed as a process that consists of four phases (*warning, impact, inventory* and *reaction*) and is governed by a tendency to amplify and to de-amplify itself eventually. According to Cohen, amplification occurs with respect to both deviance and in reaction to deviance. Briefly put, the deviation amplification sequence goes through the following stages: *initial deviance, societal reaction, increase in deviance, increase in reaction*, etc. (Cohen, 1993: 142). By the same token, the societal reaction goes through the routine of: *sensitization, diffusion, escalation, dramatization* and *exploitation* (Cohen, 1993: 142).

As a rule, de-amplification signals that the societal reaction managed to offset the transgression; marginalize and stigmatize the folk-devils to the extent that they are not seen as a threat anymore. The de-amplification might occur also as a result of some sort of normalization of the deviant behavior. Yet this type of normalization is what I would call an "arrested normalization" for the reason that it appears to be conditioned to a certain age or to a certain environment.

> In mass phenomenon such as the Mods and Rockers a form of de-amplification sets in: the amplification stops because the social distance from the deviants is made so great, that new recruits are put off from joining. The only joiners are the very young or the *lumpen* who have access to few other alternatives. These are the ones who might fight with the ferocity of a group who knows it is being left behind. In the meantime, the original hardcore might mature and grow out of deviance (Cohen, 1993: 202).

Furthermore, the author views as very angry the processes of marginalizing and stigmatizing the folk-devils. As a matter of fact, they can be regarded as components of shaming. Both Cohen (1993: 61) and Hall et al. (1994: 32) document that, at the peak of moral panic, the judgment response to the crime takes the form of judicial admonitions. And that the court becomes the place of what Garfinkel (1956) described as *degradation ceremonies*. This degradation ceremony is a public demarcation of the "atypical actor" from the "background that is overtypical" (Cohen, 1993: 61). The act is more than mere delimitation – it is condemnation, which in its own term legitimizes the moral panic.

To return to the topic of de-amplification (the marginalization of the transgression or its arrested development), its outcome might be an impression that the moral panic was an exaggerated societal reaction. And more than the actual facts, it is the very use of the term *panic* in the designation of the phenomenon that might leave such an impression. In their critical assessment of the term moral panic, Cornwell and Linders (2002) use, for example, a definition which condenses it to an exaggerated and disorganized reaction. They argue that phenomena which are usually described as moral panic (they operate with the concrete examples of moral panic over the usage of LSD) are in fact very organized and active social reactions. This notwithstanding, I see no reason why fear cannot coexist with a rigorous reaction or preventive steps against that which is feared. Furthermore, I think their criticism overlooks the fact that even Cohen warns us that the moral panic should be graded not according to the rigorousness of the assessment of folk devils, but according to the adequacy of the societal reaction.

> The argument is not that there is "nothing there" when somebody is labeled mentally ill or that this person has no problems, but that the reaction to what is observed or inferred is fundamentally inappropriate [...] Ultimately, I am pessimistic about the chances of changing social policy in regard to such phenomena as the Mods and Rockers. More moral panics will be generated and other, as yet nameless, folk devils will be created. This is not because such developments have an inexorable inner logic, but because our society as present structured will continue to generate problems for some of its members – like working-class adolescents – and then condemn whatever solution these groups find (Cohen, 1993: 203-204).

An interesting discussion about the evolution of societal reactions towards folk devils is given by Johannson (2000: 33). The author regards for example the moral panic over folk devils in the 1960s and in the 1970s as "expressions of a narrow and restricted view on youth or culture". And he sees an evolution of this moral panic from episodes of conservatory reactions – as the ones studied by Cohen – to moral panic over counter-modern subcultures. More explicitly, regarding the contemporary agenda of moral panic, Johannson (2000: 26-33) distinguishes between *postmodern media panics* (soft and transitory media products) and *moral panics* (anti-democratic and anti-modernist movements which often turn violent). And with respect to the societal reaction to them, Johansson (2000: 33) finds that in the former case they amount to "*media spectacles*", while in the latter they resort less to action and more to a kind of "*moral contemplation* where the outcome is hard to predict". What is more, the anti-modernist character of these – the author claims – generated moral panic which may become a safeguard of a democratic society.

Another discussion put forward by Cohen is that of the *commercial and ideo-logical exploitation of deviance.* Closely related to these two is also the pattern of exploitation that holds the deviance up to ridicule. However, for the purposes of this paper the term *ideological exploitation* is more important. It indicates the employment of a deviance discourse that serves the interests of a certain religious or political ideology (Cohen, 1993: 139-141). In the case of the scandals over mass protests which are going to be briefly presented in section II.1 – *The Dynamics of Scandal during the Ceauşescu Regime*, we will see that the communist regime resorted to ideologically exploiting the deviance of "hooliganism". What is more, given that the ideological exploitation takes the form of public denuncia-tion, the disclosed and condemned deviance is required to live up to the expectations of something indisputably threatening to the society. The more gains a successful ideological exploitation brings to the exploiter, the more problematic it becomes when the deviance turns out to be less threatening than presented (Cohen, 1993: 141).

The introduction of moral panic benefits the preceding discussion on scan-dal. I want to show that in cases of scandals over mass protests, Romanian communist authorities resorted to a signification of the first-order transgression that entailed elements of the misrepresentation of its political origins as criminal. This scenario, as will be documented, was implemented, for example, in the case of the *Bern affair* in the 1950s.

The term *signification of first-order transgression* paraphrases one of the signifying events/issues/problems used by Hall et al. (1994) and Hall and Jefferson (1991). As a matter of fact, these two studies are concerned with a certain type of signification, the so-called *signification spiral* – i.e. "a way of signifying events which also intrinsically escalates their threat" (Hall et al., 1994: 223). The self-amplifying sequence is galvanized mainly by two mecha-nisms: *convergence* and *thresholds*.

Convergence designates the activity of "linking by labeling of the specific issue to other problems" (Hall and Jefferson, 1991: 77). Generally speaking, three types of convergence can be derived.

Real movement	Example	Signification
1. actual convergence	homosexuals – Gay Liberation Front (GLF)	potentially accurate
2. some convergence	GLF – Marxist Left – "Red" conspiracy	increasingly contains a purely ideological dimension
3. no convergence	students – hooligans	purely ideological

Table 1   *(Hall and Jefferson, 1991: 78)*

The refashioning of a real convergence into ideological convergence might imply some, or even all of the following conversions: misrepresentation, escalation, translating/transposition (for example of a political issue into a criminal one). In this case, the signification – which Hall et al. (1994: 224-245) sometimes refer to as resignification – designates the process of the inflection of the real convergence in an ideological one (Hall et al., 1994: 224, 225)[12]. The thresholds circumscribe symbolically the limits of societal tolerance. According to Hall et al. (1994: 224, 225) these are: permissiveness, legality and violence.

At this point the discussion turns upon "moral panic as a form of moral regulation", and more explicitly upon "moral panic as the *volatile local manifestation* of what can otherwise be understood as the *global project of moral regulation*" (Hier, 2002: 329).

> For projects of moral regulation are always socially constituted in that they involve one group of persons seeking to act upon the conduct of others in some manner (Hier, 2002: 326).

The list of patrons governing this sort of regulatory project includes not only the state, but also civil society and the self. In other words, moral regulation is a process of subjectification which should lead eventually to the internalization of codes of moral conduct that are shared by the regulator (Hier, 2002: 329). If the definition in terms of subjectification pertains, moral panic designates a crisis in the process of regulation, which occurs either due to a fissure in the dynamics of moral

---

12   "The resignification process thus also simplifies complex issues – for example, by 'making plain' through elision what would otherwise have to be substantiated by hard argument (e.g. that all student protest is mindlessly violent). Thus the movement's 'essential hooliganism' comes to pass for substantiated truth. Such significations also carry, embedded within them, concealed premises and understandings (for example, those referring to the exceedingly complex relation between politics and violence). Finally, by signifying a political issue through its most extreme and violent form, signification helps to produce a 'control' response – and makes that response legitimate. The public might be reluctant to see the strong arm of the law arbitrarily exercised against legitimate political protesters. But who will stand between the law and a 'bunch of hooligans'?" (Hall et al., 1994: 224).

governance, or because of the incapacity of the process to pursue. After it gains visibility, the crisis as such leads to a moral panic if the phenomenon is problematized and depicted as the responsibility of folk devils "which are understood to embody a more general state of social/moral harm" (Hier, 2002: 329). In other words, there is a public concern with the problem, but there is also a public denunciation and clear identification of the cause(s) of the crises – a fact which renders moral panic both as an "individualizing" and a "socializing" process; not only pointing to a problem, but also providing a solution (Hier, 2002: 330).

As compared to moral regulation – which is an inclusive and a full-scale process – moral panic consists of a prompt intervention on a certain group of people. Moral regulation is a process of subjectification, whereas moral panic is one of "dislocation". Following the work of Graham Knight, Hier (2002: 330) also conceptualizes moral panic in terms of a "moral economy of harm". This hypothesis should be viewed as one of the main statements of Hier's article. Accordingly, what constitutes moral panic is not "the objective assessment of harm stemming from some activity or behavior", but the fact that this assessment has its cohorts of followers and true believers.

> What this concept implies is not that moral panics unfold based on the objective assessment of harm stemming from some activity or behavior, but how effectively claims making is able to tap into the "feeling-passion" or "common sense" of those who are subject to the ideological contents of panic discourses and, in the words of Hay [...], become subjects through it (Hier, 2002: 330).

In the analysis of the Romanian case-studies, I concentrated on how different audiences reacted to the scandals, not on how scandals themselves erupted. Such an approach in "the nature of a particular set of reactions" also navigated studies of Cohen (1993: 15), Hall and Jefferson (1991), and Hall et al. (1991) on moral panic. In my turn, I would maintain the interest regarding these reactions in spite of criticism coming from some researchers like Cornwell and Linders (2002), who show that the phenomena usually described as moral panic involve a huge deal of *active* and not solely *reactive* efforts of social and institutional actors.

The distinction between the *effects* of the event and the *reactions* is, to a certain extent, easier to demarcate in cases of scandal than in cases of moral panic. Briefly stated, in my interpretation, the scandal as disruptive publicity of transgression (Adut, 2005) is more easily located. For one – a scandal is a singular event, further – the public nature of the disclosure and the evolution of externalities are more or less spotlighted. The matter however, arises in that there are but a few who enjoy the side scenes of the process, and that many others remain suspicious of having been swindled. Put otherwise, the dramatization of the scandal raises the issue as to whether the plot eventually disclosed to the public scrutiny is what the scandal ultimately condenses to. And the matter becomes even more complicated as we advance from the first- to second-order transgression of a scandal. Conclusively, in case of scandal, at the original level of the first-order transgression, the distinction between the emergence of the event (i.e. the public transgression) and the reaction to it should be easily pointed out.

As far as moral panic is concerned, the matters are more sophisticated given that there are cases when the reaction to a certain crime or to distinguishable "social types" (Cohen, 1993: 10) forgoes the appearance of that specific type of crime or of that specific social type (Hall et al., 1994: 181). In other words, where scandal is viewed as part of *scandal dynamics*, the moral panic should be viewed as part of a *general moral panic*.

To simplify, the scandal deals with the publicity of an individualized transgression, irrespective of the fact that it also popularizes it (a circumstance which might effect provocation eventually). The transgression as such (after it was made public) is viewed as an *exceptional violation of the norm*. In the case of moral panic, the violation of the norm is not perceived as a singular occurrence, but as a *recurrent transgression of certain groups or social types*. Subsequently, these "particular events (such as demonstrations)", these "particular disapproved forms of behavior (such as drug-taking or violence)", and these "social types" such as "folk devils: visible reminders of what we should not be" are pinpointed and stigmatized and become persona of popular fears and resentments (Cohen, 1993: 9-10).

Another differentiation between scandal and moral panic pertains to the phenomenon of class distinction. For scandal to break, either the norm offender should be of high status, or the publicity of the transgression should affect a salient individual or institution. In this latter case, the transgression should be drafted as illustrative of social phenomena that pertain to high-status individuals or organizations. In comparison, moral panic targets types of norm transgression that are thought of to be generalized within certain social groups. We notice however, that in certain cases, moral panics address social groups that have been contaminated subsequently to guilt by association involving institutions characterized by exclusivity and solidarity. For this to happen, the respective institution has, however, to be vulnerable to moral attack. The sexual abuse scandals of the 2000s involving the Catholic Church are a case in point. Adut (2008: 79) shows that the allegations of sexual abuse by Catholic clergymen were perceived by Americans as constituting a phedophilia scandal, even though the ensnared priests came under accusation of having sex with postpubescent boys[13]. Thus, an important element in cases of moral panics associated with initial contamination by association of institutions is the element of the translation of transgression, and its convergence with other problems.

---

13   For a discussion of sexual (moral) panics see Herdt (2009).

3. The "Anthropological Essence" of Scandal *

The anthropological essence of scandal – to paraphrase Kurczewski's (2009b) discussion of "the anthropological essence of the rite of passage" in reference to social transformation – reveals itself in the rituals of shaming and criticism that are part of scandal and scandalizing as cultural phenomena of affirming groups' identity and norm entrepreneurship. Then, it also becomes evident in the taboo status of specific topics that manifest pollution potential and for this reason are prevented from being openly brought up and debated in the public sphere. Such a link to taboo has been strongly demonstrated in the case of sexuality, sex talk and modalities of representing and discussing sexuality in the public sphere (see Kulick, 1996; Kulick, 2009; Kulick and Klein, 2009). As shown by Adut (2008: 175-223), the proliferation of sexual scandals in the United States has evolved on the background of sexual liberation and the decline of modesty in openly discussing sexuality and sexual behavior in public.

If it comes to the anthropology of scandal it seems that its prospects have received more consideration within sociology, than within the potential subject of anthropology of scandal as such. We could test this hypothesis on two dimensions: the sociology of law and the sociology of organizations.

Thus, the work of Gluckman (1963), Malinowski (1989) and Turner (1975) on gossip, rumor, scandal and public denunciation, social drama, and that of Douglas (1992) on taboo and pollution effected by transgression (as discussed in terms of transmitting danger by contact) has been mainly reviewed in the framework of Adut's (see 2008: 9, 19-20) sociology of contemporary scandals, and of the sociology of organizations' accounts of organizational efforts to rebuild reputation following an ethics scandal (see Sims, 2009). Yet, these have failed to lead to autonomous ethnographic accounts of mechanisms of scandal and related rituals in modern society. This is not to say, of course, that anthropological records of scandals are totally absent. The anthropological field itself has witnessed strong recent contributions: scandal and resistance theory (for discussion of scandals as resistance and shaming among Brazilian transgendered prostitutes see Kulick, 1996; Kulick, 2009; Kulick and Klein, 2009); the anthropology of public policy (for occurrences of scandal with no sanctions (shaming) involving the *shadow elite* see Wedel, 2009); and the transductive account of scandal (for global dairy scandal see Tracy, 2010). Still, it could not

---

*   This section is a more elaborated version of the paper *The "Anthropological Essence" of Scandal: Ritualization of Party Moots on Mass Protests in Late Communist Romania* to be published in the edited volume comprising the proceedings of the conference *Anthropology of Law: Synthesis*, Faculty of Humanities, Charles University in Prague, Prague, May 21-22, 2011.

escape notice that the reflection on the ritualization of scandal has continued within sociology rather than anthropology.

We witness here an opposite situation to that discussed by Kurczewski (2009b: 541-542) with regard to conventional sociological framings and conceptualizations of social transformation that pass over the "need for ritualization", ritual components, and the overall dramaturgical structure of transformation. The situation is antithetical for the reason that it seems that – for the time being – it is sociology which seems more fitting to investigate the implications of ritualization, publicity and taboo in modern episodes of scandal, as compared to anthropology. Thus, from the above named anthropological studies, it is only Kulick and Klein's (2009; see also Kulick, 1996; Kulick, 2009) research on scandalizing acts involving Brazilian transgendered prostitutes that exploits the connection between sex, taboo and identity in the public sphere, as well as being that which offers an ethnography of shaming strategies. Whereas Wedel (2009), for example, although intuitively pointing to the shadow elite's impermeability to shaming, social pressure and legal sanctions, does not approach the matter from an anthropological perspective, although I believe that the author would have the conceptual tools to do so (see also Mica, 2011a).

When I am referring to the ritualization of scandals, I point to particular rituals of shaming, public reprimand, criticism and attribution of fault that are the quintessence of scandal. Not only do they figure as components of scandal, but even the anticipation of the costs of shaming and public reprimand on third parties plays a key role that aligns social reactions and arrangements within its dynamics (see Adut, 2005; Adut, 2008). The anticipation of the externalities of shaming and public reprimand might even prevent its outburst.

Thus, the publicity of a transgression (see Adut, 2004; Adut 2005; Adut, 2008; Malinowski, 1989; Pospíšil, 1971) – in some cases its severity (see Kurczewski, 2003) –, taboo (see Douglas, 1992; Adut, 2008) and rituals of shaming/public reprimand (see Gluckman, 1963; Adut, 2008; Malinowski, 1989; Pospíšil, 1971) emerge as main constituents of scandal. For the purposes of this book, I will focus on the component of shaming and public reprimand. This brings us to the anthropology of law. As already mentioned, an alternative path arriving at the anthropology of law, which could be further followed up on, is that of reputation repair tactics – a line of research that was taken up in the study of the sociology of organizations. The anthropological input of these latter studies is that they focus on what Turner (1975: 39) depicted as *redressive action* in the development of *social drama*. Even though they cut out and concentrate on a certain phase of the scandal dynamics, these contributions suggest the anthropological intuition of the importance of rituals coming full circle (see, for example, Sims, 2009).

Regarding the anthropology of law, I will in the ensuing chapters follow up on the work of Malinowski (1989), Pospíšil (1971) and Kurczewski (2003: 163; 2009b). The point to be made is that both classic and more contemporary approaches within this field pose the theoretical framework and vocabulary to take up scandal as an autonomous object of study.

Although neither Malinowski nor Pospíšil have developed an explicit theory of scandal, from the would-be anthropology of scandal perspective their work intersects in the focus on publicity and public reprimand. It should be also stated that Malinowski – as already shown in the first part of this chapter – did however elaborate novel insights into scandal and has used scandal-mongering as a source of information in his fieldwork in north-western Melanesia (see Malinowski, 1989; Malinowski, 2002). Regarding these two authors, the insights into publicity and public reprimand are an integral part of an "anthropological definition of law" (see Malinowski, 1989) and of the analysis of legal phenomena (*decisions*) (see Pospíšil, 1971) respectively[14]. Per Malinowski (1989: 24-32, 55), "reciprocity in primitive social organization" (sociological dualism), and the ceremonial character of transactions – "which entails public control and criticism" – constitute the two forces allowing for the binding character of rules of law – the *binding obligations* (which are distinct from religious commandments and rules of custom). In his formulation of an anthropological definition of law[15], this is based on mutuality and publicity.

> "Civil law", the positive law governing all the phases of tribal life, consists then of a body of binding obligations, regarded as a right by one party and acknowledged as a duty by the other, kept in force by a specific mechanism of reciprocity and publicity inherent in the structure of their society (Malinowski, 1989: 58).

The treatment of publicity incorporates elements of social control and criticism (in the case of public assessment of one's behavior), and also that of the meta-norms of a public reprimand of one's transgression. The aforementioned discussion refers to the fact that there is taking place a constant monitoring of conduct of people conforming to normative and economic expectations that society holds for them. This evaluation might lead to both positive (generous gifts, praise, and gratification) and negative sanctions (humiliation, opprobrium, etc.) (Malinowski, 1989: 36, 41-42, 52-53, 65). This approach to publicity drives Malinowski quite close to Gluckman's (1963: 311-313) assessment of gossip and scandal (in the sense of scandal-mongering) as mechanisms of group unity

---

14   For comparison between Malinowski and Pospíšil see Kurczewski (2009a: 57).

15   This is civil law actually – "But we could find the legal aspect in any other domain of tribal life" (Malinowski, 1989: 33).

against other groups, and of equality inside the group. The issue of public reprimand concerns the reaction to scandal – namely the conditions of its occurrence. As shown in the previous section, Malinowski (1989: 80) overtly establishes that the publicity of a transgression – and not "'the group-reaction' and the 'supernatural sanction'" – constitute the "active principle" in the outburst of scandal. On the basis of Malinowski's insights into the significance of a public reprimand followed by a suicide, we see that the rituals of shaming are subjected to meta-norms, and that they offer closure.

In contrast to Malinowski, at Pospíšil the element of publicity in relation to public assessment is less developed, whereas that of public reprimand (as a nonphysical sanction) is discussed at length. The "mutuality of rights and duties" (i.e. the *obligatio*) is listed as the third attribute of law – the other three others are: legal authority, intention of universal application, and sanction (of physical or nonphysical nature). The matter of publicity (as an assessment of one's behavior in public) might have been underdeveloped for the reason that *obligatio* is part of the authority's decision; it is a statement about a social relation that is two-dimensional. As Pospíšil (1971: 85) states, it is "a new phenomenon created by the authority" and it should not be taken as representing "the actual, objective social relation or obligation existing or incurred previous to the decision". Thus, by passing into decision, the mutuality of rights and duties seems to have lost its dynamism. This notwithstanding, Pospíšil (1971: 86) recognized the importance of publicity when making a point about the distinction between attitudes towards the religious and legal taboos of the Kapauku Papuans themselves[16].

The section on public reprimand and shaming discusses nonphysical sanction in terms of its efficiency as a social control. The author does not point to the conditions in which such shaming is brought about, other than the fact that it occurs subsequent to an authority's *decision*. Pospíšil's (1971) inventory of differentiated physical and nonphysical punishment traditions illustrates his thesis regarding the efficacy of *public reprimand* and of other mechanisms of shaming (ostracism, ridicule, gossip, etc.). The insistence on "psychological and social sanctions"

---

16   "Interestingly enough, Kapauku Papuans themselves have different attitudes toward the two sets of taboos which I have separated into two contrasting categories by the attribute of *obligatio*. They talk freely about violations of the purely religious taboos. Indeed, some individuals even boast about their disregard of supernatural prohibitions in order to demonstrate their bravery and courage. The violation of what we may call 'legal taboos', on the contrary, is kept secret, since one does not boast in public about one's crimes punishable by the society" (Pospíšil, 1971: 86).

should be viewed in light of the author's criticism of the underestimation of these and the overall focus on physical punishment "in our society".

I have overviewed these aspects to show to what extent mechanisms of scandal have made their way into the anthropology of law, irrespective of the fact that scandal has not yet been taken up as an object of study in this field. This discussion should be perceived at a general theoretical level. The next sections in the book concentrate on the particular research topic of scandals over mass protests in late communist Romania. I focus on the dynamics of the fault attribution and the phenomenon of the guilt/fault admittance during party meetings that were held at the institutional level in the aftermath of mass protests. The "anthropology of law" dimension reveals itself in the ritual character of this dynamic and in the symmetry of public reprimand – that is attribution of fault (by the norm audience), admittance of guilt/fault (by the norm offender) and sometimes the exclusion/shunning (of the norm offender). Thus, the logic of scandal comes full circle.

The presence of rituals of shaming and of acknowledgement of fault attests to the idea that scandal has consummated its potential. If this is so, then the impact of scandal on the normative structure of society should be traced to one of the following scenarios: the establishing of a new moral consensus (see Kurczewski, 2003: 163); the reaffirming of the existing moral consensus; or the "solidification of existing yet underenforced norms" (see Adut, 2004). Thereupon, in accordance with Kurczewski's (2009b: 541-542) dramaturgical ritual approach to social transformation, we could conclude that scandal is "a passage" as well. This dramaturgical ritual approach has been developed by the author with regard to the ritual symbolization of social transformation "as passage" from the old to the new regime. It incorporates and combines elements from the dramaturgical perspective in sociology with cultural anthropology (more explicitly in reference to Turner's social drama). In our case, the rituals of attribution of fault and the admittance of guilt/fault provide for the "ritual symbolization" of the passage from the old to the new normative "regime". This dramaturgical ritual approach to scandal is compatible with the perspective on scandal advanced by Kurczewski (2003) in a previous study on the perceived level of corruption among the Polish political elite which was briefly presented in the foregoing section in relation to scandal as a factor of evolution.

> Aside from details, the main thing is that scandal arises if someone is shocked by someone else's conduct and provoked to an outburst crossing over the customary line of tolerant silence. But only some scandals "succeed" in provoking a majority consensus in public opinion. If this happens, it means that a new moral consensus has been reached and a transgression tolerated until then is now publicly defined as a public evil (Kurczewski, 2003: 163).

Here, the consequences of scandal are traced to the establishment of a new moral consensus. Yet, we should recall that depending on its progress and direction, the scandal might lead not only to contamination, but also to provocation. Without going too much into details, as a general hypothesis it could be stated that it is the strategies of blame and stigma management, and the dynamics of social and political anticipations and arrangements that influence its evolution.

With regard to the particular case of communist scandals, the anthropology of law should bring its input not so much in order to demonstrate that we could talk of scandals in a communist setting, but in order to investigate the ritualization of reputation repair tactics and scapegoating put forward by communist authorities; and scandal as *legal action* initiated by the norm offender (see Kurczewski, 2009a: 57-61)[17]. As stated, the ritualization of response tactics in the aftermath of scandals over mass protests constitutes the focus of this book.

As already mentioned, the sociology of organizations is the second discipline where we find treatments which build upon anthropological insights into the dynamics of scandal. Illustrative in this regard is Sims' (2009) synthesis of types of redressive actions taken up by organizations as reputation repair tactics in the aftermath of a scandal. In an early phase, the author combines Turner's social drama with Edgar Schein's leader mechanisms for building or changing culture. Next, the theoretical combination evolves by including *single* and *double-loop redressive actions* for conserving or rebuilding reputation.

Sims' study resonates with similar studies in shifting stigma to subgroups or an employee in cases of corporate scandals (see Warren, 2007), or in reputation repair tactics and strategies of blame management (see Capelos and Wurzer, 2009; McGraw, 1990; McGraw, 1991). These theoretical approaches are quite thorough, and I believe that they would certainly prove to be a comprehensive and solid approach to the study of organizations during the Ceauşescu regime. This notwithstanding, the present book chooses to insist rather upon the first dimension – that which is closer to the anthropology of law, for the reason that it seems to better capture the anthropological essence of scandal with regard to the shaming practices, and the internal dynamics of the phases in its development.

---

17   The dynamics of the ritualization of scandal notwithstanding, the potential of the anthropology of scandal (in its legal dimension) consists of the possibility of interpreting scandal and shaming as *legal action*. This approach could be theoretically constructed based on Kurczewski's (2009a: 57-61) definition of legal action – which has been advanced following Leon Petrażycki's *nexus iuris*. From the empirical point of view, Kulik's (1996; 2009) and Kulik and Klein's (2009) discussion of the performative dimension of shaming by Brazilian transgendered prostitutes and its political consequences could be framed as an intuitive application of this approach.

The need to explore such internal progression has also been pointed out in the studies of scandal within the sociology of organizations. For example, Capelos and Wurzer (2009) have made an inventory of strategies of blame management and scandal response tactics put forward by the United Nations. Their findings indicate that concessions – as public responses – are preferred over other types of accounts (such as justification, excuse and denial) (see Capelos and Wurzer, 2009: 86). As a possibly related (subsequent) area of study, the authors pointed to the investigation of motivations that led the UN staff to preemptive resignation[18].

It is to the exploration of this particular research topic of yielding to pressures within the dynamics of scandal to which the present book wishes to bring its contribution.

4. Scandal and Reintegrative Shaming

As stated in the foregoing passages, I have chosen to build upon the anthropological essence of scandal, more explicitly in relation to its anthropology of law dimension. The following section has two parts. Within the limits of the first, I discuss rituals of shaming and public reprimand on the background of Turner's (1975) reintegrative phase in the development of the social drama. Recalling Turner at this stage is revealing because it points to the need to classify types of shaming which occur within the dynamics of scandal, and to a general reflection regarding the opportunity for one to engage in certain types of shaming in spite of others – i.e. with respect to their contribution to the reintegration of the norm offender. Paradoxically, the application of the Turnerian perspective to the analysis of shaming coincides with the development of a somehow similar term within restorative justice – i.e. *reintegrative shaming* (see Braithwaite, 1992). The discussion in the second part of the section elaborates this matter.

When discussing the redressive action phase in social drama, Turner (1975: 39) has pointed to an array of mechanisms ranging from personal advice and informal mediation or arbitration to institutionalized formal juridical and legal machinery, and public ritual. It is noteworthy that such redressive mechanisms might lead to the escalation of crisis in particular cases (for an inventory of

---

18   "A related area that can be further explored is the motivations of the UN staff leading to their preemptive resignation. Earlier we posed the question of whether this is a self imposed or an organizationally imposed exit strategy in light of a scandal. Case studies of particular scandals that examine internal UN memos and documents, as well as interviews with the implicated officials can shed light to the motivations that drive their behaviour" (Capelos and Wurzer, 2009: 86-87).

literature on the topic, in relation to Turner's social drama see Sims, 2009). Yet, I believe that there is still a need for exploring the social phenomena accounting for the success/failure of such actions.

If it comes to the fourth phase in the social drama, two scenarios are envisaged by Turner (1975: 41): "the *reintegration* of the disturbed social group" or "the social recognition and legitimization of irreparable schism between the contesting parties". This phase is usually accompanied by a realignment of the social relationships and components of the field, as well as by changes in the intensity of norm enforcement. It is to be observable that scandal's impact upon the normative structure of society fits quite well the aftermath of social drama as depicted by Turner. Therefore, sociological accounts of scandal as social drama do pertain (see, for discussion, Sims, 2009).

When viewing the *reintegration vs schism* scenario through the lense of the ritualization of scandal (i.e. the components of shaming, public reprimand, acknowledgement of one's fault), we see that this might find its homologue in Braithwaite's (1992) conceptual pair, *reintegrative vs stigmatizing shaming*. As a starting point, it could be stated that these two notions might constitute the main types of a would-be classification of shaming practices involved in the dynamics of scandal. As this is still an incipient discussion at this stage, one could only speculate as to which of these ideas is more beneficial to the logic of scandal. Still, it suffices to observe that, for several reasons, there is a theoretical inclination – or a hope – to look for the reconciliatory aspect in shaming.

As mentioned in the foregoing sections, the importance of shaming in scandal – be it reintegrative or stigmatizing – derives from its very logic. If the shaming component fails to be satisfied, then the scandal escapes its rituals and this might lead to a frustrated audience vis-à-vis the lack of scandal efficacy. It might be actually stated that shaming is one of the intended consequences of scandal, and that there is a general expectation that the norm offender will be subjected to shaming and shame-induction. The following quotation from Wedel's treatment of the destiny of the members of the Chubais-Harvard flex net does a good job catching the importance of the shaming and shame-induction components.

> For both Shleifer and Hay, these troubles have amounted to little more than a slap on the wrist, albeit a costly one. Any damage to the reputation of Shleifer, the much better known of the two, seems to be inconsequential in the circles that matter. As Harry P. Lewis, professor and former dean at Harvard, opined in 2006, "Most of Shleifer's economist colleagues [have] gathered around him supportively ... In fact, no one seems ashamed of this affair at all" [...] (Wedel, 2009: 145).

Shaming also allows us to measure the intensity of scandal. Adut (2008: 127, 129) noted the "negative relationship" between the intensity and the frequency of scandals, and – we could generalize – also the relationship between the "anticipated collective costs" of scandals and their frequency. The issue of anticipated costs leads to the hypothesis of a positive relationship between interdependency and reintegrative shaming (in the framework of reintegrative shaming conferences) and, by extrapolation, also in the aftermath of scandal – to be discussed later on.

In the following section, I will present general aspects of the theory of reintegrative shaming, and depict some of the lines of criticism that have been brought to this practice. Regarding the latter aspect, I will concentrate on what might be termed as the *guilting vs shaming debate*. The point of this synthesis is to gain familiarity with the notions of shame, shaming and shame-induction; as well as to show how difficult it is to theoretically capture the opportunity as well as the effectiveness of processes of shaming and shame-induction. Then, I will turn to case-studies of reintegrative shaming as a tool of informal as well as formal settlement of dispute in the Chinese context. The aim is to prepare the terrain for a discussion of reintegrative shaming practices in relation to research contexts which did not develop what Ahmed and Braithwaite (2005) have termed the "discoursive consciousness" of this process.

Before continuing the discussion, it should be stated however, that the present book does not aim to bring a contribution to the debates and constant revision of reintegrative shaming theory within the field of restorative justice programs. As a matter of fact, some elements of this theory are captured and, to a certain extent, even itemized to fit the purposes of scandal theory. This is also reflected in the topics related to reintegrative shaming which have been selected for discussion.

In practical terms, reintegrative shaming might be seen as the theoretical framework governing the Reintegrative Shaming Experiments project that has been conducted in the Australian Capital Terrritory since 1995 (RISE). In theoretical terms, it is an approach associated with the name of Braithwaite within the larger restorative justice field. The main elements are: confrontation of the offender with the consequences of the crime – "shaming without degradation"; public support in avoiding stigmatization, and "explicit commitment to ritual reintegration" (Ahmed and Braithwaite, 2004: 299-300). It is this last phase that draws attention to the opportunity of incorporating elements of this framework within the scandal theory (as social drama).

To first begin the discussion: *what is shame?* I will present some arguments in the wider criticism of reintegrative shaming theory. It is noteworthy that this is just one of the related debates which have flourished. Furthermore, it should be understood not only in relation with reintegrative shaming, but also in the general context of the theoretical rivalry between so-called guilt and shame theorists.

It would seem that there are as many reasons to differentiate between guilt and shame as there are reasons to regard them as almost indistinguishable from one another in an emotional amalgam, which among other emotional ingredients may also list remorse. As illustrations of this latter tendency, I would mention Tangney (1995: 1140) with her notion of "'shame-free' guilt" and also the study of Harris, Walgrave and Braithwaite (2004: 200) which operated with the term of "shame-guilt". This latter term – in my interpretation – is rather meant to accommodate the reintegrative shaming theory with the criticism that was advanced by several guilt-theorists.

Elster (1999; see also 2007) makes a point about a difference in nuance between shame and guilt. Briefly stated, shame pertains to the person rather than to the act, and in the case of shame, antagonism denotes *contempt or disgust* whereas in the case of guilt it indicates *anger* (for discussion of shame and guilt with regard to belief–emotion connections, and emotions and action tendencies see Elster 2009a; Elster 2011). "Correlatively, shame is 'characterological' or 'global' rather than 'behavioral' or 'specific'" (Ronnie Janoff-Bulman in Elster, 1999: 151). A similar global/specific algorithm in differentiating between shame and guilt is also at work in the study of Hosser, Windzio and Greve (2008) on "guilt and shame as predictors of recidivism". Accordingly, the emotion of guilt is the one inhibiting recidivism. Guilt, in comparison with shame – which is an emotion correlated with social withdrawal – is viewed as being more adaptive and reintegrative (Hosser, Windzio and Greve, 2008: 140). Another criterion of differentiating between shame and guilt is the extent to which they reflect the internalization of social norms. This model is employed, for example, by Polish sociologist Pawlik (2004) when discussing shame, guilt and fear.

Elster (1999: 157-158), inspired by Robert J. Levy, signals the phenomenon of the "control of shame" that is supposed to take place in certain societies. This is actually a discussion of the criticism "metanorms" of certain norm violations. Closely related to the same topic of the control of shame, is another discussion. Following Nick R. E. Fisher, Elster (1999: 163) presents the so-called "hybristic person". The term *hybristic* derives from Greek *hybris* and designates intentional shame-induction in others "for the sheer pleasure of doing so".

There is still further reason why the Greeks were more ready to induce shame in others: They enjoyed it [...] Here I shall only indicate the importance of *hybris* – the deliberate infliction of shame on others, for the sheer pleasure of doing so – in Greek society [...] The hybristic person enjoys humiliating others. He derives pleasure not merely from seeing other people being ashamed, but from making them feel ashamed and from their knowledge that he enjoys it. Moreover, the behavior typically takes place before third parties. The hybristic person wants others to know that he can humiliate someone and get away with it (Elster, 1999: 163).

In the following passages, I will discuss both the processes of guilt-induction, shame-induction and shaming on the one hand, and the social emotions of guilt and shame on the other. Briefly stated, the former addresses three verbs, whereas the latter addresses two nouns. Regarding the notion of shame for example, the distinction between the verb and the noun – i.e. between "shaming" and "shame" – was debated by Russell (1998). He discusses Braithwaite's *shaming* in contrast with Elias' notion of *shame* (see also Elias, 1994). The same difference is also made evident in the study of Hosser, Windzio and Greve (2008) on guilt and shame as predictors of recidivism. In this case the authors contrast their usage of the notions of guilt and shame – i.e. a psychological perspective of guilt and shame as "moral emotions" – with Braithwaite's usage of the notion of shame not as an emotion but as a "collective attitude" towards the offender.

Mainly, guilt-induction, shame-induction and shaming are activities to which the offender of a social norm or of a standard behavior is subject, whereas shame and guilt are social emotions. Furthermore, one can hardly point to any theoretical findings stating that guilt-induction, shame-induction and shaming invariably result in the induction of feelings of guilt and shame (or vice-versa) – as these behaviors might as well induce emotions of anger or indifference. By the same token, feelings of guilt and shame are not invariably effected by guilt-induction, shame-induction and shaming.

On the basis of the literature review, one could operate with a distinction between guilt-induction and shame-induction *processes* on the one hand, and guilt-induction and shame-induction *events* on the other. With respect to the former, the name of Braithwaite and his theory of social (and state) control by way of reintegrative shaming should be mentioned. While, in connection with the latter, the discussion is expected to draw on shameful and "guiltful" – i.e. shame-inducing and guilt-inducing – events. This topic was touched upon by Tangney (1995) and by van Stokkom (2002).

Until a future enfranchisement of the notion of "guilting" in the theoretical literature on the topic, we are but left to deal solely with the notion of guilt-induction. However, with respect to shaming, a possibility exists to employ both the notion of *shaming*, as Braithwaite (1992) did, and that of *shame-induction,* used for example by Tangney (1995) and (to a certain extent) by van Stokkom (2002). Although it has not been debated yet – at least not to the best of my knowledge – I can only assume that there is also room for differentiating between *shame-induction* and *shaming*, at least to the extent that shame-induction seems to be one step ahead in inducing the emotion of shame. As an argument in my defense, I would point to the appearance of the notion, "shame-inducing event". Taking the discussion further, we might also wonder about would-be distinctions – if there are any – between shaming and guilting on the one hand, and between inducing shame and inducing guilt on the other. But then again, both Elster (1999: 327) and van Stokkom (2002: 352) argued convincingly that shaming is not a self-fulfilling prophecy.

This discussion exceeds the scope of the present study; I rather seek to make an introduction into the processes of guilt-induction, shame-induction and shaming. For this purpose, it is noteworthy to recall that Braithwaite in *Crime, Shame and Reintegration*[19] (1992: 58) made a connection between shaming and a specific case of what I refer to as bullying and/or mobbing – see part IV – *The Ritualization of Party Moots during the Ceauşescu Regime*. Braithwaite reports of a practice of Cuban and Chinese courts, where "ordinary citizens verbally denounce wrongdoing as part of the trial process". Rephrasing Braithwaite, this could be depicted as a "culturally specific" modality of shaming, although at this point he does not specify whether we are dealing with a case of reintegrative or disintegrative shaming. Still, it also might be that this is a matter of nuances and of excesses. After all, later on in his book he makes reference to people's courts as "romantic and potentially oppressive notions" (Braithwaite, 1992: 180).

I will proceed with Braithwaite's notions of guilt induction and shaming. He primarily operates with the notion of shaming, rather than shame-induction. Furthermore, he is much less concerned with drawing a strict line between guilt-induction and shaming in his work, as he considers them as more or less two sides of the same coin; the coin being "criticism by other people" who have moral claims against the offender (Braithwaite, 1992: 57; for discussion on guilt and shame in Braithwaite see Botchkovar and Tittle, 2008). Additionally, we could regard Braithwaite's concern with the occurrence of the process of shaming in the restorative justice conferences as being the reason why he frames the process of shaming as part of guilt-induction and not the other way around. The author's line of argument goes as follows:

> Developmental psychologists sometimes like to make distinctions between socialization by shaming and by guilt induction [...] Shaming, according to this distinction, follows transgressions with expressions of the lower esteem the offense has produced in the eyes of external referents like parents and neighbors; guilt-induction responds to transgressions with admonitions concerning how remorseful the child should feel within herself for perpetrating such an evil act. The distinction is rather too fine for our theoretical purposes because "guilt-induction" always implies shaming by the person(s) inducing the guilt and because, as we will argue later, in broader societal terms guilt is only made possible by cultural processes of shaming.

---

19   This book advanced restorative justice conferences as supplementary processes in the current criminal justice system. Thereupon, the Australian National University unfolded the Reintegrative Shaming Experiments (RISE) (Gavrielides, 2008: 167-168).

> For our purposes, to induce guilt and to shame are inextricably part of the same
> social process [...] But you cannot *induce* guilt without implying criticism by others.
> In other words, from the perspective of the offender, guilt and shame may be distin-
> guishable, but guilt *induction* and sham*ing* are both criticism by others. Equally, the
> old distinction between shame and guilt cultures has no place in my theoretical
> framework because the consciences which cause us guilt are, according to the theo-
> ry, formed by shaming in the culture (Braithwaite, 1992: 57).

I quote Braithwaite at length because the excerpt provides a good illustration of
the elective affinities that came into view in the field of the sociology of
emotions with respect to the emotions of shame and guilt. For example, van
Stokkom (2002: 348) distinguishes between so-called *shame-theorists* and *guilt-
theorists*. Accordingly, shame theorists are displeased with the Western prejudice against shame and the preference for the social emotion of guilt. Guilt-
theorists try to prove that guilt is the moral emotion that should replace shame in
the field of restorative justice conferences. More explicitly, they argue that in
comparison to shame, guilt serves a more adaptive function and that for this
reason it should be assigned to the social work that usually has been entrusted to
the social emotion of shame (van Stokkom, 2002: 348).

Returning to the cited fragment, Braithwaite (1992: 57) seems to claim that
any process of guilt-induction involves shaming. And that although he shortly
afterwards says that these are "inextricably part of the same social process" – i.e.
criticism – one could hardly uphold that there is no prejudice working against
guilt-induction. After all, Braithwaite seems unhindered in stating that, as in the
case of shame, the feeling of guilt is also induced by "cultural processes of
shaming". In other words, a clear picture does not emerge from his work, as to
whether guilt-induction and shaming are *forms* of criticism by others, or if they
are purely and solely this criticism. A first reading would suggest that shaming
is a typical criticism by others, and that – depending on certain circumstances –
it can induce either shame or guilt. But as stated, the text is rather unclear with
respect to this matter. One would find it difficult to raise objections, though,
given that this is a line of inquiry that Braithwaite does not want to follow, being
instead more concerned with the distinction between integrative and disintegrative shaming rather than between guilt-induction and shaming.

Still, Braithwaite's choice of the notion *shaming* did not prove so unfortunate after all. Although contested and debated from several angles, the theory of
social control by the way of reintegrative shaming managed to land on its feet.
The notable retouches that were brought – I have in mind especially the field of
the so-called "guilt-theorists" – concerned the replacement of the social emotion
of shame with those of guilt and remorse. It has also been admitted that in the
course of the restorative justice conferences, these latter emotions do often occur

– and that one should further encourage them to appear – not as a result of the processes of shame-induction and guilt-induction, or better stated: not as a result of shaming and guilting as such. van Stockkom (2002: 352) even points to theoretical findings which argue that the notion of shaming should be applied to Braithwaite's notion of "stigmatizing shaming" – specifically of the type which is disintegrative – and that there are reasons to doubt whether shaming is the engine driving the restorative justice conferences.

To recapitulate, the theory of reintegrative shaming would still provide a useful algorithm if it is rid of the notion of shaming, and if the key to these conferences is not looked for in what kind of processes induce one emotion or another, but in the emotions that actually arise. To put it more simply, this implies that the focus is not anymore on the processes of inducing certain emotions but on the emotions themselves. Additionally, there is also non-negligible empirical evidence pointing to the fact that the appearance of feelings of guilt and remorse is much more efficient in inhibiting the relapse of crime than is (the appearance of) shame. Yet, one could also argue that except for a recommendation for the softening of the parameters of the theory of reintegrative shaming (focus on guilt-induction and maybe remorse-induction instead of shame-induction), these theories fail to correspondingly address the processes which induce these emotions. What is more, Braithwaite's notion of reintegrative shaming recalls to such an extent that of guilt (as it is conceptualized by guilt theorists) that one might wonder whether his distinction between stigmatizing shame and reintegrative shame does not overlap at certain points with the differentiation guilt theorists make between shame and guilt.

I would further argue that a considerable amount of the criticism regarding the theory of reintegrative shaming was due to the fact that Braithwaite's initial theory overestimated the process of shaming, which in fact he elevated to the level of shame-induction without making a clear distinction between the two. Even in the above quotation, Braithwaite does not discuss the equation *shaming–guilting*, rather *shaming–guilt-induction*. In their turn, the so-called guilt theorists reacted to Braithwaite's theory with notions such as guilt-induction (which allegedly appeals to responsibility and is more integrative) and shame-induction (which is expected to have more negative effects) without taking notice of the fact that the issue of guilting and "remorsing" are still unresolved. Braithwaite's theory holds the considerable advantage of discussing the processes of disintegrative and reintegrative shaming, and it is expected to open debate on other processes such as, for example, *guilting* and *remorsing*. According to van Stokkom (2002: 355), New Zealand's restorative justice conferences were found to not appeal to the process of shaming. And hence "as [Allison] Morris states [...] one wishes he had termed his theory 'reintegrative remorse'". Yet, if all of the above pertains, there are reasons to expect inquiries into the would-be processes of guilting and "remorsing" on the one hand, and of guilt-induction and "remorse-induction" on the other. What is more, I believe it is just a matter of time until we witness a conceptual refinement of shaming–guilting and shame-induction–guilt-induction respectively.

Before opening the discussion regarding the applications of the reintegrative shaming theory to other fields, I would like to present Braithwaite's response to issues raised by his critics. Braithwaite – one might speculate – indirectly provides his answer in an article written with Harris, Walgrave and Braithwaite: *Emotional Dynamics in Restorative Conferences* (2004). In a few words, I would signal a more determined focus on the notion of shaming and on the definition of this notion in terms of criticism by others. Notably, it is specified that the process of shaming – i.e. criticism – does not necessarily have to target the infliction of shame and guilt. Hence it is a definition which is closer to the process of criticism (which could be even merged in an acceptable way with empathy) than to that of shame and guilt induction respectively. Moreover, the authors integrate the emotions of guilt and remorse in the amalgam of emotions that is affected by the process of shaming. The novelty of the article is in the introduction of the notion of *shame-guilt*. Seemingly, this is a compromise effected subsequent to a careful evaluation of the dominant criteria of differentiation between the two emotions.

In the following analysis, I will return to the societal implications of the theory of reintegrative shaming not confined solely to the circle of the restorative justice conferences. As a theory of social control, its elements are useful in shedding light on mechanisms that surface in other areas – although still connected, to a certain degree. Notable in this respect, is the study of Trevaskes (2004) on expressive sentencing in trials and "mass sentencing rallies" in Chinese criminal courts. According to the author, the purpose of this anti-crime campaign is to startle would-be criminals and to educate the public (Trevaskes, 2004: 6). These campaigns – which are considered to be the result of a mass-line legal culture developed over fifty years of socialist rule in China – implied the return to the active practice of open trials and the abandonment of closed trials and kangaroo courts in the post-1978 period (Trevaskes, 2004: 9-10). The trials became what Trevaskes – following Lin Zhun (former vice-president of the Supreme People's Court) – calls "classrooms for law propaganda". What is more, they unfold as "a shaming ritual which symbolically reflects the relationships between the state, the criminal and the masses" (Trevaskes, 2004: 15)[20].

---

20   "As a shaming ritual, the rally is presented in a format that emphasizes the emotive acts
       of public humiliation and moral indignation. Primarily a deterrence and educative

In addition to Trevaskes, an interesting contribution to the understanding of the Chinese case is made by Chen (2002) in the study of applications of the labeling theory and the reintegrative shaming theory to the case study of social control in this country. The analysis of the type of social control which is prevalent in China has led him to conclude that it is more appropriate to address this phenomenon in terms of reintegrative shaming than to use the labeling perspective.

In comparison with the guilt theorists cited above, these two articles create room for the discussion of Braithwaite's reintegrative shaming theory with respect to the process of shaming and not in connection to the emotions that are affected by this or by any other process (shame, guilt, remorse etc.). To recall van Stokkom (2002: 355) quoting Allison Morris: "one wishes he had termed his theory 'reintegrative remorse'" – i.e. not "reintegrative remorsing theory" but "reintegrative remorse". The focus in both articles is on the behavior of *shaming* – but this could also be *guilting* or even *remorsing* for that matter. They provide a discussion as to why, at the societal level, certain behaviors are admitted, or even encouraged. From this angle, we could view the guilt theorists as having an agenda which tries to contain the behavior of shaming during the restorative justice conferences.

Returning to the Chinese case, Trevaskes (2004) makes the point that the purpose of shaming is not primarily to induce shame in the offenders, but to substantiate the power of the court and to educate the masses. Hence, regarding both restorative justice conferences and the social control of society at large, I would conclude that there is an issue pertaining to the encouragement of certain attitudes regarding specific violations and an issue of the restraint of others.

The relevance of these Chinese case-studies – to employ the Mertonian (1968) distinction – rests in drawing attention to the importance of the *latent functions* of reintegrative shaming, and not just to those which are *manifest* (i.e. the scope of reintegration as such). At the most general level of discussion, the latent functions of reintegrative shaming would be to show that the norm audience is able to orchestrate such rituals. In case of rituals of reintegrative

---

mechanism used during anti-crime campaigns, the main messages of the rally are first, that the state is able to effectively control crime and second, that crime does not pay. Messages of general deterrence and public condemnation of crime, intended to reach criminals and would-be criminals in the audience, are designed to frighten and to present a warning to those who commit crimes that they will be captured, prosecuted, publicly humiliated, and (in many cases) executed. To the law-abiding citizen present in the audience, the act of sentencing and public shaming is intended to fulfill the retribution function of the law as well as carrying a message of reassurance that social order is safe in the hands of the judicial organs" (Trevaskes, 2004: 14).

shaming following episodes of scandal, these provide legitimacy and reproduce the existing normative order.

The next monograph that I believe to be relevant for discussing reintegrative shaming in relation to scandal is Lu, Zhang and Miethe's (2002) analysis of interdependency, communitarianism and reintegrative shaming in China. Interestingly, these authors were less concerned with the general hypothesis of reintegrative shaming – that is, to what extent reintegrative shaming leads to a reduction in the likelihood of reoffending. Instead, they tested the "intermediate prediction" according to which "interdependency and communitarianism enhance reintegrative shaming" (Lu, Zhang and Miethe, 2002: 190). The results of their survey of residents in contemporary China indicate that the impact of interdependency on reintegrative shaming is context dependent. As such, if it comes to family, interdependency shows no relationship to shaming practice; but in the neighborhood, interdependency is a strong determinant of reintegrative shaming. Without going into details accounting for this particular state of affairs, it suffices here to say that this study raises an important question into the kind of interdependency and social relations that favor the support for reintegrative shaming practices. Furthermore, it offers a sequel – and to a certain extent also a possible reformulation – to reintegrative shaming theory by showing that if interdependency favors reintegrative shaming practices, and if reintegrative shaming techniques reduce the likelihood of reoffending, then – by implication – "higher compliance to societal rules may be achieved through communal efforts to build and consolidate interdependent relationships" (Lu, Zhang and Miethe, 2002: 192).

The relationship between interdependency and reintegrative shaming – or shaming for that matter – might pose an interesting puzzle in the context of scandals as well. Wedel's (2009) observations regarding the occurrence of scandal with no sanctions and the ability of the so-called shadow elite to escape the consequences of shaming in the aftermath of scandal show that overlapping and mixed interdependencies of actors in various social and professional networks offers them the possibility to escape the rituals of shaming. Although the intuition regarding the way overlapping and mixed interdependency influences shaming practices is still under-theorized, dispersed studies in the theory of organizations and public policy indicate the hypothesis that membership in distinct networks affects the norm offender's response to shaming and might leave the norm audiences of a certain social network or group frustrated because the shaming rituals did not come full circle.

With regard to scandals occurring during communism, a study of the relationship between interdependency, outburst of scandal and (following) shaming practices should investigate variations according to status characteristics, perception of status enhancement in communist society, membership in the communist party, possibilities for professional and career development within and outside the officially sanctioned opportunities etc. Furthermore, the study of interdependency should be undertaken in the following domains: regional and local levels of party membership, formal and informal institutional framework, regional and local political activism and trade unionism culture, geographical location, environmental NGOs and church organizations (both inside and outside the country under analysis), diaspora etc.

Conclusions

This chapter has sought to delineate the theoretical angle guiding the analysis of the dynamics of scandals during the rule of Ceauşescu, within the limits of this book. This perspective is primarily founded on Adut's framing of scandal as the disruptive publicity of transgression, and Nałkowski's and Kurczewski's insights into scandal as a factor of evolution. As I have shown, the study of scandals in communism could be undertaken within the scandal approaches developed in two distinct areas of research: legal anthropology and organizational sociology. I have chosen to proceed with the first. Subsequently, a dramaturgical perspective on shaming practices and reintegrative rituals in scandal (developed in the Turnerian paradigm) was shown to correspond to Braithwaite's reintegrative shaming approach in restorative justice programs. After a review of points of criticism that have been brought to reintegrative shaming theory with regard to the process of shaming and its purported effects, I have tried to highlight those points of the theory that – irrespective of the restorative justice agenda – could be incorporated into scandal theory.

PART II
SCANDAL AND COMMUNISM

Perhaps, the first inquiry which could be raised with respect to the scandals of the Ceauşescu regime is regarding the appropriateness of locating the phenomenon of scandal in a non-democratic setting.

The reason why a symbiosis between scandal and a democratic regime could be regarded more genuine is mainly due to the animation of institutions such as (boundless) public opinion, (free) mass media and social norms based on consensus. According to Thompson (2008: 575-576), in cases when political scandals do appear in authoritarian regimes, they are usually restrained from being blown out of proportion and are confined to the political field. In cases when they spread outside the realm of politics, it usually happens by word of mouth or via underground media sources.

In the opinion of certain authors, the short wait of an instant translation from some institutions to the communist context hampers the chances of the occurrence of real scandals. A fair argument, which – if accepted with no common sense of the situation – might however lead one to consider Central and Eastern Europe under communist rule as completely scandal-free. This seems to be for instance the rationality at work in an interesting study by Esser and Hartung (2004) on political scandals as a reflection of political culture in Germany. The paper provides an analysis of scandals and political culture focused on democratic West Germany and united Germany after 1989. Esser and Hartung attempt to provide insight into the political culture of Germany by reviewing existent and *nonexistent* types of scandals. They present a typology:

1. "scandals formative to the development of political culture";
2. "scandals linked to the particular history of Germany";
3. "scandals that happened elsewhere as well";
4. "scandals missed in Germany" (see Esser and Hartung, 2004).

Discussing the fourth index – i.e. scandals missed in Germany – the authors notice the absence of sexual scandals. This issue is also investigated by Waisbord (2004) with respect to the dynamics of Argentinian scandals. It could be argued, that the distinction between the conclusions of the two studies arises from differences in political culture. In the case of former West Germany and united Germany, the shortage of sexual scandals is attributed to the fact that media coverage of private and intimate spheres are both prohibited by law and considered taboo (Esser and Hartung, 2004: 1064-1065). It is worthy of note that both articles compare the frugal presence of sexual scandals in their country to the much more flamboyant traditions of Britain and the United States. In case of Argentina – without going into too much detail – Waisbord (2004: 1076) points to two possible explanations. The first hypothesis places a strong emphasis on cultural aspects. Accordingly, the puritan soil of Britain and the United States seems more fertile for sexual scandals. Hence, the absence of puritan culture in a Catholic country like Argentina interferes with the advancement of more promiscuous scandals. Another theory – as an alternative, or an addendum – could be taken into consideration. The post-1960 sexual scandals in the United States are collateral to the progression of cultural wars in this country. Thereupon, the absence of cultural wars in Argentina goes hand in hand with the lack of sexual scandals in this country.

Esser and Hartung point to mechanisms and legacies in the dynamics of scandal which arise from the fact that numerous scandals in the democratic West Germany are offspring of its National Socialist past. By the same token, several scandals in the unified Germany are related to the former German Democratic Republic (Esser and Hartung, 2004: 1048). While it might not influence their findings, it is my conviction that the authors are too eager to neglect the possibility of scandal in the democratic West Germany in connection with the German Democratic Republic or vice-versa[21]. Notable (counter)examples in this regard are the 1963 defection of a Stasi officer Ullrich Altmann and the 1979 defection of Werner Stiller. I am quite certain that a researcher would find other examples of diplomatic scandals. Contacts of West German politicians with secret service agencies and the leadership of the German Democratic Republic (or the other way around), human rights scandals, and sports scandals are possibilities that come to mind, absent from Esser and Hartung's inventory.

I stipulate that considering such events one can speak of scandal also in the context of the Communist Bloc. The fact that the institutional taxonomy of the scandals in the communist regimes in Central and Eastern Europe was altered does not imply that these regimes were completely scandal-proof. The regimes' monopoly in counterfeiting scandals or overall features of scandal when staging state-controlled campaigns and show-trials does not refute the existence of phenomena we can describe in terms of scandal. The review of literature on national indexes of scandals and national affinities with certain types of scandal sketches out their development as a process. It also indicates that communist Romania was not only subject to a certain scandal dynamic, but also that the regime had to improvise, invent and mimic mechanisms for dealing with such episodes.

---

21   "In this study, scandals are understood in the sense of being possible only in open and democratic societies with a free press. Because in communist East Germany, scandals simply could not exist (the public sphere and the press were under state control), this analysis concentrates mainly on the events in democratic West Germany and the reunited Germany (since 1989). It will be shown that the roots of important scandals in West Germany can be traced back to National Socialism and important scandals of the united Germany to the communist GDR" (Esser and Hartung, 2004: 1048).

Literature on the topic allows us to speculate that diplomatic and human rights scandals were most discomforting for the Romanian communist regime, as was the scandal (or reactions *in terms* of scandal) to the fertility policy of Ceaușescu's Romania. On this last topic, is interesting to note that when the 1966 Anti-abortion Decree was implemented, Ceaușescu's demographic policy received an overall favorable review in the West. An interesting annotation to Western reactions to Ceaușescu's anti-abortion policy is made by Kligman (2000: 65) when she briefly discusses the "politics of abortion during the cold war" [*sic*] [*author's translation*]. According to the author, at the passing of the Anti-abortion Decree in 1966, the only country overtly manifesting its discontent was the Soviet Union, whereas in the West the Decree almost passed unnoticed (Kligman, 2000: 65). Later on, the fertility policy was welcomed as part of the same package of initiatives depicting Ceaușescu as a new type of communist leader: anti-Soviet and anti-colonialist (anti-imperialist). Reportedly, Ceaușescu presented the issue of fertility control as closely connected to the envisaged strategies of development and the right to auto-determination (Kligman, 2000: 127). The success story was, however, one which was less and less believed. By the mid 1980s, the Western powers were ferociously condemning the policy. In conclusion – as this case study indicates – scandal, both as an event and as a process, is politically blind and easy to manipulate.

Regarding scandal in communist Romania, it has to be stated that there had also been cases that worked to the advantage of the state. Romania's declaration of its right for self-determination in 1964 and Ceaușescu's condemnation of the Soviet-led invasion of Czechoslovakia in 1968 can be examples of such scandals. One has to note though, that in these specific cases Romanian society played the role of a kibitzer rather than a norm audience. In the long run, still – the roles of norm audience, kibitzer audience and norm offender are interchangeable. For example, in the instances of human rights scandals, the norm audience was the Romanian society, whereas the kibitzer audience was composed of external observers.

The foregoing literature review brought us to Adut's (2005; 2008) definition of these events in terms of the "disruptive publicity of transgression". The employment of this perspective in the analysis of several scandals over mass protests which have erupted during Ceaușescu's regime places the "original sin" of the sequence of scandals in the public demonstrations of the "working people". In this way the scandal perspective perceives scandal as an agent structuring a progression of reactions, and not as a (scandalous) behavior that was reacted to in the first place. To make the distinction more clear: in the former case the element of publicity is inevitable for understanding the reaction of the norm audience (and also the fact that the publicity of the transgression summons the norm audience into reacting) and for the contamination of third parties. While for the latter case, the publicity of the transgression is of secondary importance (or is self-evident), as what is important here is the gravity of the conduct that was reacted to, and not the fact that a certain conduct (which was going on for some time) was suddenly made public and, thus, that triggered reaction.

Such an understanding of scandal (that focuses on the threshold of public acceptance of transgressive and deviant behaviors, and less on their sudden publicity – in the sense that the publicity is regarded as implicit, not as secondary) is formulated by Kurczewski (2003: 163) – see also the discussion in section I.3 – *The "Anthropological Essence" of Scandal.*

For the study of mass protests during communist regimes, the distinction between the two types of scandal perspectives becomes more clear when differentiating between scandals over mass protests on the one hand (*scandals as publicity*), and scandals triggering mass protests on the other (*scandals as conduct*). Yet, the distinction should not be essentialized, given that the latter type is usually triggered by the former. The category of scandal as publicity – over mass protests – pertains to those phenomena when the first-order transgression is the public manifestation of people's dissatisfaction and resentment. In this case the norm audience is the communist authorities. The grouping of scandals as conduct – over mass protests – consists of behaviors, events, or decisions which have provoked the mass protests. Here, the norm audience is the people.

In order to illustrate this type of occurrence, the Polish experience of scandals triggering mass protests is particularly interesting for the reason that it reveals the engagement in the dynamics of scandals of a non-human actor: *meat.* The non-human character of meat intersects the scandal perspective advanced in this book with *actor-network theory.* Given that it is not the purpose of this study to bring a contribution in this field of research, it suffices to say that the actor-network theory (sociology of translation) is appealing for the reason that it allows the introduction of non-human actors in the analyses. As such, Callon (1986) describes and interprets the failure of three marine biologists to develop a successful conservation strategy for the scallops of St. Brieuc. Callon traces the mechanisms by which the three biologists try to build up and maintain a network of relationships, by which they define the problem of the actors and establish who these actors are and what their roles are.

A similar endeavour might be depicted in the case of meat, or more generally of the food market in communist Poland. According to Kurczewski:

> the political history of People's Republic of Poland is also a history of control over supply of meat to Polish tables (Kurczewski, 1993).

The communist regime introduced a redistribution of food instead of allowing the market to do so. The economists were reticent in front of social pressures for implementing the rationing of meat for the reason that this might lead to a revival of market practices (Kurczewski, 1993: 310). Furthermore, the communist authorities resisted the measure as they perceived it as a tool of social control over state institutions and of advancing legitimate demands. For the people, food and more particularly meat rationing in the 1980s represented a "collective right to just distribution as enacted by the people against the Party State, based upon collectivist doctrine" (Kurczewski, 1993: 296). The battle for strategies of meat redistribution is extensively documented in Kurczewski's book – *The Resurrection of Rights in Poland* (1993, see also Kurczewski, 2004). The main thesis advanced in the chapter on *Self-Limited Freedom of Market: Food Rationing*, is that although it would be certainly an overstatement to catalogue the events of the 1970's as food riots, the increase in food prices (in the background of increasing social aspirations) acted as a catalytic agent in the outbreak of the mass protests. If engaging the previously discussed scandal perspective, the hypothesis might be also understood in these terms: *increase in food prices acted as scandals as conduct*. Complicating things even more, if employing elements of actor-network theory in analysis, the deciphering of the dynamics of scandal over the increase in food prices should list meat – a non-human actor – along with the norm offender, the norm audience, and the kibitzer audience as actors in the analysis. And this is for the reason that the dynamics of scandals over mass protests emerge as a part of the battle between different actors for implementing a distribution strategy of meat during the communist regime in Poland.

The listing of meat as the main actor in the analysis of the dynamics of scandals – and not that of food – is due to the fact that meat consumption is a generic indicator of the possibilities one has to access food in a given society (see Kurczewski, 1993: 300).

The following sub-chapter will illustrate certain dynamics of scandals in communist Romania. Its purpose is to exemplify a model of analysis in terms of norm audience, kibitzer audience, first- and second-order transgressions, externalities, etc. The review of the case studies concentrates on the chain of reaction to scandals and it focuses exclusively on the logic of the contamination of third parties. This fact enables a thorough exposure of the course of contamination – that is of *scandal as publicity* –, yet leaves us vulnerable when depicting the mechanism of the eruption of several scandals in communist countries – that is, of *scandal as conduct*.

1. The Dynamics of Scandal during the Ceauşescu Regime

Compared to the foregoing chapter, the following part assumes a more down-to-earth approach. Its purpose is to draw up a list of scandals in communist Romania. The typology is based on literature on the topic of communism and relevant press items. The main methodology utilized was the research of historical accounts, press releases and internet sources. There is, however, a limit to this endeavor, as historical and sociological research of those matters was given a green light only two decades ago. The problem lies not as much in the relatively brief time-frame, as in the fact that the obstacles on the path of research were only partly removed. As matters currently stand, a lot of energy is spent not on building a certain casuistry of social processes and phenomena of the communist times, but rather on facilitating access to resources – such as the communist and *Securitate*[22] archives.

This fact notwithstanding, there is literature dealing with what can be viewed as scandals, or with *scandal-like dynamics* regulating events of a seemingly different nature. Among the events that incorporate dynamics of scandal, Adut, in his study, named:

> religious heresies, publicity stunts, political purges, artistic provocations and contro-versies, acts of civil disobedience, causes célèbres, electoral campaigns, moral cru-sades, Goffmanesque interactional disturbances, and whistle-blowing incidents (Adut, 2005: 244).

In the foregoing sub-chapter, I have indicated that an exhaustive inquiry into the dynamics of scandal in a socialist society should necessary account for the phenomenon of interdependency in several domains such as: regional and local levels of party membership, formal and informal institutional framework, regional and local political activism and trade unionism culture, geographical location, environmental NGOs and church organizations (both inside and outside the country under analysis), diaspora, etc. As such a comprehensive undertaking falls outside the purposes of this paper, I would at this point make reference only to some structural elements regarding the party membership. This is particularly important because it indicates that the level of interdependency in this domain was quite high.

According to Stoica (2005; 2006b), the Romanian Communist Party (R.C.P.) was proportionally the largest Communist Party in Central and Eastern Europe. Stoica (2005: 686) estimates that up to 33 percent of Romania's employed population were members of the party. His studies provide a compre-

---

22 *Securitate* was the State Security Department (secret service) of Communist Romania.

hensive analysis of the personnel policies of the R.C.P. Briefly stated, the conclusions are the following:
- women were underrepresented within the ranks of both party members and party functionaries;
- "some ethnic 'others'" such as Germans, Gypsies, Russians, Ukrainians, Turks and Tatars were disfavored in the application process;
- peasants were considered to posses the "proper" social background;
- while enjoying a significant presence within the ranks of the party, the category of well-educated individuals had less access to higher party ranks. Regarding this issue, Stoica (2006b) recalls Vlad Georgescu's observation that in the late 1970s and in the 1980s, Romania was ruled by the least educated elite in its modern history.

Furthermore, although not completely immune to political dissidence – as already mentioned – the communist regime in Romania managed to prevent attempts to organize a dissidence movement at the level of the society. As a matter of fact, at least the mid-1960s did witness bulky waves of popularity for the regime in response to its international initiatives which appeared to forecast a destiny for the Socialist Republic of Romania apart from the Soviet Union. The Plenary of the Central Committee of the Romanian Workers' Party (April 15-22, 1964) adopted a declaration that reproved the Soviet claim for leadership of the communist international movement (Jowitt, 1970). The historiography of Romanian communism usually traces the political antipathy between the Soviet Union and the Popular Republic of Romania back to this point. After 1965, the Popular Republic of Romania became the Socialist Republic of Romania. On October 21, 1964, Gheorghe Gheorghiu-Dej[23] requested that the KGB – through the Soviet ambassador in Bucharest – withdraw its advisers from the country. The request was fulfilled in December of that same year.

As a result of a succession crisis after the death of Gheorghe Gheorghiu-Dej in early February 1965, Ceauşescu[24] became the first secretary of the Central Committee of the Romanian Workers' Party (Betea, 2001a; Betea, 2001b) and – slowly but surely – set out to seize political power in the country (Câmpeanu,

---

23   Gheorghe Gheorghiu-Dej (1901-1965) – general secretary of the C.C. of the Romanian Communist Party [R.C.P.]/Romanian Workers' Party [R.W.P.] from October 21, 1945 until April 19, 1954; first secretary of the C.C. of the R.W.P. from October 1, 1955 until March 19, 1965; President of the State Council from March 25, 1961 until March 19, 1965 (C.N.S.A.S., 2004: 291-292).

24   Nicolae Ceauşescu (1918-1989) – prime secretary of the C.C. of the R.W.P. after Gheorghe Gheorghiu Dej's death in 1965; President of the Socialist Republic of Romania from March 29, 1974 until December 22, 1989 (C.N.S.A.S., 2004: 140-142).

2002; Tismăneanu, 2003). The 1965 Constitution proclaimed the Socialist Republic of Romania and stipulated the principle of "socialist legality". In a few years' time, Romania initiated and maintained relations with countries such as Israel (with which it did not break off diplomatic relations in 1967), and the Federal Republic of Germany.

It can be stated that communism in Romania was baptized anew on two occasions in 1968. In April the Plenary of the Central Committee (C.C.) of the Romanian Communist Party (R.C.P.) posthumously rehabilitated Lucreţiu Pătrăşcanu[25]. This communist politician and leading member of the party (also a lawyer, sociologist and economist) was imprisoned in 1948 as a "national deviationist" and friend to war criminals. He was ultimately executed in 1954 (Betea, 2006). The same Plenary expelled Alexandru Drăghici – the Minister of the Interior during the reign of Gheorghiu-Dej – from the party. Both acts were meant to symbolically condemn the past abuses of the regime (Dennis Deletant in Oprea, 2002: 35-39; Neagoe-Pleşa and Pleşa in Dobre, Neagoe-Pleşa and Pleşa, 2006: IX-X). The condemnation of the Warsaw Pact invasion of Czechoslovakia later the same year was also perceived as such a renewing event.

Thus, Romanian society in the late 1960s did exhibit a certain enthusiasm for its communist state. However, this sentiment started to fade in the following decade. By the summer of 1989, Ceauşescu, vividly enjoying the personality cult built around him, managed – at the expense of the society – to fully pay off the foreign debt.

Except for the political longevity of the communist dictator, another noteworthy element of the communist regime in Romania is the promotion of his wife – Elena Ceauşescu[26] – and other members of his family to high echelons of power. Eventually, the regime collapsed after a series of violent events which started in Timişoara in December 1989. On December 25, 1989 Ceauşescu and his wife were sentenced to death by a military court and executed by a firing squad.

The scandal-relevant elements of the Ceauşescu period are the low frequency of scandals directly in contestation of the political regime at the level of the society and their correlatively high intensity. What also stands out, at least as far as the most notorious mass political protest is concerned – the 1987 Braşov revolt, for example –, is the predominance of reintegrative shaming rituals of the norm

---

25   Lucreţiu Pătrăşcanu (1900-1954) – Minister of Justice from March 6, 1945 until
        February 24, 1948 (C.N.S.A.S., 2004: 456-457).

26   Elena Ceauşescu (1919-1989) – member of the Political Executive Committee of the
        C.C. of the R.C.P. from November 28, 1974 until December 22, 1989. Member of the
        Permanent Bureau of the Political Executive Committee of the C.C. of the R.C.P. from
        January 26, 1977 until December 22, 1989 (C.N.S.A.S., 2004: 138-139).

offenders (party officials and protesters alike). Also worthy of note is that within the contemporary mainstream and amateur Romanian historical discourse, the absence or occurrence of political protest (i.e. of "spontaneous changes" – to use Rychard's (1993) terminology) is retrospectively used to account for the repressive character of the communist regime in question (see discussion in *Introduction*). In my interpretation – among other elements – the high intensity of scandals over mass protests that have occurred during communism has largely benefited and supported the proliferation and reproduction of this historical discourse.

Below, I list occurrences of such phenomena in communist Romania and classify them according to the role played by the regime, as well as first- and second-order transgressions.

Romanian communist authorities	First-order transgressions	Second-order transgressions
Norm audience	1. scandals over mass protests 2. scandals over public criticism of Ceauşescu 3. diplomatic scandals 4. scandals over the defection of intelligence officials 5. scandals over the defection of sportsmen	1. scandals over deficiencies of party control – mass protests
Kibitzer audience	1. scandals over the reaction to first-order transgressions in the Communist Bloc	1. scandals over the reaction to second-order transgressions in the Communist Bloc
Norm offender	1. human rights scandals 2. Radio Free Europe scandals 3. sports scandals 4. others	1. human rights scandals

Table 2

It goes without saying that the above table (2) is neither complete, nor the only one that can be drawn up. I claim, however that it is analytical enough for the purposes of this study. I focus my analysis exclusively on the mechanisms discernible in the evolution of scandals, and less on drawing a general profile of the scandal dynamics during the Ceauşescu regime. My research is primarily concerned with the representative character of *convergence, contamination, provocation* and *scandal as a factor of evolution* in the case studies under review. The interest in drawing a picture of the scandal dynamics is only minor. Thus, specific case studies are illustrative for the interplay of the mechanisms of scandal. What could be stated is that, indeed, scandals over mass protests have been a precarious occurrence. And to the understanding of this occurrence, this book is intended to bring its contribution.

On a side note, it should be added that all of the examples enjoyed – and still do enjoy – a high status of notoriety in Romania. One could say, however, that there is a need for elaboration via an addendum table that would comprise a typology of incipient affairs and scandals which are either less publicized, or even forgotten nowadays. By the same token, there also ought to be a table displaying a typology of state campaigns and show-trials that the communist state tried to misrepresent as real scandals at that time.

In the following table (3) I assign concrete examples to the above typology.

Romanian communist authorities	First-order transgressions	Second-order transgressions
Norm audience	1. – the 1977 Jiu Valley strike – the 1981 Motru strike – the 1987 Braşov revolt – the Banat Action Group (1972-1975) – the 1977 Caransebeş affair 2. – the 1977 Paul Goma letter – the 1978 Károly Király letters – the 1979 overt criticism of Ceauşescu by Constantin Pârvulescu – the XIIth Congress 3. – scandals over the defection of members of the diplomatic corpus – scandals over accusations of espionage, persona non grata declarations 4. – the 1969 defection of Dan Iacobescu – the 1978 defection of Ion Mihai Pacepa 5. – the 1981 defection of Marcel Răducanu – the 1984 defection of Béla and Márta (Martha) Károlyi and Géza	1. – the castigation of party leaders and activists – Jiu Valley, 1977 – the castigation of party leaders and activists – Braşov, 1987

	Pozsár – the 1988 defection of Miodrag Belodedici – the 1989 defection of Nadia Comăneci	
Kibitzer audience	1. – the reaction of Ceauşescu to the Warsaw Pact invasion of Czechoslovakia, 1968	1. – the sports scandal in Los Angeles, 1984
Norm offender	1. – scandals over individual protests (cases of individual dissidents) – scandals over mass protests – scandals over the use of the army as a labor force 2. – the attack on Emil Georgescu – the attack on Radio Free Europe in Munich, 1981 3. – the sports scandal in Prague, 1977 4. – scandals over Ceauşescu's policy of fertility – scandals over Ceauşescu's *systematization* – the Transcendental Meditation affair [*Afacerea Meditaţia Transcendentală*][27]	1. – scandals over individual protests (cases of individual dissidents) – the Goma affair – scandals over mass protests

Table 3

In my interpretation, each of these scandals can be examined in terms of norm offender, norm audience, kibitzer audience, externalities (contamination and provocation) and scandal as a factor of evolution.

I now present in some detail several of the above cases. The purpose of this overview is to give a glimpse of the broader field of scandals and affairs in communist Romania. This discussion brings us closer to the main subject of the book – the reaction of communist authorities to scandals over mass protests during the rule of Ceauşescu. However, given its purpose, the analysis is relatively asymmetrical and deals in more detail with the cases in which the Romanian communist authorities constituted the norm audience.

---

27   For a discussion of this episode see Jela, Strat and Albu (2004).

First-Order Transgressions

Norm Audience: Romanian Communist Authorities

1. Scandals over Mass Protests

– The 1977 Jiu Valley Strike and the 1987 Braşov Revolt

Before discussing these two events in terms of scandal, I will briefly present their aftermath. In the case of the 1977 Jiu Valley strike, waves of people sent "from the center" just kept on coming to the Valley. They were to establish "order and discipline" (C.N. in Barbu and Chirvasă, 1997: 55). A punctual purge took place at the political and administrative level – almost all of the first secretaries of the mines were replaced. Waves of dismissals shook even the highest echelons of power (C.N. in Barbu and Chirvasă, 1997: 38, 49). However, from the government, only the then Minister of Mines was incriminated (*** in Barbu and Chirvasă, 1997: 91). Furthermore, fifteen miners were charged with "offenses against good morals and turmoil of public order" [*ultraj contra bunelor moravuri şi tulburarea liniştii publice*] (interview I.V., 2006). The sentences ranged between two and five years of prison to be carried out by labor in other socialist units [*executarea pedepselor aplicate prin muncă corecţională în alte unităţi socialiste, prin efectuarea unor activităţi productive*]. A wave of forced relocation also followed (Spiridon, 2008: 240-241; Barbu and Chirvasă, 1997: 136-176; interview P.P., 2006).

Following the 1987 Braşov revolt, two weeks of interrogations singled out sixty-one individuals to face the charges of "offenses against good morals and turmoil of public order" [*ultraj contra bunelor moravuri şi tulburarea liniştii publice*]. Simultaneously, purges were carried out in the administrative and police apparatus of the city (Spiridon, 2008: 241-242; Oprea and Olaru, 2002: 221-240).

According to tables (2) and (3), these two scandals find their place in three distinct categories. In both cases, we are dealing with at least two directions in the development of the original scandal. One dimension is inside the country, whereas the second one can be located outside. Both of these progressions of externalities can be regarded as second-order transgressions. The first chain reaction, for example – the internal – determined the sequences of investigation and castigation of party leaders and activists. Thus, the first-order transgression – namely that of the protesters – also exposed serious deficiencies within the local party community. Therefore, the first-order and second-order transgressions maintain the same norm audience – i.e. the Romanian communist authorities. In comparison, in the parallel progression of the original scandal – the external – the dynamics of the scandal transformed the status of the Romanian state authorities from offended norm audience to norm offender. Briefly stated, the way the communist regime reacted to mass protests inside the country aroused the disapproval of several kibitzer audiences on the outside. These audiences tried to mobilize and transform themselves in order for them to constitute a norm-audience in the second-order transgression.

As noted in the *Introduction*, convergence plays an important role in the dynamics of scandal. The concept, derived from the theory of moral panic, denotes the process of the "linking of the specific issue to others by labelling, either explicitly or implicitly" (Hall and Jefferson, 1991: 78). In this case, convergence links mass protest to hooligan behavior.

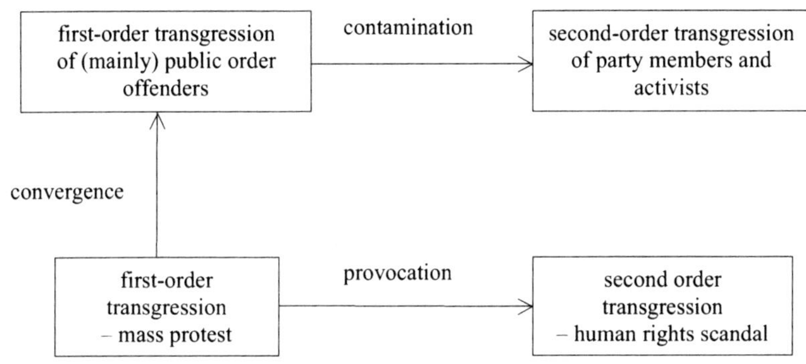

Scheme 1

– The 1981 Motru Strike

Due to its informal designation – the *bread strike* (or the *bread revolt*) [greva pâinii] – the case of the October 1981 mass protest of the Motru miners seems more appropriately addressed using the perspective of *scandal as conduct*, as this was presented in the foregoing section of this chapter. The mass protest was set off after the issuing of Decree no. 313 from October 17, 1981[28] on the rationing of bread. Furthermore, the pattern of repression against the leaders of the strike was similar to the one engaged in the case of Jiu Valley 1977.

---

28   *Decretul nr. 313 din 17 octombrie 1981 privind unele măsuri referitoare la întărirea autoconducerii și autoaprovizionării teritoriale, precum și la asigurarea autoaprovizionării în bune condiții a populației cu pâine, făină și mălai* [Decree no. 313 from October 17, 1981 concerning some measures regarding the strengthening of territorial auto-management and auto-provision, as well as the assurance of auto-provision in proper conditions of population with bread, flour and maize].

The fact that the *bread strike* was triggered by rationing calls for a comparison with the Polish dynamics of mass protests, where food rationing was eventually forced upon the administration by the population subsequent to the outburst of strikes in reaction to the increased food prices throughout the 1970s, and eventually also at the beginning of July 1980. The divergent dynamics point to a differentiation in the way of perceiving the administrative rationing of goods with regard to Romania and Poland during the reign of their respective communist regimes. As such, in the case of the 1981 Motru strike, we might be dealing with what Kurczewski (1993: 302) terms as the "negative definition"[29] of the introduction of rationing. Meanwhile, the Polish dynamics rather point to a perception in terms of a "social contract"[30] of this administrative measure (Kurczewski, 1993: 303). The main difference is not that in the latter case rationing food is considered to be opportune as such, but that it is perceived as less evil in the given social context of food scarcity.

– The Banat Action Group [Aktionsgruppe Banat] (1972-1975)

This was a group of young German language writers affiliated with the Student House of Culture in Timişoara. Among its members, here are some worth remembering: Gerhardt Ortian, William Totok, Richard Wagner, Ernest Wichner, Anton Sterbling, Rolf Bossert, Anton Bohn, Werner Kremm and Johan Lippet. Their works were openly challenging and rejecting the official ideology.

---

29   "Direct administrative rationing of goods, in which we are interested here, is a set of politically determined conditions of entry for an individual consumer into possession of a specific amount of the good in question. If we look into the legal literature on the procedure, the negative definition seems to be the only one at our disposal [...] Socialist legal literature on the issue is shamefully lacking, and those few authors who diverted their attention to this otherwise basic social fact are divided" (Kurczewski, 1993: 302)

30   "Social contracts of this type are usually theoretical constructs of an abstract character, to be presented to students or to clarify a point to the general reader. In the case of food-rationing in Poland which started in 1981 one may, however, point to the reality of such a contract taking place. The introduction of meat-rationing led to the mushrooming of rationing for other items forced upon the administration by participants in the long strike on the Baltic Sea coast in summer 1980 that ended in the signing of an agreement between the government and the Inter-Factory Strike Committee. One should remember again that the strikes in 1980 were started in reaction to the increased meat prices at the beginning of July 1980, in a situation where, due to the developing crisis in the food market, the state had introduced the new system of so-called commercial shops where supposedly better-quality meat was sold for much higher prices, while people were queuing for hours for food" (Kurczewski, 1993: 304).

– The 1977 Caransebeş Affair

This refers to the episode of the arrest of three members of the Caransebeş Baptist Church, in 1977. The intervention of the police came after the church meeting had been interrupted by members because of disagreements concerning sympathies with the Christian Committee for the Defence of Freedom of Religion and Conscience (ALRC) (King, 1981).

2. Scandals over Public Criticism of Ceauşescu

– The 1977 Paul Goma Letter

This episode pertains to the human rights movement initiated by writer Paul Goma. He is one of the most prominent and contested dissident writers of communist Romania. Goma started challenging the political regime by the time he was in high school, and the two years he spent in the Jilava and Gherla prisons (after contesting the Soviet intervention in Hungary in 1956) constitute the subject of some of his best known novels.

His 1977 open letter was read on Radio Free Europe. It called for the respect of human rights by the communist government, and for Romanians to sign Charter 77. As will be documented in the next chapter, this movement seems to have occasioned the first manifestation of discontent in Jiu Valley. As a result, Goma was excluded from the Writers' Union of Romania and was subjected to stalking, arrests and beatings by the *Securitate* organs. On November 20, 1977, Goma and his family left Romania and went into exile in France.

The offering of the possibility to emigrate by communist authorities (in order to silence the movement) was anticipated by several of his followers (Cătănuş, 2008: 260). Therefore, it is said to have led to the occurrence of the so-called *paşaportari* [passport holders] phenomenon. This denomination pointed to the instrumental character of contesting the regime by several signatories – among whom was also Goma – of an open letter addressed to the first follow-up conference after the Helsinki summit to be held in Belgrade. After the 1989 Revolution, the *paşaportari* hallmark on the 1977 common ambition to disclose the evils of the political regime was still vehiculated and served as an argument for diminishing the significance of the initiative of the signatories of the "Open Letter Addressed to the Belgrade Conference". It is noteworthy that at this time the criticism came from contesters of Goma within the Romanian literary and journalistic field, and has to be understood also as a result of Goma's severe criticism of the weakness shown by the literary field during the Ceauşescu era.

– The 1978 Károly Király Letters

In 1978, Károly Király – prominent member of the R.C.P. – sent letters of protests to the leadership of the party concerning the oppression of the Hungarian minority in Romania. The Committee for Human Rights in Romania (New York) further distributed them in the Western press. The Károly Király letters were also circulated at the first Helsinki follow-up meeting in Belgrade in 1978 (Király, 1994).

3. Diplomatic Scandals

– Scandals over the Defection of Members of the Diplomatic Corpus

According to Olaru and Herbstritt (2005: 124), a policy reform was introduced following the repeated defections of members of the diplomatic personnel. The result was the clogging of the Romanian Ministry of External Affairs and diplomatic missions with officers of State Security.

4. Scandals over the Defection of Intelligence Officials

Usually these officers were judged for treason and convicted in absentia. According to Olaru and Herbstritt (2005: 54-58), Military Unit 0544/R of the Romanian State Security had been in charge of their liquidation.

– The 1969 Defection of Dan Iacobescu

Dan Iacobescu, considered to be "number two" in the *Caraman network* (see discussion on affairs later on in this sub-chapter), defected to the United States *via* England. His defection resulted in the disclosure of the whole network. Iacobescu was tried in absentia by a Military Tribunal and sentenced to death (Levant, 2007).

– The 1978 Defection of Ion Mihai Pacepa

Subsequent to the defection of Pacepa, the Department of State Security had to be completely reorganized (Pacepa, 1988; Olaru and Herbstritt, 2005: 111, 193; Pelin, 2007: 16, 17).

5. Scandals over Defection of Sportsmen

– The 1981 Defection of Marcel Răducanu

Marcel Răducanu of *Steaua Bucharest*, was voted the best Romanian football player in 1979 and 1980. Reportedly, his 1981 defection to Dortmund was considered a desertion, as Răducanu was also a captain in the Romanian Army. Subsequently, he was sentenced in absentia to six years in prison (Cimpoiaşu, 2006).

– The 1984 Defection of Béla and Márta (Martha) Károlyi and Géza Pozsár

In 1981 the Károlyis (coaches of Nadia Comăneci) along with Géza Pozsár (the choreographer and dance coach of the women's national team) defected to the United States during the "Nadia 1981" exhibition tour (Maha, 2007).

Béla and Márta (Martha) Károlyi were founders of the centralized gymnastic training system in Romania in the late 1960s and early 1970s. Károlyi established a boarding school in Oneşti, at which Nadia Comăneci was one of the first students. Nowadays, they enjoy international fame, having built successful coaching careers in the United States. For instance, the United States Elite Coaches Association twice named Pozsár the "Best Choreographer of the Year" (see Pozsar's Gymnastics, ***).

Their defection led to the reinforcement of the "security" of athletes who, reportedly, were kept under the close scrutiny of the State Security, which feared their defection.

– The 1988 Defection of Miodrag Belodedici

Miodrag Belodedici (winner of the European Cup in 1986 with *Steaua Bucharest*) defected to the Socialist Federal Republic of Yugoslavia in 1988. In 1991 he won the cup again, this time with *Red Star Belgrade* (Belodedici in Comşa and Saiu, 2007). He was found guilty of treason and sentenced in absentia to ten years of prison. Furthermore, UEFA suspended him for one year, so he was able to play only in friendly matches. Belodedici himself recalls this year as one of the best times in his life (Belodedici in Comşa and Saiu, 2007). After the Romanian Revolution of 1989, all charges were dropped, and Belodedici returned to Bucharest.

– The 1989 Defection of Nadia Comăneci

During the 1976 Olympics in Montreal, Nadia Comăneci became the first gymnast in Olympic history to be awarded a score of 10.0 – in a total of seven times during the Games.

The possibility of Comăneci's defection was a major a concern, especially after the defection of her coaches in 1981. After 1984 – when she officially retired – Comăneci was forbidden to leave the country. Exceptions were made, however, in the case of socialist states.

> My life drastically changed after the Károlyi defection. I was no longer allowed to
> travel outside Romania. Whenever the Gymnastics Federation put me on a list to
> travel for some kind of exhibition tour, the list came back with my name crossed
> out. I was cut off from making the small amount of money that had really made the
> difference in my family's life. I started to feel like a prisoner. In reality, I'd always
> been one (Nadia Comăneci in ***, 2004) [*author's translation*].

At the time of her defection, Comăneci worked as a coach in the Romanian
Gymnastic Federation. Despite constant surveillance, she eventually managed to
defect to North America *via* Budapest and Austria in November 1989. She ran
away with the help of Panait Constantin, a controversial character to whom she
reportedly paid $5,000 and who is said to have abused her – speculations about
their relationship inflamed the scandal even further.

According to Nicolae Vieru (in Maha, 2006) (the then president of the
Gymnastic Federation) her defection was followed by a large-scale investigation
and a great party meeting.

Kibitzer Audience: Romanian Communist Authorities

1. Scandals over the Reaction to First-Order Transgressions in the Communist Bloc

– The Reaction of Ceauşescu to the Warsaw Pact Invasion of Czechoslovakia, 1968

The events that took place in Czechoslovakia in 1968, as well as those which
occurred in Poland in 1981 and 1989 should be referred to as *crises* rather than
scandals, even if Ceauşescu's reaction to them was inevitably governed by the
latter.

Each of these three episodes highlight moments of Romania's evolution
within the Warsaw Pact. According to Olteanu, Duţu and Constantin (2005: 49-
50), in 1956 the Romanian authorities supported the Soviet intervention in
Hungary. During the 1961 Berlin crises and the 1962 Cuban missile crises they
adopted a cautious attitude. In 1968, Ceauşescu went as far as to publicly
condemn the Soviet invasion. Eighteen years later he similarly criticized the
Russian intervention in Afghanistan. Soon afterwards, in 1981, Ceauşescu
disapproved of a would-be military intervention in Poland; he also did not take
part in the Sino-Soviet split. All of these actions can be explained by the desire
to protect the principle of national sovereignty.

Compared to the widely publicized reaction in 1968, Ceauşescu's opinion
on the Polish crises in 1981 and in 1989 were confined to a much smaller circle

and did not reach the public opinion (although there were speculations and leaks, his stand on the issue was not a matter of public debate). As in the case of Czechoslovakia, in the Polish crises Ceaușescu seemed to go against the main stream within the Warsaw Pact – there were however some major differences. In 1981 the possibility of a Soviet military intervention in Poland was discussed in two closed meetings of the Military Committee comprised of Warsaw Pact member states' defense ministers. The subject of these two meetings was the situation in Poland and a hypothetical telegram from General Jaruzelski to the defense ministers of the members states, reportedly asking for support in resolving the Polish internal crisis (Scurtu, ***; *Shorthand Record of the Meeting of the Executive Political Committee of the C.C. of the R.C.P. of December 13, 1981* in Deletant, Ionescu and Locher, 2004: ***; Constantin Olteanu in Olteanu, Duțu and Constantin, 2005: 208-220).

It could be concluded that in 1981, as in 1968, Ceaușescu remained loyal to his norm of "non-intervention in the domestic affairs of other states". The same thing does not however, pertain to his attitude in August 1989. At the news of the appointment of Tadeusz Mazowiecki as Prime Minister, Ceaușescu felt compelled to send telegrams to his counterparts and draw their attention to the dangers socialism was facing both inside and outside Poland (Olteanu, Duțu and Constantin, 2005: 75-77; Scurtu,***). He also called for an urgent meeting of the communist leaders in order to discuss the threats the appointment carried to "the principles of socialism". According to historical evidence, Ceaușescu's initiative was dismissed by the other communist leaders as being anachronistic (Olteanu, Duțu and Constantin, 2005: 75-77; Scurtu, ***).

For the purposes of this study, the stance of the Romanian government towards the 1968, 1981 and 1989 crises is important for two reasons. First, it illustrates the present discussion about scandals in communist Romania. Second, it contextualizes Ceaușescu's feedback to crises which took place in his own country. It seems reasonable, however, to apply the scandal perspective only to the events of 1968. Analogous to the Los Angeles sports scandal of 1984, in this case Romanian authorities acted as kibitzer audience on the one hand, and as norm offender (or as implicit norm offender) on the other.

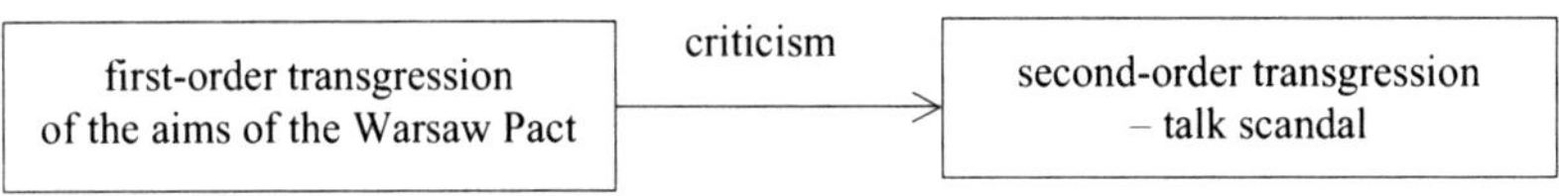

Scheme 2

Scandal as a Factor of Evolution

Speaking in terms of scandal as a factor of evolution (Nałkowski, 1952: 19-25; Kurczewski, 2003: 163-164), the following should be noted:

– Subsequent to the invasion of Czechoslovakia, Romania ceased to allow military exercises of foreign armies on its territory. The policy went further, as the Romanian army also did not take part in military exercises on foreign territory. Furthermore, in order to obviate a similar invasion of Romania, authorities introduced stipulations regarding the dislocations, crossings and temporary stay of Soviet troops on Romanian soil, as well as its own troops in Bulgaria (Olteanu, Duţu and Constantin, 2005: 47). More explicitly, these were to depend on concrete Romanian-Soviet and Romanian-Bulgarian conventions. Foreign military troops were also interdicted from transit across Romanian territory (Olteanu, Duţu and Constantin, 2005: 77; Deletant, 2004: ***).

– After Ceauşescu's speech condemning the invasion, Patriotic Guards were formed. This paramilitary formation was to be used in the event of a potential Soviet-lead attack.

– Reportedly, the Warsaw Pact invasion of Czechoslovakia had implications regarding the relationship between Ceauşescu and the Hungarian minority. According to Deletant (2004: ***), strong criticism of Hungarian and Soviet leaders made Ceauşescu cautious with respect to the Hungarian minority. In order to prevent a hypothetical attack by the Soviets under the pretext of the minorities' unrest in the country, Ceauşescu started a popularization campaign. In late August he toured major urban areas of significant Hungarian population, delivered tailored speeches and made promises to Hungarian counties Harghita and Covasna. In September, he visited counties on the borders with Hungary and Yugoslavia (Deletant, 2004). The foundation of the Council of Working People of Hungarian Nationality and the Council of Working People of German Nationality in late 1968 is most likely not a coincidence (Bachman, 1989: *Mass Organizations*).

Norm Offender: Romanian Communist Authorities

1. Human Rights Scandals

– Scandals over Individual Protests (Cases of Individual Dissidents)

Primarily, this category refers to the cases of the dissidents: Doina Cornea, Paul Goma, Vasile Paraschiv, Radu Filipescu, Gheorghe Calciu-Dumitreasa etc. (see, for example, Paraschiv, 2005).

– Scandals over the Use of the Army as a Labor Force

Here, I address the particular case of the employment of the military in coal mining in Jiu Valley between 1977 and 1989.

The Army was brought to Jiu Valley as a work force in September 1977 after the miners' strike (addressed in one of the case studies of the research). This decision was linked to workforce redistribution, to a large extent affected by the August events. Many work contracts had been canceled after the strike – absenteeism and poor discipline usually serving as official reasons. According to some testimonies, the number of contracts canceled ranged into the thousands (interview P.P., 2006). Opinions are divided as to what extent the measure was indented solely as a means of the *political hygienization* of the Valley. It seems plausible, however, that the high level of workforce turnover in the region demanded some measures to be taken (interview V.A., 2006; interview I.A., 2006; Aldescu, 2001: 340-359). Such steps became imperative following the strike. Furthermore, it is highly probable that the instability and indiscipline of the workforce was regarded as a major factor facilitating the protests. By the same token, bringing in the army, so soon after the 1977 events, was often interpreted as a strategic measure to discipline the Valley (Goma, 1999).

The disclosure of the policy of using the army as a labor force was not a single scandal. Rather, it came in the form of a persistent information campaign by Radio Free Europe, BBC and Voice of America, coupled with complaints of families who lost their sons in mining accidents (Aldescu, 2001: 350). The circulation of these letters of grievance posed a problem to the regime, as they tried to act as a "publicly recognized form of appeal" addressed to the *central* authorities against *local* ones. According to Kurczewski (1993: 175), the effectiveness of such letters depends on the central authorities' willingness to act in the interest of the one handing in the complaint. It might be assumed, that the use of this practice during communism had been a major nuisance for the regime, as it required at least *some* sort of answers.

As a result of this campaign of denunciation and letters of appeal, the authorities were forced either to abandon their policy, or at least – reduce and camouflage it. Eventually, they settled for the latter option. The notion that the large-scale use of the army as a labor force cannot ensure the continuity of professional tradition served as a pretext for limiting the practice (Aldescu, 2001: 350). And thus, it was the local authorities who were left with the problem of stabilizing the civilian labor force in the region. In June 1988, three labor battalions were disbanded. The remaining mining labor battalion was renamed a "construction detachment" [*detaşament de construcţii*]. According to Aldescu "this opened a new, final, stage of the army's participation in mining – camouflaged involvement" (Aldescu, 2001: 350; interview I.A., 2006) [*author's translation*]. However, that very same year, the authorities partially backed out of their decision and formed two additional "construction detachments".

According to Aldescu, between 1977 and 1989, a total of around 100,000 young men were drafted to work in the Petroşani coal mine.

2. Radio Free Europe Scandals

These refer to the harassment of the directors of the Romanian section of Radio Free Europe, and also to the attack on the Radio Free Europe station in Munich, on February 21, 1981 (Olaru and Herbstritt, 2005: 191; Pelin, 2007; Pacepa, 1988).

3. Sports Scandals

– *The Sports Scandal in Prague, 1977*

Ceauşescu decided to withdraw the Romanian gymnastic team from the European Championship. According to Nicolae Vieru – the then president of the Romanian Gymnastic Federation – the scandal as such broke out because Ceauşescu was watching the competition on Romanian TV.

> The scandal in Prague started because Ceauşescu also followed the TV transmission at home. Everything was evolving on the basis of certain hostilities towards our delegation. The organizers and the Czech press did not have exactly laudatory words about us (Vieru in Maha, 2006) [*author's translation*].

After defending the all-around title, Nadia Comăneci was to perform a vault. She was in the first spot up until the performance of the last competitor Nellie Kim – an Olympic gymnast from the Soviet Union who was a vault gold medalist at Montreal in 1976. Nellie Kim made a mistake, but because the exercise was more difficult, jurors awarded her higher scores and she won the gold. Though the Romanian athlete won the following uneven bars competition, the commentator on Romanian TV continued to criticize the arbiters' decision (Maha, 2006). Comăneci's straight 10,0 at beam performance was to no avail – the Romanian ambassador was already dispatched to order the team to withdraw from the competition on Ceauşescu's instructions (***, 2004).

> During the competition – I was a member of the Appeal Comity together with Madam Maria Simionescu – somebody tapped me on the shoulder: "I am from the embassy and I have received orders to communicate to you to withdraw from the contest. At 20,30 hours an airplane will be waiting for you at the airport". Initially I did not want to comply. We were about to take all other medals. So [...] I sent our methodologist, I.I., to the embassy to see what this was all about. At some point I

was called to the phone by I.: "Nicolae, gather the girls and the arbiters quickly, because this is bad. The order comes from the [B]ig [G]uy". In that moment, I froze. I understood that the order came from Ceauşescu. I got scared, it was the first time in my life that I understood what stress means [...]. At the meeting of the international forum in Switzerland this case has been discussed. I was told: "Vieru, for what you have done you should be punished". I was in Moscow with presents for the president of the international forum, Titov. I knew what was in store for me. We did our self-criticism saying that we did not have an alternative, this being an order. We got off only with a warning (Vieru in Maha, 2006) [*author's translation*].

Second-Order Transgressions

Kibitzer Audience: Romanian Communist Authorities

1. Scandals over the Reaction to Second-Order Transgressions in the Communist Bloc

– The Sports Scandal in Los Angeles, 1984

This scandal refers to the Soviet-led boycott of the 1984 Summer Olympics, exercised by Cuba and all countries of the European Communist Bloc except Romania and Yugoslavia – a reply to the American-led boycott of the 1980 Summer Olympics in Moscow.

On 12 May 1984, the Czechoslovak Olympic Committee announced that, "for security reasons", it will not participate in the 1984 Summer Olympics. The following excerpt from a 2008 article gives a revelatory illustration of the way the boycott influenced the power equilibrium in the Olympic arena.

> Like its predecessor in 1980, the 1984 Olympics may be remembered more for who didn't show up than for who did. [...] The Soviet Union-led boycott, a retaliation for the absence of the U.S. and its allies four years earlier in Moscow, left a huge athletic gap as Soviet bloc sports powerhouses like East Germany and the Soviet Union stayed home. Romania was the only Warsaw Pact nation to attend and made the most of not being overshadowed by its more powerful allies, finishing third overall with 53 medals. Nineteen countries boycotted the Games, not nearly as extensive as the 1980 boycott, but those 19 nations had accounted for 58 per cent of the medals in 1976. As a result, the host Americans benefited the way the Soviets did from the Western powers' absence in 1980; the U.S. raked in 174 medals, including 83 gold, 24 more medals than the second-place West Germans. Indeed, the Cold War and the prospect of boycotts deterred many countries from vying for the hosting rights to the 1984 Games in the first place (CBC Sports, 2008).

According to Gomoescu and Corbeanu (2006), the decision to take part in the Olympics was of political significance. By refusing to comply with Moscow's wishes, Ceauşescu set at naught the Soviet power and drove closer to America.

Therefore, if to interpret this seed of scandal, I would rate the Romanian communist authorities both as kibitzer audience and as unprovoked norm audience. More explicitly, the Romanian powers-that-be could be regarded as kibitzer audience for the reason that they *witnessed* the Soviet-led boycott *from the outside*. Furthermore, given that they did not follow it, they might be considered an unprovoked norm audience to the very first transgression – of the Americans in 1980. Thus, given the interdependency of the two boycotts, the 1984 boycott might be regarded as a second-order transgression. In the meantime, the Soviet norm audience became the norm offender. Romanian communist authorities, in their turn, also acted as norm offenders. More explicitly, by choosing to confront the Soviet power, the Romanian audience might be considered to have offended the norm of following Moscow's lead.

Similar claims can be made about Romania's decision to maintain relations with Israel after the outbreak of the Six-Day War in 1967 (as the only communist state from Central and Eastern Europe to do so).

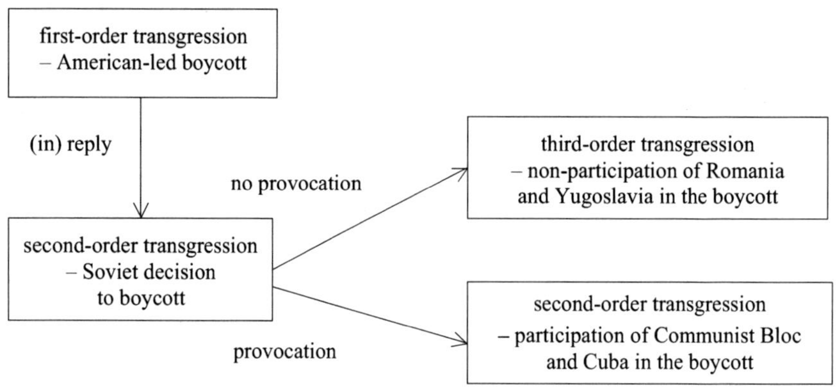

Scheme 3

Norm Offender: Romanian Communist Authorities

1. Human Rights Scandals

– The Goma Affair

The Goma affair was initiated by the 1977 Paul Goma letter episode. It pertains to the author's activity contesting the political regime in Romania that unfolded in France – after his emigration – and the boycott of this activity by the *Securitate* organs. On February 3, 1981 Goma received a parcel in his post (Oprea, 2004: 201). On January 13, 1982 Matei Pavel Haiducu, a secret agent entrusted with a mission from an industrial spy-network operating in France, received the order to assassinate Goma and Virgil Tănase – a Romanian dissident writer. Yet instead of obeying the command, Haiducu turned to the French counter-intelligence (Deletant in Oprea, 2002: 42). Both episodes made the headlines of international press and exposed the Romanian authorities as norm offenders in human rights scandals.

– Scandals over Mass Protests

Mainly, this type offers another reading of the cases which have been listed in the section: *First-Order Transgressions – Norm Offender: Romanian Communist Authorities*. The difference being that in the latter case Romania is viewed as a norm offender of human rights regulations, and consequently this violation is considered to be the subject of the original scandal; whereas in the present occurrence, the Romanian communist powers-that-be are regarded primarily as the norm audience in a scandal over an individual protest. Hence, it can be assumed that it is the way the authorities react to the first-order transgression that renders them as a norm offender in a second-order transgression.

Scheme 4

Affairs

More or less deliberately, the foregoing discussion on scandal in communist Romania did not debate the forms of *causes célèbres* and *affairs*. Given that I found it quite difficult to discuss a notorious long-running legal case that occurred in the 1970s and 1980s, I will limit myself to draw some notes on affairs in communist Romania.

First of all, as compared to scandal, *political affair* leads eventually to political crises. In other words, affair does not publicize or question only the deviant behavior, but it sheds light on certain institutional anomalies and eccentricities that might encourage people to challenge the very political formula of the society. The international reference compendium of *Political Scandals and Causes Célèbres since 1945* (Day et al., 1991) – which rather deals with "the politics of democracies" – lists the following episodes: *Shehu affair* (1981-1983, Albania), *Markov affair* (1978, Bulgaria), *Masaryk affair* (1948, Czechoslovakia), *Slansky affair* (1952, Czechoslovakia), *Imre Nagy affair* (1956-1958, Hungary), *Katyn massacre* (1940-1990, Poland), *Popieluszko affair* (1984), *Rust affair* (1987, Soviet Union), *Yuri Churbanov and the Uzbekistan cotton scandal* (1976-1990). Additionally, when talking about communism and affairs, I should also mention two other records. The first belongs to Berberova (2005) regarding *The Kravchenko Affair*[31] (1949, France). The second is the report of Fogel and Rosenthal (1999) on the *Ochoa affair*[32] (1989, Cuba).

From the more than 175 cases presented in the compendium (Day et al., 1991), only four of them are not listed as *affairs*. The compendium deals rather with affairs as *political/state affairs*. In the following section, I give two examples of episodes which could be cataloged as affairs in communist Romania. These should be read only as illustrations of communist affairs and as a preparatory exercise in investigating affairs during the Ceauşescu regime.

– The 1955 Bern Affair

The attack and occupation of the Romanian legation in Bern was conducted by the so-called *Beldeanu group*. Formed by five anti-communist activists, the group – although it was composed of civilians – managed to occupy the legation for about 40 hours before surrendering to the Swiss police. According to the declarations of the members, their purpose was to reveal evidence incriminating the legation's involvement in espionage. The group also demanded the release of several Romanian political detainees. One of the legation's employees, a driver, was killed during the attack. The group stood trial in Switzerland in 1956 and the leader of the group – Oliviu Beldeanu – was sentenced to four years in

---

31   *The Kravchenko Affair* (1949) pertains to the extended 1949 libel trial between Viktor Kravchenko and the French Communist weekly *Les Lettres Françaises*.

32   *The Ochoa Affair* (1989) pertains to the investigation, trial and execution of General Arnaldo T. Ochoa Sánchez on drug-trafficking and corruption charges.

prison. Soon after his release, Romanian State Security managed to lure him to East Berlin, where he was arrested and taken back to Romania. He was eventually put before a military tribunal and sentenced to death for treason in 1959 (Olaru, 2003; Olaru and Herbstritt, 2005: 49-54).

Romanian authorities considered the attack to be an act of terrorism which took advantage of the softness and negligence of the Swiss, who failed in their duties to protect a foreign diplomatic mission in their country. In other words, the communist authorities pretended not to hear the allegations of the involvement of their legation in espionage. Furthermore, they encouraged leaks of information linking the "terrorist attack" on the legation to Western intelligence agencies. The attackers themselves were referred to as "bandits", "criminals", "fascists" and "iron-guardists" (Olaru, 2003: 138)[33].

Thus – while convergent to a certain extent – there were two separate interpretations of the events. One speculated about the espionage activities of the Romanian diplomatic outpost in Switzerland (and about the content of the documents discovered by the attackers). The other talked about a terrorist attack and pointed to the incapacity of the Swiss authorities.

Subsequently, the outer norm and kibitzer audiences were also divided. The first group reacted to the affair as it was defined by the attackers. This was the case, for example, of the American Congress and Romanian diaspora in the West. These audiences were rather subjected to provocation as they saw in this diplomatic and political affair a good opportunity to attack the communist regime in Bucharest. They were in favor of a political trial of the attackers. A political trial, which, no doubt, would have led to a wave of second-order transgressions and turn the first-order kibitzer audiences into second-order norm audiences. Furthermore, the British kibitzer audience can be also assumed to have been in favor of this kind of framing of the first-order transgression, as it became overtly concerned and suspicious about the activities of Romanian diplomats in London (Olaru, 2003: 74, 75).

There were also audiences which subscribed to the interpretation of the first-order transgression provided by Romanian communist authorities – limiting the case to a terrorist attack. Among them, there were even the Swiss authorities. Nevertheless, according to a telegram sent by the British Embassy in Romania to London, the support previously given to Romania in the whole affair soon moved in the direction of the Swiss government and of the attackers. This was provoked to a large extent by the tendentious and noisy behavior of Romanian authorities, which went as far as an attempt to arrange for a common protest of

---

33   The notion designates members of The Legion of the Archangel Michael, known also as the Iron Guard, the main fascist movement in Romania during the interwar period.

the Western diplomatic corpus. Hence, it can be stated, we are dealing here with a second-order transgression regarding the behavior of the Romanian authorities – i.e. of the original norm audience as such.

The existence of another – although far smaller – second-order transgression should be also noted here. As opposed to the Voice of America and BBC, the first reaction of Noël Bernard – the director of the Romanian section at Radio Free Europe – was to condemn the attack. Reportedly, his stance precipitated the shortening of his mandate (Olaru, 2003: 81-82; Pelin, 2007: 45-47). This second-order transgression is linked to the original affair that was rather defined in the terms of the attackers.

Further, the second-order transgression – which is however linked to the original affair as it was presented by the authorities of the People's Republic of Romania – consists of purges and the *rotation of cadres* in the personnel of intelligence agencies, primarily in the Department of External Intelligence (Olaru, 2003: 126-132).

Scandal as a Factor of Evolution

Reportedly, there was a huge media and propaganda enterprise and the Romanian authorities also resorted to several intrigues in order to assure that in 1956 there would be a criminal trial and not a political one (Olaru, 2003: 84). Eventually a compromise between the Romanian and Swiss authorities was reached. According to Olaru (2003: 87-88), the release of passports to Romanian citizens with relatives in Switzerland and the negotiation of the contract regarding the introduction of the Diesel drive system on Romanian railways managed to ensure that a criminal trial would be provided for.

Probably the most significant change was the modification of the official policy of the People's Republic towards Romanian citizens seeking refuge in the West. And thus the *Bern affair* gave the stimulus for the policy of repatriation. According to Olaru (2003: 132-137), this policy was oriented mainly toward those who left the country after August 23, 1944. Gheorghe Gheorghiu-Dej was the initiator of this measure. The decision was presented to the other members of the Political Bureau on 23 March 1955, at the end of a meeting that discussed the implications of the *Bern affair*. Seemingly, the *Bern affair* convinced the communist authorities that it was time to mollify their aggressive policy towards the Romanian exiles in the West. Hence, it was issued *Decree no. 253/1955 concerning the facilitation of the repatriation of some Romanian citizens and former Romanian citizens and of the amnesty of the repatriated ones* [Decretul nr. 253/1955 privind înlesnirea repatrierii unor cetăţeni şi foşti cetăţeni români şi amnistierea celor repatriaţi], published in *Buletinul Oficial* on June 30, 1955.

The Romanian Committee for Repatriation with its headquarters in Bucharest and in Berlin was also established (Olaru, 2003: 133-134).

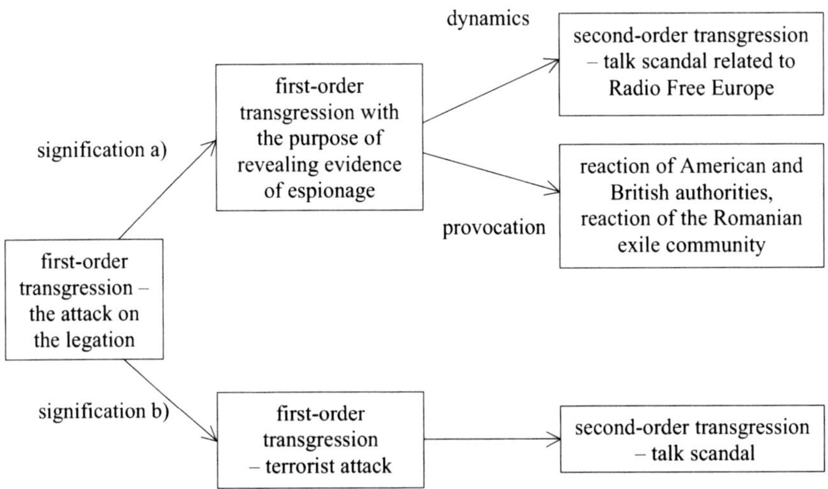

Scheme 5

– The Caraman Network

In 1958-1968, as chief of the espionage station in Paris, Mihai Caraman led the notorious "Caraman network", which managed to steal documents from NATO headquarters (Levant, 2007; Oprea, 2005).

Conclusions and Discussion

The empirical material analyzed outlines the following hypothesis with respect to the dynamic of scandal in the 1970s and 1980s. The scandal seems to be more genuine in the cases in which the Romanian authorities are involved with an external actor in the same kind of transgression (be it first-order or second-order transgression for that matter). While, in the cases in which the Romanian authorities are involved with an internal actor – as in cases of mass protests – there is a predisposition to misrepresent the scandal, more precisely Romanian communist authorities display a tendency to misrepresent or transmute the transgression into another type of transgression. However – and this is important

– the scandal as such remains, though its subject changes and it usually is convergent with the original.

The argument I tried to make in the foregoing sections was that in cases of human rights scandals and episodes of mass protests governed by scandal, the communist authorities relied on converging the first-order transgression with other types of transgressions. The convergence – although not fully ideological – involved to a large extent elements of misrepresentation and of transposition. For the most part, employing these mechanisms allowed the communist authorities to escape facing the political implications of the individual and mass protests. After the scandal broke out and the authority of the party was already null – as was the case in Jiu Valley in 1977 and in Braşov in 1987 – the only solution left to the party leaders was to "signify" (Hall et al., 1994: 224) the first-order transgression. This was certainly not a smooth undertaking. In case of Braşov in 1987 for instance, the authorities were initially exploring the hypothesis of an iron-guardist intrigue (Airinei, 2002: 271); but as it became obvious that the game was not worth the candle they eventually resorted to a less ideological plot based on "acts of hooliganism". After overcoming the difficulties of signification, the next step involved the *attribution of fault*.

Following Kurczewski (1993: 145)[34], I would argue that the establishment of the responsible party dictates the dynamics of the second-order transgression (i.e. the castigation of party leaders and activists). As we will see in the next chapter, the scandals over mass protests were usually followed by investigation and reform measures. The purpose of the investigations was first of all to trace down the responsible party and attribute fault for the eruption of the scandal.

Getting back to the issue of the scandal as a disruptive publicization of transgression, in the following chapter I will try to characterize the norms that

---

34   "It is important to remember that after the change in power and the initial improvements of Gierek's regime, that the same situation began to emerge, but this time on much higher level of investments, debts [...] and social aspirations [...]. Official acknowledgement of the crisis, amounting to a failure in what was treated as the basis for the legitimation of the system since Khrushchev and the post-Stalin era, was the most difficult thing for the Communist ruling class to do, whereas the truth had already been seen by society from the beginning. Strikers were speaking about the economic crisis as early as 1970, whereas the Communist rulers did not agree to the diagnosis until as late as summer 1980. This means that, due to censorship, not a word about the crisis (and above all, not even the word 'crisis' as such) could be published anywhere in Poland, nor used on television or radio in this period. The responsibility of the leaders was less threatening – Communists were always quarrelling and intriguing about who would be held responsible for past problems, rather than confronting the reason for the problem for which the responsibility was to be established" (Kurczewski, 1993: 145).

were transgressed in specific Romanian cases. The convergence (be it more, or less ideological) of the first-order transgression with other issues consists in actuality of the convergence of the norm that was transgressed with yet another. Therefore, the categories and the examples outlined in table (1) and table (2) should be also viewed in correspondence with the type of the norms broken.

In the words of Kurczewski (1993: 339): "A norm is not the cause of conduct [...] but it defines the cause and the effect, the agent, his or her responsibility and conduct". What is more, the discussion should rather begin with the normative (the structure which relates to and prescribes norms and standards) and with the normative language, rather than norms as such. Regarding this matter, the author discussed the phenomenon of colonization of the normative structure during communism to the point that it bears no distinction to what it had been before. With respect to Polish society, Kurczewski (1993: 388) considers that its more basic normative structure managed to be repressed by the 1950s, but that after 1956 it revived again and made itself visible in the course of several furious outbursts. What made this emancipation possible was the struggle for freedom which revealed the dissonance between the original and imposed normative structure. The new communist normative structure was set up by different mechanisms. It was decoded from hints and intentions shown to be at work in political practice and derived from the normative language of the authorities.

> The normative language of the authorities is that of propaganda and planning. Propagandist and planner use this language through creating the appearance of description. Instead of "Poland should be a country of social justice", both will say "Poland is a country of social justice". The rebellious worker rejects appearances and instead says that "Poland should be a country of social justice", and puts such a demand on the list (Kurczewski, 1993: 142).

The examination of this normative language is expected to reveal the logic of the resignification of the first-order transgression, as well as the transition from the first- to second-order transgression in cases of scandals over mass protests.

In the following chapter, when discussing the types of norms that were violated during the Ceauşescu regime, I will follow the work of Kurczewski on the topic, in the respect that I will put forward an indirect reading of the violation of these norms. More explicitly, they will be deducted from the types of responsibility which have been allocated to different collective and individual actors in the aftermath of the events. Besides a better understanding of the dynamics of scandals under Ceauşescu, I also anticipate this discussion to lead to the consideration of other issues such as conformism during communism, shaming and bullying.

PART III
THE REPLY TO SCANDALS OVER MASS PROTESTS DURING THE CEAUŞESCU REGIME

The following chapter discusses the 1977 Jiu Valley strike and the 1987 Braşov revolt in terms of scandal. It performs an investigation into the shaming and reintegrative practices present especially in the aftermath of the 1987 revolt. The presentation of the two episodes is somehow asymmetrical; in the case of the 1977 strike I insist rather on the scandal relevant aspects, while in the case of the 1987 revolt the reintegrative angle is brought to the fore. The broad picture will however gain its equilibrium after reading part IV – *The Ritualization of Party Moots during the Ceauşescu Regime.*

1. Jiu Valley 1977

Jiu Valley is Romania's main mining region, situated in a valley of the Jiu River between the Retezat Mountains and the Parâng Mountains, in southwestern Romania, Hunedoara County. The region counts six main cities and towns: Petroşani, Lupeni, Petrila, Aninoasa, Uricani and Vulcan; their population at the moment amounts to approximately 170,000 inhabitants.

The situation of the miners' stratum in Romania was absolutely dependent upon the roller-coaster vagaries of heavy industry's performance in the Romanian economy (Baron, 1998; Baron, 1999). Thus, it experienced a long and erratic decline, from being one of the top-rated occupations in the region to one of the most poverty stricken, leading to the escalation of mass "hungers strikes" since the end of 1999 (Bruha, Ionaşcu and Jeong, 2003: 5-18; Dobrescu and Rughiniş, ***; Kideckel, 2001; Kideckel, 2008).

As far as the communist period is concerned, the state made a point of developing heavy industry. Mining was, thus, one of the highly favored professions at the time. Nevertheless, their position as the "vanguard of proletariat" did not impede the miners from being the most active groups of workers protesting against the communist regime. The legend around their highly developed workers' stratum consciousness begins at some point in 1929, when the Lupeni strike took place (Istrati, 1969). This event was appropriated later on by the communist propaganda. More specifically, the official communist discourse presented the strike as the first episode when the working class had opposed the bourgeoisie exploitation in the inter-war period in Romania.

In the early years of post-communism, the miners from Jiu Valley once again became the protagonists of political events – the miners' marches on Bucharest (*mineriads* [mineriade]) (Vasi, 2004).

The Strike and Its Context

With respect to the 1977 strike, it can be stated that the metaphorical "quiet before the storm" was rather absent, the strike being unleashed in a context of circumstances and facts in which the communist regime had all the reasons to doubt that it will manage to complete the year on good terms.

First, there was the tragedy of the Bucharest earthquake of 4 March, 1977, felt throughout the Balkans (especially in Bulgaria), which killed about 1,570 people, wounded more than 11,000 and destroyed 80% of the town of Zimnicea (Roseti, 2007; Ţiu, 2008). According to Ilie Verdeţ[35] – first deputy chairman of the Council of Ministers [*prim-vicepreşedinte al Consiliului de Miniştri*] at the time of the strike – in spite of the evidence of the disastrous effects of this adversity in the social-human and economic fields, Ceauşescu did not loosen the reins in his striving to accomplish the Plan. On the contrary, he was determined to meet its targets as if nothing had happened (Verdeţ in Barbu and Chirvasă, 1977: 207).

Another significant occurrence, this time on the scene of the Romanian political dissidence, is the human rights movement initiated by writer Paul Goma. This movement seems to have occasioned the first manifestation of discontent in Jiu Valley. Some time before the strike – on 23 March 1977 – miner D.B. went to Bucharest to sign the appeal for human rights that was penned by the writer. As initially he did not find him at home, D.B. left Goma a note that was subsequently read at Radio Free Europe (A.B. in Barbu and Chirvasă, 1997: 11-13; A.B. in Barbu and Boboc, 2005: 159-160). After his deed was thus publicized D.B. "was degraded to a hauler and afterwards they put him as superintendent in the wood deposit. They immediately called a meeting in the courtyard of the mine and in the presence of everybody they poked fun at him" (A.B. in Barbu and Chirvasă, 1997: 13; A.B. in Barbu and Boboc, 2005: 161).

The second act of rebelliousness that "foretokened" the "mutiny on the Jiu Valley" was the so-called "thorny confession" written by the miner G.D., a memoir addressed to the Central Committee of the party, Ministry of Mines and Romanian television (Cecilia Sibişan and Adriana R. Mocanu in Barbu and Chirvasă, 1997: 180-181, 214-215). The author got his answer in one of the

---

35   Ilie Verdeţ (1925-2001) – member of the Political Executive Committee of the C.C. of the R.C.P. from November 28, 1974 until June 24, 1986; member of the Secretariat of the C.C. of R.C.P form March 22 until July 24, 1965, from November 28, 1974 until November 23, 1979, and from October 8, 1982 until November 14, 1985; Prime Minister from March 30, 1979 until May 22, 1982 (C.N.S.A.S., 2004: 614-615). Eventually marginalized, he served as head of the Central Auditing Commission (Tismăneanu, 2003: 268-269).

trials held in the aftermath of the August strike. He was sentenced to two years of prison.

What eventually added fuel to the fire was the Law no. 3/1977 (enacted on June 30) which ended disability pensions for miners and raised the retirement age by two years[36] (Velica and Velica, 2002). According to one witness directly involved in the events, the turmoil could have been avoided if the terms of the law had been previously discussed with the miners, as it was usually done before (C.N. in Chirvasă and Barbu, 1997: 22, 24)[37].

A so-called "*Securitate* version" of the origins of Law no. 3 and, implicitly, also the strike is also available. It belongs to one of the experts who, together with General Emil Macri, orchestrated the settlement of the 1977 Jiu Valley case – i.e. general Nicolae Pleşiţă[38]. His account diminishes the importance of the

---

36   *Lege nr. 3 din 30 iunie 1977 privind pensiile de asigurări sociale de stat şi asistenţă socială* [Law no. 3 from June 30, 1977 regarding state social insurance and social assistance pensions], published in *Buletinul Oficial*, no. 82, August 6, 1977.

    "The Bill stipulated that members of Group I can retire at 52 years of age. Regarding other groups it stipulated: Group II retires at 57 (at request at 52), Group III at 62 (at request at 60). The miners no longer could retire at 50. Thus 'the conscription' was prolonged by 2 years. The second issue: according to the old labour law, workers from Group I who got sick were entitled to obtain another position which their health allowed them to take up, remaining in the previous wage-class. Although one was working at a new work place, he was paid as [he used to be] in the older one. But the new Law did not allow for something like this. You were to be remunerated according to the job you did. Another issue: Group II employees could not work but half from the labour time [...] In Jiu Valley there were 5,000-5,200 miners in this situation. [...] This made 5,000 people very unsatisfied. On the other side, all the miners had to work two additional years. A lot of retirement dossiers were given back. There was a general dissatisfaction" (C.N. in Barbu and Chirvasă, 1997: 23) [*author's translation*].

    See also Constantin Dobre (in Barbu and Boboc, 2005: 193) and Velica and Schreter (1993: 188).

37   "I was certain that there will be reactions to Law no. 3. But I could not envisage their amplitude. I knew that something is going to happen when I saw the law in [its] projected form. When I read the law, I realized something was not alright. You did not have to be an expert to realize that this law did not bring good things. That is why I requested this law to be discussed with the people. We used to discuss, before, the laws with the people. [...] I required this from the first secretary at the county level – Ilie Rădulescu. He consulted [with people] at the higher levels and told me it is not necessary. 'Now people are enlightened' he said and he was right" (C.N. in Barbu and Chirvasă, 1997: 22) [*author's translation*].

38   "I consider myself to be in resistance since the year 1977 when I was told to go with a *Securitate* battalion and to do what the members of the Peasant Party did in Lupeni in

economic factor, while the strike is presented as an effect of power politics that unfolded at the highest echelons of the party and of *Securitate*. Accordingly, the main characters of the intrigue are: Nicolae and Elena Ceauşescu, Ilie Verdeţ, Janos Fazekas (Fazekas János)[39] and Emil Bobu[40]. Emil Bobu – the then Minister of Labor – managed to convince Elena Ceauşescu that workforce shortages in Jiu Valley could be remedied by extending miners' retirement age. Although the project was disapproved by Verdeţ, Fazekas and Trofin, Elena Ceauşescu managed eventually to impose the contentious regulation (Pleşiţă in Patrichi, 2001: 106-109). Ceauşescu – who initially showed reluctance towards the measure – approved the publication of the new law. The apprehension of Verdeţ, Fazekas and Trofin regarding a possible uprising of the miners were confirmed.

Another peculiar element of the account regards the notorious sequestration of Verdeţ by miners. Accordingly, the dignitary who was sent on the spot from the capital let himself fall into the hands of miners in order to teach a lesson to those who ignored his advice. Reportedly, when informed of his duplicity, Ceauşescu degraded Verdeţ. Eventually, in 1986, his career was sunk in the so-called "elephants' grave" – the Central Auditing Commission (Nicolae Pleşiţă in Patrichi, 2001: 108). In another interview Verdeţ recognizes that he disapproved of the bill and that, presumably, this was the reason why Ceauşescu sent him to the Valley[41]. He also confirms the existence of the rumors according to which he was involved in agitating the spirits in the Valley; then again, Verdeţ states that these rumors were spread by the *Securitate*.

There were several elements which rendered the 1977 strike scandalous. One such element was detaining Verdeţ along with C.N. (the mayor of Petroşa-

---

1929 when they shot the miners. I did not place any soldier in the Valley" (Nicolae Pleşiţă in Patrichi, 2001) [*author's translation*].

39   Janos Fazekas (Fazekas János) (1926-2004) – member of the Political Executive Committee of the C.C. of the R.C.P from November 28, 1974 until May 21, 1982 (C.N.S.A.S., 2004: 256).

40   Emil Bobu (born 1927) – member of the Political Executive Committee of the C.C. of the R.C.P. from November 28, 1974 until December 22, 1989 (C.N.S.A.S., 2004: 102-103).

41   "When the Pension Law was mooted by the political committee, I was against it. I said: it is not right to do something like this, we did not have any motivation. I was supported by two members of the leadership of the party, the rest agreed [with the bill]. Probably this was the motivation why they sent me here, [i.e.] because I did not agree with the law. Subsequently, it was sought via *Securitate*, via different people to prove that I was to blame. And this especially in the context in which Ceauşescu could not imagine Verdeţ coming to Jiu Valley, Verdeţ – who is a miner – and not being able to enlighten the miners" (Ilie Verdeţ in Barbu and Chirvasă, 1997: 206) [*author's translation, author's emphasis*].

ni) in lodge number two of the porter at the mine in Lupeni (D.F. in Barbu and Chirvasă, 1997: 106-107; Constantin Dobre in Barbu and Boboc, 2005: 204-208). The well-known sequestration ended once the news of the arrival of Ceauşescu in the Valley had been made official.

Another noteworthy element of the 1977 strike is the fact (or perception) that the *Securitate* and the police did not overtly "interfere". In other words, although both were present, the appeasement of the conflict was attempted in a politically friendly manner. According to Verdeţ, helicopters were prepared to liftoff and railways had been blocked in order to prevent the departure of miners to Bucharest (Ilie Verdeţ in Barbu and Chirvasă, 1997: 211). C.N. claims that the local party leaders had enough flair and did not call for the assistance of the Patriotic Guards (C.N. in Barbu and Chirvasă, 1997: 30-31).

In response to the miners' demands, Ceauşescu came to the Valley on the third day of the strike. After a short visit to Petroşani, he went to Lupeni where, reportedly, he was being awaited by 35,000 miners who had come to welcome him. Being caught in the grip, Ceauşescu promised to fulfill the demands and the scandal was thus settled. At the end of the meeting, a more "enterprising" miner even suggested that Ceauşescu be granted the title of "honorary miner". After Lupeni, Ceauşescu went back to Petroşani where a popular meeting was held in his honor.

In the aftermath of the strike, the waves of people sent "from *the center*" just kept on coming and coming to the Valley (C.N. in Chirvasă and Barbu, 1997: 55). There was a punctual purge at the political and administrative level – almost all the first secretaries of the mines were replaced – as well as at the highest echelons of power (C.N. in Barbu and Chirvasă, 1997: 38, 49).

> After a few days we have started a series of measures. It started from the top. The Prime Minister was replaced; the Minister of Mines was replaced. On the local level first secretaries were replaced, unionists, and U.C.Y. [the Union of Communist Youth] activists. Only I and the functionaries from Vulcan [...] remained ... They also replaced the first secretary at the county level (C.N. in Barbu and Chirvasă, 1997: 38) [*author's translation*].

Fifteen miners were sentenced for "offences against good morals and turmoil of public order" [*ultraj contra bunelor moravuri şi tulburarea liniştii publice*]. According to the official point of view, these acts occurred in no connection with the strike as such (Spiridon, 2008: 240-247; P.P. in Barbu and Chirvasă, 1997: 115; interview P.P., 2006; Barbu and Chirvasă, 1997: 132-176; Barbu and Boboc, 2005: 11-15, 21-145). The sentences ranged between two and five years of prison to be carried out by work in other socialist units [*executarea pedepselor aplicate prin muncă corecţională în alte unităţi socialiste, prin efectuarea unor activităţi productive*]. Waves of deportations also followed.

C.N., the then first secretary and mayor of Petroşani – among the few who made a hairbreadth escape from the early purge – recalls that, allegedly, there were two fronts of action: the political and the state, respectively[42]. And thus what can be regarded as the *after-strike affair of the party immunity* had begun. Reportedly, everything was based on the existence of two party resolutions which have been known only to *les connaisseurs*, resolutions which were proverbial gold mines in situations of crises like this one. The first one establis- hed that "no party member could be investigated while having his membership card upon him", the second that: "all those sent to court, who were party members, could not be sentenced without me being informed. I would moot the issue and decide whether the trial was to continue or not. If it was decided that no, [then] the man was not tried" (C.N. in Barbu and Chirvasă, 1997: 54, 55)[43] [*author's translation*].

Several important "round tables" took place debating what happened in the Valley in 1977. First, on September 3 of that same year, there was a meeting of the State Council. The first secretary of the county – who by the time of the strike was

---

42   "All party members who took part in the strike in an active manner were sanctioned. If you had taken out all of them, you would have had nobody to talk to. The active ones [...] all these were mooted. Those who were mooted were excluded from the party. There might have been an exception that I do not know about. I do not know. [...] I do not know even today how many of them there were. 40-50. I do not know. [...] They got excluded on the party line. [...] This was another issue on the state line. Here I cannot draw a conclusion. It is noticeable that the measure was taken at the central level, that it was an indication that these people are to be sent to the counties of origin. But here the party did not interfere anymore. This was done by the state organs. The party organs together with the state organs were to secure them a working place, accommodation etc. [...] I have no idea how many of them there were. And the justice organs, the police took almost all the participants of the strike. They took them irrespective of who they were. They prepared files and send them to court. They were convicted. I do not know how many of them there were" (C.N. in Barbu and Chirvasă, 1997: 46) [*author's translation*].

43   In order to have a glimpse of the "immunity bubble" created this way, it is revealing to consider the case of the chief engineer at I.M. Aninoasa during the 1977 strike. After the strike the party performed genuine stunts in order to obtain the collective's approval for his exclusion from the party, he was reproached for having facilitated (provided trans- port) the departure of miners from Aninoasa to Lupeni during Ceauşescu's visit to the Valley. Eventually, after unsuccessful attempts of exclusion he received only a vote of blame/censure [*vot de blam*], which had its unpleasant repercussions for quite a period of time (V.A. in Barbu and Chirvasă, 1977: 58-67) [*author's translation*].

      "If you got excluded you were destroyed. The party membership card was at that time like today's parliamentary immunity. All those who got excluded were finished. Then the justice had a free hand" (V.A. in Barbu and Chirvasă, 1977: 64; interview V.A., 2006) [*author's translation*].

on sick-leave – was seriously criticized (C.N. in Barbu and Chirvasă, 1997: 38-40). Another plenary took place on October 26, 1977. Although it was not designed to discuss the Valley events, a member of the Central Committee inquired about them. Obviously, he was irritated by the fact that the members of the committee had not been informed of the strike and had to find about it on Radio Free Europe. Reportedly, they were given the version that appeared in the official newspaper *Scânteia*. Subsequent to this meeting, the Minister of Mines was left with a vote of blame/censure [*vot de blam*] (C.N. in Barbu and Chirvasă, 1997: 43-45).

There are several elements that make the Jiu Valley strike of 1977 truly unique. First, as above stated, the police and *Securitate* did not overtly interfere in the strike. Second, it seems that, although it was later on strongly denied by the victims, C.N. and Verdeţ were kept hostage until the arrival of Ceauşescu. Finally, there was no violence during the strike[44].

According to Verdeţ, Ceauşescu's interpretation of the event was that it happened subsequent to the "bad work of propaganda" and "the decisions of the party not being popularized" (Ilie Verdeţ in Barbu and Chirvasă, 1997: 206) [*author's translation*]. There is no "official story" of the strike, only of Ceauşescu coming to Petroşani. *Scânteia* reported of Ceauşescu's "work visit" in Jiu Valley:

> in order to analyze on the spot – together with cadres responsible for the economy, representatives of the local party and state organs and [with representatives] of the working people – the way of introducing the decisions of the XI-th Congress of the Party in this sector of our industry. During this visit, the general secretary was accompanied by the comrades Gheorghe Oprea[45], Gheorghe Pană[46], Ilie Verdeţ, Constantin Băbălău[47], the Minister of Mines, Petroleum and Geology (*Scânteia* in Barbu and Chirvasă, 1997: 86) [*author's translation*].

---

44   Reportedly, the local high political echelons realized from the beginning that bringing out Patriotic Guards would have resulted in a real carnage (C.N. in Chirvasă and Barbu, 1997: 31) [*author's translation*].

45   Gheorghe Oprea (born 1927) – member of the C.C. of R.C.P from July 21, 1972 until December 22, 1989; member of the Political Executive Committee of the C.C. of the R.C.P. from November 28, 1974 until December 22, 1989 (C.N.S.A.S., 2004: 442).

46   Gheorghe Pană (born 1927) – member of the Political Executive Committee of the C.C. of the R.C.P. from November 28, 1974 until December 22, 1989 (C.N.S.A.S., 2004: 447, 448).

47   Constantin Băbălău (born 1926) – member of the C.C. of the R.C.P. from August 12, 1969 until November 23, 1979 (C.N.S.A.S., 2004: 86).

The Leader

The story of the "overnight" leader of the 1977 strike was a subject of castling between two seemingly contradictory rumors. Both accommodate perfectly the intrigues of a so-called *popular power regime*. On a side note – the present day brings a contender for the role. Miron Cozma, the leader of 1990s miners' marches claimed recently to have been also "the backstage leader of the revolt of August 1977" (Mihu, 2007a).

Immediately after the events of 1977, a quite persistent rumor had it that the two leaders of the protesters – Constantin Dobre and Jurcă – were killed (***, 1979; ***, 1981). Jurcă is a name that appears quite frequently in the columns of Romanian diaspora publications dealing with the strike. He was even granted the role of the "co-pilot" of the strike. Curiously however, Jurcă almost disappeared in the accounts that surfaced after the 1989 revolution. Regarding Dobre, after a wide circulation of the rumor about his death, another version surfaced according to which he was allured by *Securitate* into its ranks (Cesereanu, 2004).

According to journalist G.C. (interview, 2005), Dobre was determined to leave to the city of Craiova in many respects due to the pressure exerted upon him by his colleagues at work. Accordingly, Dobre – like many strikers – was reproached by the unfulfilled demands of the strike:

> G.C. – So, first of all he [Dobre] was determined to leave. How should I put it … There was no acting in force, i.e. to grab him by his sleeve and to take him I don't know where. But the small cavils at the work place, the small troubles caused with the colleagues determined quite many of them to depart … to leave the scene – to put it like this. Among these [miners who left] was also this Dobre who was determined to leave, because his colleagues did not stand him anymore. His colleagues did not stand him [Dobre] anymore because of the 29 demands that he put forth – being the number one organizer of the strike – not all were fulfilled. [...] But the people [...]: "Man, you did the strike in vain, look this was not done, that was not done". And so on and so forth [...] And by all means, many of these [people] had to leave because of small frictions at the workplace (interview G.C., 2005) [*author's translation*].

The foregoing excerpt indicates that the leader of the miners might have left Jiu Valley subsequently to *work related stalking* and/or to *whistleblowing retaliation bullying* – i.e. two types of *workplace bullying* which are documented at large in part IV – *The Ritualization of Party Moots during the Ceauşescu Regime.*

Then again, according to Verdeţ, in November 1977, Dobre was already at the Academy of Ştefan Gheorghiu[48] "having been sent to school" by the Inspectorate of the Ministry of Internal Affairs, Craiova (Ilie Verdeţ in Barbu and Chirvasă, 1997: 209). And from the reproduction by T.R. – secretary of

---

48   Ştefan Gheorghiu was a leading party cadres training institution (Lupu, 2007: 265-277).

propaganda at the Municipal Party Committee, in charge of the Eastern part of Jiu Valley – of a conversation with Gheorghe Pană (that took place in the summer of 1978 in Neptun) we learn that Dobre might have had an unsuccessful attempt to visit Ceauşescu in order to complain about the selective and unsatisfactory implementation of the miners' demands (T.R. in Barbu and Chirvasă, 1997: 75). Reportedly, Ceauşescu rid himself of the miner by sending him off to the Minister of Labor – Gheorghe Pană. From sources which are less suspicious towards Dobre, we find out that in 1988 he studied in Craiova for a PhD in international relations (Rus in Spiridon, 2003: 63). According to the statements of P.P. – the attorney of the miners in the exoneration process of those sentenced in 1977 – Dobre appeared again in the Valley during the December 1989 Revolution, shortly after Ceauşescu's escape attempt. Reportedly, as he was welcomed with suspicion, the 1977 leader had to withdraw in a hurry, though only for a short time, as the very next day Dobre appears on National TV "speaking in the name of the miners" (P.P. in Barbu and Chirvasă, 1997: 113).

Dobre's accounts of his own destiny became more and more public in the last few years. It might be not at all a coincidence that their proliferation juxtaposes with the precipitation of heated debates in the field of transitional justice in Romania. A certain evolution is noticeable, the leader becoming more and more talkative regarding his past in the last years. Thus, in his first detailed chronicle about the 1977 events, Dobre does not make further elaborations either regarding his hypothetical regimentation or regarding the circumstances in which he left the Valley (Constantin Dobre in Barbu and Boboc, 2005: 180-270). While in the next book of Boboc and Barbu (2007: 217-352), large excerpts from the 2005 testimony of Dobre are followed by the reproduction of informative notes and reports from the archives of the communist State Security Department. Dobre proves more generous in declarations given to the Romanian media.

L.M.: You are accused of having betrayed the cause.
Constantin Dobre: I did not know what "Ştefan Gheorghiu" was. I was working as an unskilled [worker] at IRA Craiova and I wanted to finish a faculty. One [guy] who left from us, from the enterprise, became a journalist and he was writing articles in a party newspaper. Seeing what he was writing, I also wanted to become a journalist. I went to the editorial staff, I gave a sample, but I failed. After three-four days, the first-secretary – Miu Dobrescu – called me and told me that I can study only at "Ştefan Gheorghiu" [and] that it is a state institution, but not a party one. And I took [an exam] to the economic section, no [obligatory] attendance.
L.M.: While there, you have met Virgil Măgureanu[49]?
C.D.: Yes, a person whom I have honestly believed, and who compromised me in an abject way (Mihu, 2007a) [author's translation].

---

49   Virgil Măgureanu was the director of Romanian Information Service (1990-1997).

Also his revelations from the *Gardianul* daily in 2006 are worth mentioning: "Măgureanu asked me to assassinate General Macri" (Constantin Dobre in Badea, 2006) [*author's translation*]. In 2007, Dobre reappears in the spotlight in order to correct erroneous information from the report of the Tismăneanu Committee[50] regarding his death in the aftermath of the strike. Eventually the information was rectified, without however, the mistake publicly acknowledged by the authors of the report (Admin, 2007). Seemingly, the origin of this inaccuracy is the persistence of some rumors about Dobre in certain circles and the exile press in the aftermath of the strike. As already stated, one of these was the death of the strike leader (***, 1979; ***, 1981). Inside the country, an even more persistent gossip proclaimed that Dobre turned into a collaborator of the party and *Securitate* soon after the events of 1977.

In August 2007 excerpts from his surveillance file – code name "Dodu" – were made public (Mihu, 2007b). These have been published in the most recent book of Boboc and Barbu (2007).

I recalled elements of the biography and the rumors circulating about the former leader of the miners in 1977 as they – in their own turn – draw a story of a scandal. In comparison with other scandals, the one generated by the appearance of erroneous information regarding Dobre's death in the 2006 Tismăneanu report is obviously a scandal of much smaller proportions. This notwithstanding, the misstatement was big enough to be remembered in the field of transitional justice in Romania for quite some time (see Administrator, 2007; Florin, 2007). What should be noted is that the scandal would probably have been more ample in the absence of rumors regarding the would-be betrayal of Dobre. The following scheme (6) represents an extension of scheme (1) from the foregoing section. What is worthy of consideration, is that it features a junction with the 2006 scandal regarding the condemnation of the crimes of communism in Romania by President Traian Băsescu. This condemnation was based on the findings of the contentious Presidential Committee for the Analysis of the Communist Dictatorship in Romania.

---

50   In 2006, political scientist Vladimir Tismăneanu was given six months by the presidential committee, dubbed the Tismăneanu Committee after its president, to certify the illegitimate and criminal nature of the communist regime in Romania, and whether there is an illegitimacy to be established per se (see Stan, 2007; Stan, 2009; Cesereanu, 2008; for a broader picture of disclosure, lustration and decommunization measures in Romania, see Grosescu and Ursachi, 2009; Mica, 2008b; Mica, 2009b; Stan, 2002a; Stan, 2002b; Stan, 2004; Stan, 2010; Stan and Turcescu, 2005).

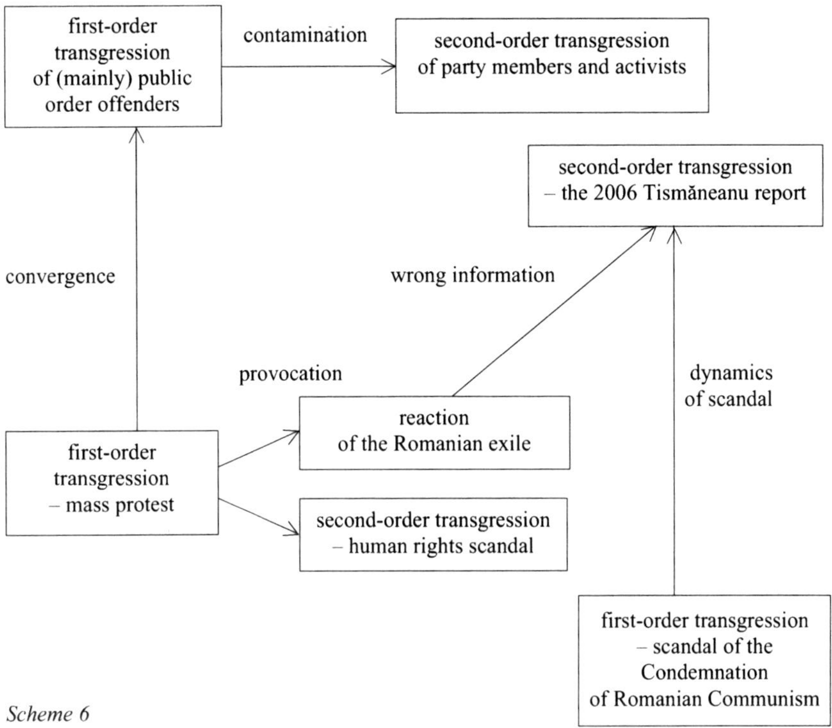

Scheme 6

The Reception of Ceauşescu – Activists and Journalists on Alert*

There are reasons to approach the 1977 Jiu Valley miners' strike from a scandal perspective. As several of the testimonies recall, notwithstanding the fact that the demands of the miners had, by and large, an economic character, the protest of the miners turned inevitably political by the very fact that it was put on display.

The present study focuses on "the visit of comrade Nicolae Ceauşescu to the Valley". In the following sections, a "less official" account of this visit is offered. More explicitly, if I were to employ Goffman's (1990) concepts, I will present elements of the "backstage"[51] activity prior to the visit of Ceauşescu to

---

*   For an earlier version of this section's treatment see Mica (2008a).

51   "A back region or backstage may be defined as a place, relative to a given performance, where the impression fostered by the performance is knowingly contradicted as a matter

Petroşani and Lupeni. As stated before, this visit made the job of the party leaders at the location twice as hard – the responsibility of keeping the miners in check was doubled by having to prepare a smooth and warm welcome for the President of the country. As the interviews given in Jiu Valley in summer 2006 show, Ceauşescu's visit was a very important event in the quieting of the scandal.

The visit can be divided into three episodes. The first was the meeting with the Petroşani party activists; second – the meeting with the miners in Lupeni in front of lodge number two (main scene of the protest); finally – the meeting with the Popular Assembly back in Petroşani.

Before moving on, however, I will make a small parenthesis regarding the vanishing of party's authority during the scandal. The matter is significant, as the activists of the local party establishment were the ones expected to prevent the scandal. The party activists had been mobilized, but they failed to do anything due to the fact that the "miners did not accept being led by anyone at that point" (interview V.A., 2006) [*author's translation*].

The local party activists and party leaders, who had been usually more feared than respected, found themselves helpless when facing the protesting miners. Delegations assembled on the spur-of-the-moment had to be sent from the capital to the rescue of local party activists, whose authority collapsed. The party members lower in rank tried to maintain control over the miners with the help of those miners who held party positions themselves (interview V.A., 2006).

Reportedly, party activists were already "chased like rabbits" throughout Lupeni after the first communication failure with the striking miners when they were faced with the additional task of "dressing Lupeni up" for welcoming Ceauşescu and mobilizing people to come to the popular assembly.

> Because this was the problem of the activists – to bring people. "And you are going to go to this-and-that place!" And eventually ... because there were few of them and they were shitting their pants. Because they were all afraid: "What if it does not turn out well?" And they will be kicked out ... (interview I.D., 2006) [*author's translation*].

---

of course [...]. Here grades of ceremonial equipment, such as different types of liquor or clothes, can be hidden so that the audience will not be able to see the treatment accorded them in comparison with the treatment that could have been accorded them. Here devices such as the telephone are sequestered so that they can be used 'privately'. Here costumes and other parts of personal front may be adjusted and scrutinized for flaws. Here the team can run through its performance, checking for offending expressions when no audience is present to be affronted by them; here poor members of the team, who are expressively inept, can be schooled or dropped from the performance. Here the performer can relax; he can drop his front, forgo speaking his lines, and step out of character" (Goffman, 1990: 114-115).

As compared to the party activists, the effective mobilization of the journalists took place when the "work visit" of Ceauşescu in the Valley was confirmed. They were supposed to help in preparing the welcoming of the Comrade. Up to that point, however, the journalists were not assigned any role by the party. Apart from the concern with the lack of subordination among the miners, there was also the issue of the shortage in human resources. As it was summer, many activists, even superiors of the local party establishment, were on vacation. The shortage in journalists and activists was supplemented by those sent to the Valley from the city of Deva (interview I.D., 2006), while the ranks of the assembly meeting were filled with people coming from all over the Valley.

As said before, the visit of Ceauşescu was planned for three acts in two locations. The group of journalists and activists who gathered the evening before Ceauşescu's arrival at the House of Culture was divided into two groups. The city of Petroşani was shared out to the first group, whereas Lupeni was allotted to the second. In the following sections I will deal with each episode separately.

The meeting with the *aktif* [activ] (body of party cadres) took place at the House of Culture, where around 800 people were amassed. The purpose of this meeting was to update Ceauşescu on the recent developments in Jiu Valley. Still, there was no mentioning whatsoever about the events in Lupeni. The job of the journalists was to prepare the speeches. There are interesting accounts of this practice. The details are described by a former journalist of the local newspaper in Petroşani (interview I.D., 2006). He himself was charged with writing speeches for two miners – one from Lupeni, other from Petrila. Reportedly, they were chosen by the local party secretaries. The journalist made some phone calls in order to get to know the whereabouts of the two miners. The Lupeni miner was "set", while the profile of his colleague from Petrila was still pending. It is important to note that the features of the miner were the ones which granted, at the end of the day, some personality to a speech, a practice which had already become a discursive triteness in the early years of the communist era.

Well, this has been in my whole career as a journalist the most awkward job ever. This was it! It was the newspaper of the party, and everything that they – the activists – did not do, it was supposed to be done by us. Everything that was to be written had to be written by us. Including telegrams, and ... and we had to ... I had to prepare two speeches. A miner from Petrila. "Who?" "Get in touch with the secretary from there and he will tell you who" [...] So. This was my mission. And I went to the office, and made phone calls. "Hey, who will you give from Lupeni to deliver a speech tomorrow?" "We were told [about the one from Lupeni]" "What about [the one] from Petrila?" "I still don't know!" [...] So, because I said at some point: "Comrade! I have worked 20 years in the mine! Brigade leader! I have a family! I have five children! All of them are happy! They live! The wife works at the knitting factory, or somewhere". So, these elements were needed. Apart from those trite expres-

> sions, "Much-beloved! Highly esteemed!", this was the big problem! It had to be
> individualized in a way (interview I.D., 2006) [*author's translation*].

Early the next morning the speeches were written. Everything proceeded smoothly, only the miner from Lupeni was panic-stricken before the show. And thus, the intervention of "somebody from the C.C." (Central Committee) was needed, who had to talk with the miner and to convince him to give the speech. In fact, the crippling stage fright that the miner had suffered was caused by the fear of a would-be reprisal from other miners. During the speech his hands were shaking. Overall, five people took the floor. After the meeting with Ceauşescu ended, the journalists had to keep an eye on the miners who had been entrusted to them (interview I.D., 2006).

The meeting was about two hours long. As stated above, there was no mention of Lupeni. Ceauşescu held his usual speech. At a certain moment during the meeting, while he was skimming through the pages of a thick dossier, he was approached by a local activist and given a note. It seemed that the miners from Lupeni were getting impatient, and that it was time for Ceauşescu to leave (interview I.D., 2006).

It can be stated that the meeting went on without any incidents. But the most difficult part for the party activists, the "work visit of the comrade" to Lupeni, was still ahead of them. The activists and journalists came up against several intricacies. When they met the previous night to prepare the speeches, a group of miners rushed upon them in the middle of the night. Miners captured activists and journalists and restrained them at the legendary lodge number two. The purpose was to thwart any design of staging "the welcoming of the comrade". By the same token, the miners also hampered the process of decorating Lupeni with flags – reportedly, only two flags were put up (interview I.D., 2006).

Upon his arrival, the miners besieged Ceauşescu who was thus left solely in the company of one or two functionaries (which was later called "change of protocol"). Protesters also impeded him in delivering his speech, so Ceauşescu had to move on to negotiations with the miners (represented by the miner Constantin Dobre) during which, he promised the on-the-spot adoption of necessary measures, granting – among other things – a six hour workday.

After the meeting, Ceauşescu went back to Petroşani, where people from all over the Jiu Valley had been gathered for the meeting. The evidence so far collected on the issue does not indicate whether "changes of protocol" had taken place in Petroşani in this final phase of Ceauşescu's visit to Jiu Valley.

Conclusions

I attempted in the foregoing text to reconsider the historical moment of the 1977 strike of the Jiu Valley miners by means of exploration in terms of a scandal. I consider the approach to have proven its usefulness particularly when addressing the strategies employed by the local and central party establishment in dealing with the episode of miners' protest. I tried to show that "dealing with the strike" for the local and central establishments inevitably took the form and the stakes of "dealing with a scandal"; a scandal, which – if not carefully handled – could go around as a scandal generator both inside and outside the country (the mobilization of the diaspora, for instance). The quieting of the protest took place on different levels. From this overall mobilization of forces, I focused on the preparations of the party activists and journalists for the visit of "comrade Nicolae Ceauşescu" in the Valley. I considered it the most significant moment, given that *Scânteia* camouflaged the direct negotiations with the miners that were forced upon Ceauşescu as a voluntary "work visit" of the President.

However, there is a need for an extension of the analysis of the strike in terms of scandal outside the boundaries of the country. The international scandalous potential of the strike was linked to its echo in the exile community. Therefore, analysis of the punctual reaction of the state to this particular scandalous event should be corroborated with an analysis of the response of the state – if there was any – to the reactions in terms of scandal – if there were any – of the diaspora.

2. Braşov 1987

In the following section I will make a first presentation of the regime's actions to restore its authority and reinforce "the normative structure" challenged by the workers' manifestations.

The analysis is carried out based on a body of six interviews which were conducted in Braşov in 2006. These are supplemented by available historical evidence. Given the profile of my interviewees – the then norm offenders – the study does not reveal an institutional logic per se, but the institutional logic as it was perceived by its clients. On the basis of these testimonies, I have reconstructed and further analysed the consequences of participating in the events for the protesters.

From the testimonies at my disposal, I can sketch the following plot. In the aftermath of the revolt, waves of people were taken for interrogations by the Braşov police. A large group was selected, who in turn was taken to Bucharest for almost two weeks of additional interrogations. This careful selection yielded sixty-one people who were eventually tried. Many of the workers had been beaten in both police stations. Reportedly, hundreds of statements had been given and it is said that their character was clearly molded according to whether the investigators were tracing a *political revolt* or – as it later on turned out to be the case – an *act of hooliganism*. More explicitly, at the beginning the investigators seemed to acknowledge the political character of the revolt and were set to look for its organizers (interview D.I., 2006). The investigators in Bucharest moved towards convincing the workers to acknowledge that they have been part of an act of hooliganism. In the beginning, the workers were threatened with the maximum penalty for their deeds, while in the end they were told that Ceauşescu decided to grant them clemency, and that they are not going to serve too much time (interview D.I., 2006). Those interrogated were asked (or demanded) to sign a statement of commitment in which they were to ask for clemency and pledge to undergoing rehabilitation by reintegrating into another "working unit". Within a short period of time they were taken back to Braşov for the trial.

Surprisingly enough, according to the evidence collected on the issue thus far, the trial was conducted in a genre that recalls what Braithwaite (1992) refers to as reintegrative shaming – see section I.4 – *Scandal and Reintegrative Shaming*. The self-criticism from the part of the offender, followed by the granting of clemency by the victim (the state/the communist regime) fits the profile of a successful reintegrative shaming – a degradation ceremony with a happy ending. As stated, this sort of shaming is linked to the name of Braithwaite and it constitutes the basis for the so-called *restorative justice conferences*. To put it plainly, the therapeutic effect of the reintegrative shaming (both for the victim and for the offender) is that it does not place the offender in the middle of stigmatizing bubbles which would later on bring up a de facto deviant status. Moreover, in the present case, the offended (the state) gives him the chance to rehabilitate himself by reintegrating into society. What in the case of the Braşov trial constitutes the engine of this process is the self-criticism that the defendants displayed and the clemency eventually granted to them by the regime. It is also indicative to note that in the perception of the defendants, the accusers act as "representatives of the people". While it is the prosecutor who presents the charges, "reliable working men" are the ones issuing moral indictment. On the basis of the evidence at our disposal, it could be stated that in the whole scenario accusers have acted as stigmatizers and as voices of moral indignation.

It is interesting to note that the trial took place after more than two weeks of interrogations and continuous pressure. Thus, at first blush, it should make everybody happy: the defendants – as they were granted clemency, and the state – as it is asked for forgiveness.

The elements pertaining to what Braithwaite defines as *reintegrative sha-ming* could be also viewed as components of what Goffman designates as a *corrective process*. By definition, scandal sets about a sequence of face-saving practices. Goffman (1982: 20-23) points to four phases in the classical corrective process (together they constitute an *interchange*):

– challenge ("participants take on the responsibility of calling attention to the misconduct");

– offering ("a participant, typically the offender, is given a chance to make amends for the offense and re-establish the expressive order"). Typically, this "move" implies either an interpretation of the meaning of the event (in the sense that the transgression is signified as being less threatening or as a mistake) or a focus on the offender (attenuating circumstances are found);

– acceptance ("the persons to whom the offering is made can accept it as a satisfactory means of reestablishing the expressive order and the faces supported by this order. Only then can the offender cease the major part of his ritual offering");

– thanks ("the forgiven person conveys a sign of gratitude to those who have given him the indulgence of forgiveness") (Goffman, 1982: 20-23).

The Branding (Degradation) Ceremonies [*şedinţe de înfierare*]

The trial of the sixty-one was preceded by purges in the political and administrative apparatus. Subsequent to these purges, thirteen managers and other cadres from the Braşov plant were transferred to working units in other cities. All this happened under the formal label of dismissed (from office) (Oprea and Olaru, 2002: 224-228). Furthermore, two others received suspended sentences of, respectively, two years and one year and eight months (Oprea and Olaru, 2002: 228). As will be documented in the next chapter, the purges unfolded during the so-called *party moots on mass protests* – i.e. meetings of symbolic blame-giving that consisted mainly of the *attribution of fault* and of the *acknowledgment of one's guilt/fault*.

The trial of the sixty-one was preceded by several *branding (degradation) ceremonies* [şedinţe de înfierare]. These ceremonies were meetings of degradation and stigmatization. A word by word translation from Romanian into English would stand for *branding ceremonies* solely. And indeed, the formula covers the two possible usages of the term in the Romanian language. The first stands for the placement of a brand on an animal with a hot iron. The second indicates an activity of condemning and blaming in public, giving the sanction of "stigma of public opinion or moral blame"[52] (Malinowski, 1989: 66-67).

I decided to use the term *branding/degradation ceremonies*, in order to point to the fact that these are in fact *degradation ceremonies* (Garfinkel, 1956). In his article *Conditions of Successful Degradation Ceremonies* (1956), Garfinkel does not explicitly use the words: "stigma of public opinion or moral blame" (Malinowski, 1982: 66-67), or branding. He talks instead about a process of unmasking the motives of the "perpetrator" and the reconstruction of the perpetrator's identity by the denouncer.

> The work of the denunciation effects the recasting of the objective character of the perceived other: The other person becomes in the eyes of his condemners literally a different and *new* person. It is not that the new attributes are added to the old "nucleus". He is not changed, he is reconstituted. The former identity, at best, receives the accent of mere appearance. In the social calculus of reality representations and test, the former identity stands as accidental; the new identity is the "basic reality". What he is now is what, "after all", he was all along (Garfinkel, 1956: 421-422).

Public denunciation is a process of *shame induction*. The aim is to reinforce group solidarity at the expense of one member of the collective who becomes ostracized. This is obviously a type of shaming which, following Braithwaite (1992), could be termed as *not reintegrative* (*disintegrative, stigmatizing*). There are several elements which point in this direction. These could be depicted from Garfinkel's distinction between shame and guilt. Garfinkel's definition of a *status degradation ceremony* is one which focuses on the perceptions and representations of the situation of the denouncer and by the audience as such. Accordingly, "the public identity of an actor is transformed into something looked on as lower in the local scheme of social types" (Garfinkel, 1956: 420). However, there is little discussion about the real effect of the degradation ceremony on its subject, or of the perpetrator's contribution to the whole performance. Does the perpetrator feel ashamed? Does he eventually feel guilty? The one-sided focus on the emotional involvement of the denunciator and of the witnesses is also evident in the types of the conditions which are considered to be necessary for the emergence of a successful degradation ceremony:

1. the event and the perpetrator must be presented as "out of the ordinary";
2. the event and the perpetrator must be "typed";

---

52   This must be understood as "the sanction of tribal punishment, due to a reaction in anger and indignation of the whole community. By this sanction human life, property, and last though not least, personal honour are safeguarded in a Melanesian community, as well as such institutions as chieftainship, exogamy, rank and marriage, which play a paramount part in their tribal constitution" (Malinowski, 1989: 65-55).

3. the denouncer must represent the public interest;
4. the denouncer must deliver his speech in the name of the ultimate values of the group;
5. "[t]he denouncer must arrange to be invested with the right to speak in the name of these ultimate values";
6. the witnesses have to be convinced that the denouncer is a supporter of these values;
7. the denouncer and the witnesses must perceive a distance between them and the perpetrator;
8. the perpetrator "must be placed 'outside', he must be made 'strange'" (Garfinkel, 1956: 422-423).

The following analysis of so-called party moots on mass protests reveals that all these *moots* incorporated elements of degradation ceremonies which targeted perpetrators who were not present; and that, indeed, the above terms and conditions are all fulfilled. The combined sequence of *party moots* (for the party leaders and members) and *branding (degradation) ceremonies* (targeting the protesters in absence) leads eventually to a *reintegrative shaming ceremony* – but this might be also termed as a *reintegrative shaming moot* – of the perpetrators (i.e. the protesters). The eight conditions for a successful degradation ceremony proved necessary and sufficient to carry out such a moot because of two reasons. First – as we will see – the party members and leaders involved were ready to admit their fault. Furthermore, the degradation ceremonies targeting the protesters are staged in the absence of the perpetrator; hence, their approval is not needed. However, this does not pertain to the trial of the sixty-one – as documented, their adhesion was warranted by a signed letter of commitment. In conclusion, the more accurate term for the above list would be conditions of *successful degradation ceremonies with regard to the perpetrators and the witnesses*, and not *conditions of successful degradation ceremonies (in general)*.

In Romania during the late communist era these branding (degradation) ceremonies could have been held in the presence of the persons indicted, or in absentia. For example, at the time of the outburst of the Romanian 1989 Revolution, party secretaries of all levels were called in the middle of the night to meetings where they were expected to point their fingers and denunciate the riotous element demonstrating on the streets of Timişoara. At the factory level, these sorts of meetings used to be held, for example, after somebody managed to illegally emigrate using a tourist leave. Such situations were uncomfortable, as the party secretary denunciating the respective person in a branding (degradation) ceremony was usually same one who had recommended the person as a "reliable element" to be granted the passport to leave the country for tourist purposes. This indicates that these meetings might have quite easily turned against the very persons presiding over them.

The meetings – even at the time – were believed to have been staged. Their purpose was of an incriminating nature and in some cases they led to the exclusion of party members found guilty of "aiding the participants of spiteful acts".

> D.I.: The moment I was arrested, there was clearly a meeting being organized and I was excluded. So, the first measure was ... if you were a party member, the meeting was quickly held, a proceeding was quickly prepared, by means of which they were clearly delimiting themselves from his [the offender's] deeds. He was excluded from the organization. And he was given the sack.
> A.M.: Have you attended this meeting, or was it held in your absence?
> D.I.: No! [This one] not! As I told you! If a meeting had been held for me it was clear ... I was already arrested. So I could not attend a meeting of this kind. [...] So, I did not have the right to attend [it]. I did attend one of the meetings where they took C. I had taken part in such meetings before. And it was brief. "V.C., whatever ..! To stand up now [...] U.C.Y.-ist [member of the Union of Communist Youth]". So they were these party sort-of-things. The president of the party organization from there [offender's local organization]. Two-three words, briefly: "The element, whatever ... so-and-so ". After which immediately: "Who is for his exclusion, please raise your hand". It's recorded in the proceedings.
> [...]
> A.M.: How many people participated, let's say, in the exclusion of V., for example?
> I.D.: Well, however many there were in that organization. If there were 20-25 people, from which seven from the first shift ... the seven of us participated, to put it like this. Sometimes the others too ... (interview D.I., 2006) [*author's translation*].

Another noteworthy element is that the sessions were held in front of an audience. Their public was of a different nature than the one from the trial, for example. As certain interviews revealed, there were cases when the participants had to be persuaded to vote for the proposed exclusion. In other words, if we speak of a certain conformity of the public during branding (degradation) ceremonies, it has to be taken with a grain of salt – because the successful outcome of the staging was not always granted. In some individual cases the vote did not go the party's way.

> And, by surprise – they were also left astounded – nobody raised his hand to support the expulsion (E.T. in interview E.T. and F.P., 2006) [*author's translation*].

In this matter, the accounts of E.T. and F.P. are revelatory. E.T. was the chief of U.C.Y. (Union of Communist Youth) in its sector at the time of the revolt, and he participated in the events. The next day a U.C.Y. meeting was held in his shop with the audience comprised of young men (U.C.Y. members). E.T. and

F.P. were pointed out at as "unreliable elements". According to their testimonies, the goal of the meeting was to expel the two from the organization.

> I was presented. "Look what so-and-so did! Look! He stained the values of the workers from Braşov, wonderful constructors of auto-trucks ...!" (E.T. in interview E.T. and F.P., 2006) [*author's translation*].

Yet, it seems that there was some kind of solidarity that impeded the U.C.Y. members to vote for the exclusion of the two. And thus, in spite of the gallery of diatribes and criticism, the working people did not vote for their expulsion.

> You could unload two trucks of invectives on somebody, but in the end it had to be voted, and recorded that – let's say – 50 of 92 have voted for [the exclusion] (E.T. in interview E.T. and F.P., 2006) [*author's translation*].

Depending on the context, and (seemingly) on the position of the person indicted, the expulsion failure could either be hushed up or not. In the above cited case, for example, after two unsuccessful vote attempts, E.T. and F.P. were asked to leave the room and the expulsion was voted in their absence. They were arrested and interrogated shortly thereafter.

The branding (degradation) ceremonies seem to have evolved in two steps. The first is the incrimination of the persons indicted and the second is the vote for their exclusion. From the testimonies at our disposal it can be inferred that the incrimination was carried out by party secretaries (at the level of the plant) or by shop foremen (also party members). Their stand was, more or less, voluntary. It would seem that some of them have been driven into these sessions given their position in the party, whereas others obviously considered the incriminating sessions as a means to propel their own careers.

> F.P.: I remember ... him crying [...] We used to have [him as] a friend. He was the chief of the U.C.Y. at the level of the shop.
> E.T.: Yes ...
> F.P.: He was presiding at ...
> A.M.: So the one presiding was crying?
> F.P.: Yes. So he was the chief of the U.C.Y. at the tool depot. Thus, practically, he was above E. [from the point of view of his function]. And he was obliged to read ...
> E.T.: To indict.
> [...]
> F.P.: You realize ... The shop foreman asked for the maximum penalty (interview E.T. and F.P., 2006) [*author's translation*].

There still remains an issue as to what extent these branding (degradation) ceremonies did or did not have the effect of a degradation ceremony (Garfinkel, 1956) on the indicted ones, i.e. on the perpetrators. According to Łoś (1988: 75), the "peer justice" performances did have the humiliating impact of degradation ceremonies[53]. In the case of the late communist era in Romania the fact is somehow hard to assess, given that after 1989 all these branding (degradation) ceremonies were mocked rather than remembered as humiliating. It is, however, evident that in the specific case of the 15 November 1987 revolt, they managed to thoroughly frighten the indicted (and most probably not only them). In that specific context, it seemed quite realistic for the defendants to believe that they were going to be sentenced to death, even though they envisaged that this will take place rather by being shot in the back than after a trial.

Eventually, the staged branding (degradation) ceremonies and the staged trial came down to the fanaticism of the people who were requesting the death penalty. Several testimonies point to the fact that the meetings of indictment and the trial stand out by the manner in which they were carried out and not by their palpable outcome, i.e. the exclusion of one or the other from the party, or the punishments of deportation from Braşov given to sixty-one defendants who had stood trial for hooliganism (interview M.A., 2006).

The Request of the Death Penalty

According to the empirical material, the boiling point of branding (degradation) ceremonies was the demand of the death penalty.

> There are testimonies, that the policemen were good fellows. Some of them [of the defendants] … ran away from their place of containment. They came home. They [the police] did not tell them anything. [...] They helped them. The people around them helped them. They exaggerated the whole condemnation. Why? Because they became frightened. In the meetings at the Club House death sentences were demanded. [...] Who demanded them? Their work colleagues! A fact which called off everything. The whole credit. This holds for both sides. There [you have it]! (interview M.A., 2006) [*author's translation*].

According to several testimonies, the regime would have actually executed all sixty-one of the defendants if it were not for international pressure on Ceauşescu.

---

53   "Any evaluation of the potential usefulness of social courts must include the context in which they operate. The obvious danger in any totalitarian state is the reality that such social bodies become mere extensions of the coercive state power [...] Yet another problem results from the very nature of any 'peer justice' institution. Such structure involves enormous exposure to public scrutiny and condemnation by peers; for some people, the psychological trauma of being publically shamed may have devastating consequences. All those familiar with the descriptions of the impact of 'degradation ceremonies' and informal labelling tend to be aware of the psychological and moral damage which they may occasion [...]" (Łoś, 1988: 74-75).

A.M.: And how did the trial develop? You said that the father of one of your colleagues asked for the death penalty.

D.I.: No. This was at the branding (degradation) ceremonies [*şedinţe de înfierare*]. This happened there. At the beginning. [...] So, at U.C.Y. and party meetings.

A.M.: So, you have been as well subjected to branding (degradation) ceremonies [*şedinţe de înfierare*]? Was this before you got arrested? [Or] afterwards?

D.I.: Afterwards. We were ... we had been arrested. A meeting was held. What measures to be taken on the party line, security, whatever. So, what happened there? "What are we going to do with the workers who revolted?" And there, in those big meetings, in the plenary meetings of the party ... there they called, some of them, the zealous ones of the party ... "To be condemned to death! We demand capital punishment!" I do not know what [else] ...! So, they were showing off their zeal as "big communists" (interview D.I., 2006) [*author's translation*].

According to the testimonies, it seems that the people in charge of delivering the tirades were carefully selected by party officials. They were the party secretaries at the level of the branches or workshops. It might however be the case that not all those requesting the death penalty had been chuckling. It was the case that not all those requesting the death penalty had been exonerated from their role in facilitating the outburst of the workers, if there was any such responsibility ranking on their shoulders to be established. In regard to this matter, the most notorious case is that of the technical manager of the *Steagul Roşu* factory. Reportedly, in branding (degradation) ceremonies he was among the first to demand the maximum penalty.

Or the kind of [...] (who was the economic director at that point or whatever) – the miserable – was the first to demand death. "Condemn them to death! Terminate all of them!" And so on ... He was also deported to Vaslui, or someplace (interview D.I., 2006) [*author's translation*].

The defendants faced the scarecrow of the death penalty in two instances. It was assiduously commanded by representatives of the working people during branding (degradation) ceremonies and it was present as a threat during the interrogations before the trial.

A.M.: And this issue of the death penalty? The first time ... how was first requested?

D.I.: So, the first time ... how did they categorize us? As criminals. They would read to you from the Penal Code. And they were telling you: "Let us see, D.! Hey! Where do you belong? Look! Here! What have you done? Did you shout: 'Down with Ceauşescu!?'" "Yes!" "Did you break the interceptors [from the trolley-buses]?" "Yes!" "Did you set the flag on fire?" "Yes!" "So, this makes you a criminal under paragraph ... – whatever ... So look what is written down here! The so-and-so article! Good ..." [...] "17-25 years! No! No! No! Because you are stubborn ... You did not want to recognize your guilt ... Hold on! Life in jail or death! Aaah! – he says – Look! Do you see this pen?! I can decide with one signature, whether I grant you clemency or not. Out you go! Get out! I have to think about it!" [...] And after 20 minutes they would call you in again. So it was this psychological thing. In the moment you had the pleasure of meeting this person again and you knew the alternatives he gave you ... Clearly! You immediately took the alternative. "Yes sir! Let me write more! Let me do [more]! To admit to [having done] whatever else!" This was their way of working. [...] So this was a psychological thing, to put it like this. And this came together with the fact that you were not fed [...]   (interview D.I., 2006) [*author's translation*].

The Statement of Commitment

The investigators gradually became less violent, to the point that a form of dialog was established with the defendant. Eventually we can even speak of a certain paternal attitude on the part of the investigators (interview D.I., 2006). Two or three days prior to the trial, the defendants were told how to behave. The party took care to ensure that they were properly fed and dressed. What – on the basis of the documents – was perceived as the material outcome of the two-week interrogation was the so-called *statement of commitment* – defendants' ticket out of the beatings and the interrogations to which they were subjected in Bucharest; accompanied by clemency supposedly granted by Ceauşescu himself.

> M.M.: This is what they were saying: "Good, but you have to write it somehow too ..." At the beginning, and here, in Braşov they kept on saying that we are going to be tried, we are going to be tried ... Well, afterwards they started ... and even this old investigator said that: "You are very lucky that he intervened [on your behalf]. Comrade Nicolae Ceauşescu forgave you and you are going to be treated only as a hooligan for your acts and ...".
> A.M.: And how did you interpret this affirmation?
> M.M.: Well, how should I have interpreted it?
> A.M.: [Did you interpret it] with relief?
> M.M.: I saw a door to get out of there. From that hell (interview M.M., 2006) [*author's translation*].

From collected accounts we can infer that the statement of commitment contained self-criticism in front of the state and an agreement to relocate.

> This statement of commitment has two connotations. To put it like this ... this declaration. On the one hand, we recognized that we did the wrong thing. Second, we were given clemency on the basis of this declaration. And, to put it this way, the third point was letting them send us wherever they wanted to. I mean, to leave it to their latitude. I mean: "If you consider that there is any place where I have to go to rehabilitate myself ...", whatever. I did agree. So these three things were at large what they wanted. [This was] what their goal had been. And us ... You can imagine. It had been a novelty for us ... even the fact that the work punishment, prison sentence were not the problem. The problem was that ... We recognized the deeds in

the first instance. So it was not anymore ... Well, that some of us denied them during the period of investigations ... Whatever ... So everyone tried to escape. Or we tried to put the blame on somebody else, who we knew was arrested. Thus, something [had happened]. We tried. They – now – had the teams very well done. They had pictures ... (interview D.I., 2006) [*author's translation*].

Moreover, the statement of commitment implied asking for clemency and commitment (depending on the individual cases) to repair the damages.

> A.M.: And in the end you to were given a statement of commitment to sign?
> M.M.: Commitment that ... I will carry on the activity the way I am requested at the specific place [of work]. And that I will repair the material damages etc. Not that I will do anything else. So, to inform ... I was not asked anything like this. I was only told that: "I will carry on my activity, I am going to be an element ... a reliable citizen ... they have it there (interview M.M., 2006) [*author's translation*].

From the data gathered, it is rather difficult to assess what the actual scope of the statement was. It seems, however, that it was to guarantee the protesters' commitment to rehabilitation. What is most important, it seemed to provide their agreement to relocate. After the deportation, their wives were called for (put pressure on) to either to divorce or follow their husbands. In early January 1988 a clemency decree was issued (Oprea and Olaru, 2002: 132). And if it was not for the open secret that they were political offenders, the decree would have allowed all of them to return to Braşov. Their sentences – prison terms to be executed at their work place – ranged between six months and three and a half years.

The Trial

Before the trial, as mentioned earlier, the defendants were trained in self-criticism. The training was done individually. It took place in Bucharest at some point during the last two-three days before their return to Braşov.

> A.M.: And how? How was it [the statement of commitment] presented to you?
> M.M.: So, it happened in the last days. In the last two days. [...] Yes, in a way he told us, the old man told me: "You were lucky that this-and-that, and whatever ... You are going to be treated with indulgence for what you have done, although you do not deserve it ... and so-on and-so-forth. And you are going to be tried, but you are not going to get a severe punishment. [...] But after a few years you are going to forget. You are going to forget that you have participated" and so on ... That afterwards, after this introduction somebody else came. [...] So, this is what was happening in the last days. He came with the respective statement. So I was taken over by somebody else. In the last week, he took care that we give the respective statement. He came from Bucharest. Each person came with his investigator, who ... [...] "Bear in mind this". So. He was calling us. We were writing. "Did you memorize? You are

asking for clemency that 'I will do ... I will pay for the material damages. I am pledging that ...'"
A.M.: And you were told that a trial is coming up, and that during the trial ...?
M.M.: Yes, yes. [...] And. "We ask for clemency. That we agree to repair the material damages" [...] He said. "More ... in 2-3 years you are going to get off. So. Maybe even quicker, who knows? How you are going to behave at the workplace where you are going to" and so on and so forth (interview M.M., 2006) [*author's translation*].

The trial took place under high security. According to the then chief of traffic control in Braşov, the men under his orders were told not to allow traffic in the area where the trial took place, more explicitly on the street where the Club House was located (interview T.D., 2006). The hall where the trial was supposed to take place was divided in two. The defendants sat on one side, on the other – party members and the carefully selected audience. Seemingly, the least colorful character was the prosecutor. He read the indictment after which the floor was open to the accusers who were present in the hall. It was them, who requested the death penalty.

The counselors for the defense were even less noticeable than the prosecutor – to the extent that some defendants do not even remember them. There had been about five defense lawyers and the defense of the defendants was delivered collectively.

A.M.: And about how many did take the floor?
M.M.: The floor ...? From them? I do not know if there have been three-four-five [of them]?! [...] They asked for the punishment as well. "They deserve the maximum punishment!" I mean the capital punishment. "Yes. The maximum punishment admitted by the law and whatever!" And then the lawyers intervened. I had a lawyer too. One was representing about 25 [of us]. And he said that: "The majority of them are young. They are from other parts of the country. They adapted a little bit harsher and so on and so forth ..." He was trying to show that we are not adapted. We came here in Braşov as strangers and we started consuming alcohol. This and lack of family support led us to do what we have done. This was as a defense. "And [let] the instance grand clemency!" And so on and so forth (interview M.M., 2006) [*author's translation*].

One of the original elements of the trial was the self-criticism, "self-shaming" of the accused. This implied apologizing and agreeing with the punishments inflicted upon them.

A.M.: And afterwards [after the word of the defense] each of the defendants had been given the right to speak?
[...]
M.M.: Well, yes. After they did all the indictment and so on and so forth ... they said ... I do not know if ... the punishments. But I think so. It was decided ... the instance. No, before he said that "We take the floor" and each of us was standing up

when called out: "Yes, so, Comrade President – this was the way we were addres-
sing him – I admit to committed deeds. I am asking for clemency to the instance and
I agree to pay for the material damages to different ... for what they have done ..."
It was imposed upon me. I do not know now the formula.
M.M.: And the declaration was short?
A.M.: Yes. One statement.
A.M.: Ok. Were there people crying?
M.M.: Yes. Some of us. The more sensitive. They said: "... I am sorry! I am truly
sorry! I did not want to do something like this!" I really do not remember names. I
do not remember who exactly made this declaration. Yes and he is determined to
straightened himself and to become a reliable citizen and so on and so forth (inter-
view M.M., 2006) [*author's translation*].

The testimonies recall a self-shaming rally with quite dramatic effects. Several
have cried. There is also one testimony available which recalls the whole *self-
criticism–shaming–apologizing ceremony* as having been taken place very
quickly.

A.M.: And how long did the trial take?
M.B.: "Do you recognize why you are here?" "Yes!" About half an hour – forty-five
minutes. "Do you regret the committed deeds?" "Yes!" "Three years!" These have
been the questions. "Ok! Two years and a half!" "One year and a half!" [...] So,
everything was staged. Everything was prepared. Absolutely! And the papers these
people were reading, they have it already done. Because they were reading them. So,
they were not speaking freely (interview M.B., 2006) [*author's translation*].

Conclusions

What is striking about the profile of the men selected to face trial is that they
were young and mainly without strong ties to Braşov. Perhaps, this fact made
the job of the communist authorities a lot easier. By that point, Ceauşescu's
political regime had lost its credit on the international arena to the extent that it
could have used a self-criticism itself in order to take the spots out of its coat.

The regime managed to nip the germs of protest in the bud in 1987. It seems
that the manner in which the investigations and the trial had been conducted was
indeed the decisive element. As the testimonies reveal, the punishments were
not as harsh, but still the people were put on their knees. Another factor that
might have facilitated this outcome is that the revolt was spontaneous and that
half of the defendants were whipping boys and the other half – momentary overt
political protesters. One of our interviewees recalled that, "the bulk of them did
not know what they were doing there". The statement might be interpreted as a
token of evidence for the fact that a collective organized action against communism was still pending. This might have facilitated the self-criticism endeavor of

the defendants, but it might as well have been effective as a working hypothesis for the organizers of the trial.

PART IV
THE RITUALIZATION OF PARTY MOOTS DURING THE CEAUŞESCU REGIME

The following chapter aims to answer the following inquiry of the present study: Which mechanisms governed the dynamics of convergence and contamination in the above events (as far as party members, leaders and activists are concerned)? Accordingly, I opted for the analysis of moots [*luări in discuție*] which followed the occurrence of scandal. The following introductory part on party moots on mass ptotests and moot bullying points to several distinctions between these party meetings and the Kpelle moots (Gibbs, 1963). Yet, there are common elements – i.e. the essential processes of the attribution of fault and the admittance of guilt/fault – which clearly frame the communist meetings in terms of moots.

As matters stood, the outcome of these moots has been both convergence and contamination. The term convergence indicates that the moot affected the official framing of the events which had just taken place – a signification which entailed the convergence between the protesters and hooligans. As far as contamination is concerned – it is an externality of scandal. In this specific case, contamination affected a second-order transgression of party members and activists from the first-order transgression of (mainly) public order offenders. The hypothesis to be tested in the following analysis is that the mechanisms of convergence and contamination were running concurrently during the party moots on mass protests and that they supported each other.

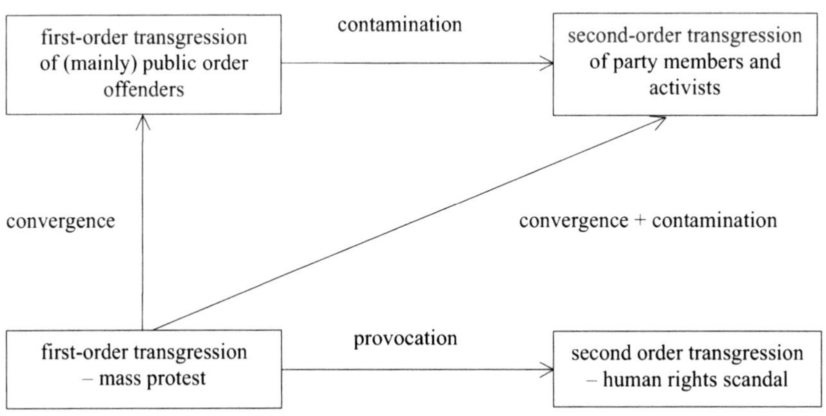

Scheme 7

The following sub-chapter applies an inverted chronology. In other words, I begin with the case of Braşov 1987, and later discuss Jiu Valley 1977. This choice is a result of the nature of the empirical material that will serve for the analysis of such phenomena as guilt-inducing, bullying and/or mobbing during the late communist era in Romania.

Briefly stated, I will try to show that in the aftermath of the 1987 revolt in Braşov, the bulk of the efforts were pointed in the direction of establishing those reproachable for the events which occurred – i.e. those who were implicated from the political and administrative apparatus on the one hand, and by the bulk of the protesters (those designated as hooligans) on the other. Equally important, establishing those who were guilty went hand in hand with those individuals recognizing their misgivings and making a pledge to improve their behavior and re-educate themselves. This harmony was reached at the expense of several dismissals and party sanctions, as far as the leaders in the administrative and political apparatus were concerned. There are also two cases of suspended prison sentences. The party sanctions include votes of blame/censure, votes of blame/censure with warning, and a few exclusions from the party [*vot de blam, vot de blam cu avertisment, excludere*]. In the case of the protesters, the authorities resorted to interrogations and tactics of intimidation. Out of the 183 interrogated, sixty-one were selected to face the charge of having committed an "offence against morals and turmoil of public order" [*ultraj contra bunelor moravuri şi tulburarea liniştii publice*] during the trial – fifty-three of whom were from *Steagul Roşu*. Twenty-six received prison sentences to be carried out at the workplace [*închisoare cu executarea pedepsei la locul de muncă*] and the others received suspended prison sentences, not exceeding three years (Spiridon, 2008: 241-242; Oprea and Olaru, 2002: 229-240). Furthermore, the few students who shortly after the events tried to uphold the cause of the revolt were also expelled from their schools.

In the foregoing section, the excerpts cited tried to provide a glimpse of the atmosphere that preceded the trial and the climate of the trial itself. Primarily, these were documented from the point of view of the arrested and/or convicted protesters. Their testimonies give non-negligible evidence attesting to the fact that the phenomena of bullying and/or mobbing have occurred on a large scale basis in the aftermath of the mass protests. In the following section, I will further substantiate this hypothesis on the basis of the transcripts and proceedings of party meetings that were held at the factory level. I seek to document that the issues on the agenda of these meetings anticipate episodes of what I would term as: *moot bullying*. In my interpretation, the encouragement of bullying and/or mobbing during communism went hand in hand with the party allegedly demanding *(issues) to be discussed with the people*. During the meetings of party cadres, an almost contagious urge to incriminate "the guilty ones (the group of hooligans)" became visible, along with demands for the most severe (i.e. capital in several instances) punishment. As scapegoating progressed, this call and wish to reprimand did not lose intensity, even though the so-called "representatives of the working people" substituted their request for capital punishment with one for the exclusion of "the guilty ones (the group of hooligans)" from their ranks. Following the lead of literature on bullying and/or mobbing I would regard this demand for the exclusion of "the guilty ones (the group of hooligans)" as a bullying and/or mobbing syndrome. Several authors point to the fact that there are instances when bullying and/or mobbing in the workplace targets the *de facto* exclusion and departure of the victim. In other words, bullying and/or mobbing at the workplace has all the chances to unfold as the mobilization of a group of people who are not content with the sole persistence of a scapegoat, but who actually will not rest until the one being mobbed is not "taken out of the game".

Conclusively, with regard to workplace bullying and/or mobbing there is one hypothesis that I want to advance herein. Accordingly, the process of scapegoating in the aftermath of both the 1987 revolt, and the 1977 strike includes elements of bullying and/or mobbing. As stated, this is a type of bullying that I would call moot bullying. I will try to show that, although in different fashion, both party cadres and protesters were subject to it. In the case of the protesters for example, the moot bullying was delivered by groups of representatives of workers demanding severe punishment of "the guilty ones (the group of hooligans)" and eventually – their expulsion from the factory.

In the following sections I will try to depict and analyze the characteristics of moot bullying in relationship with scapegoating. In comparison with the phenomena of bullying and/or mobbing, scapegoating is acknowledged on a larger scale to have occurred in the aftermath of the 1987 revolt. As far as bullying and/or mobbing are concerned, these phenomena are rather accounted for indirectly in cases when reference is being made to the so-called branding (degradation) ceremonies. In other words, the testimonies give evidence of these phenomena having occurred without naming them as such.

As it was probably already noticed, when mentioning the general phenomenon of bullying I opted for the formula of bullying and/or mobbing instead of declaring simply bullying and mobbing respectively, as it is at times hard to find a consensus regarding the distinction between these two notions. As a forthcoming section will elaborate upon the differences between these two terms, it suffices here to say that following Matthiesen's (2006) work, I could have decided for the conceptualization which regards bullying as a more aggressive phenomenon and mobbing as a somehow more subtle process. Viewed from this angle, it should come as little surprise that both bullying and mobbing have occurred in the aftermath of the events of 1977 and 1987. While all of the above pertains, I decided to follow Matthiesen's typology of bullying which includes elements such as: *conflict bullying, predatory bullying, scapegoat bullying, work related stalking, whistleblowing, retaliation bullying,* etc. (Matthiesen, 2006). Among other benefits, this choice allows for supplementing the series with one more subtype – *moot bullying*; as well as viewing it in relationship with others.

Recalling the issue of guilt that was mentioned and addressed jointly with that of shame in the second chapter of the book, we can see that the study is concerned with the phenomena of inducing and acknowledging guilt. The double *guilt–shame* and *inducing guilt–shaming* is introduced for the reason that it contextualizes – from the theoretical point of view – the phenomena of acknowledging guilt in the party meetings at the level of the enterprise after the events of November 1987 in Braşov. Additionally, it also proves useful in depicting nuances between the self-criticism of the party cadres (which is carried out in terms of *guilt*) and the criticism of "the guilty ones (the group of hooligans)" (which draws on words such as *disgrace* and *shame*).

Before opening the discussion, it should be stated that the present study is not the first inquiry into the issue of shame and shaming – both within communist regimes in general and with regard to the specific case of Jiu Valley. Wedel's book: *The Private Poland: An Anthropologist's Look at Everyday Life* (1986: 163-168), for example, discusses the oscillation of the expressions of Polish national sentiments between *shame* and *pride*. Further, the particular issue of *shame talk* in Jiu Valley was also presented in the studies of Kideckel – *Labor and Society in the Jiu Valley and Fagaras Regions of Romania, Part I: Variations in Response to the Crises* (2001) – and Friedman – *Shame and the Experience of Ambivalence on the Margins of the Global: Pathologizing the Past and Present in Romania's Industrial Wastelands* (2007a). Both articles discuss the generalization of the emotion of shame subsequent to the loss of the work-derived identity brought about by the massive layoffs in the region during the 1997-1999 period (Kideckel, 2001). Kideckel considers shame as a social emotion, but also as an activity targeting the local authorities (for example in the hunger strikers of 1999 and 2000). Whereas, Friedman's study presents "personal and critical functions of shame" – i.e. more than an emotion, shame becomes a component of the critique of a political, economic and moral order that is perceived as unjust (Friedman, 2007a: 246). Hence, shame is both the result and the critique of this decline (for discussion of these two authors see Mica, 2009a).

As already mentioned, by and large, both the 1977 miners' strike and the 1987 revolt were followed by countless moots which debated the events, the behavior of the protesters and the reaction of party cadres. These public meetings were primarily conducted by party cadres or by the so-called "working collective" [*colectivul de oameni ai muncii*]. In the case of 1987, the party meetings (both public and behind closed doors), as well as the General Extraordinary Assembly of the representatives of the working people from *Steagul Roşu*[54] are examples of such moots. I decided to refer to them as *party moots on mass protests* for the reason that they unfold subsequent to mass protests and they are orchestrated by party members. Furthermore, I would also like to distinguish this particular type of moot within the overall genre, and in particular, from concrete manifestations – such as *the Kpelle moot* for example.

According to the Merriam-Webster Online Dictionary (***) a *moot* is:

1. a deliberative assembly primarily for the administration of justice; *especially*: one held by the freemen of an Anglo-Saxon community;

2. *obsolete*: argument, discussion.

Belonging to the same family there is also the word *moot court* designating a "mock court in which law students argue hypothetical cases for practice" (Merriam-Webster Online Dictionary, ***). An established education method in Anglo-Saxon legal traditions, *mooting* was quite celebrated in the early Tudor period. While in seventeenth and eighteenth century it experienced a period of decay (due to the rise of written texts), the twentieth century witnessed the proliferation of *mooting societies* and *mooting competitions* (see Aquecheek, 2006).

The term found its application in the field of anthropology, namely in the case of the so-called *Kpelle moots*. The Kpelle people – a patrilineal group of rice cultivators who live in Liberia and in southeastern Guinea – developed an institution for the informal settlement of disputes which is based on the manipulation of rewards (Gibbs, 1963).

The Kpelle *berei mu meni saa*, or "house palaver", is an informal airing of a dispute which takes place before an assembled group which includes kinsmen of the litigants and neighbours from the quarter where the case is being heard. It is a completely *ad hoc* group, varying greatly in composition from case to case. The matter to be settled is usually a domestic problem: alleged mistreatment or neglect by a spouse, an attempt to collect money paid to a kinsman for a job which was not completed, or a quarrel among brothers over the inheritance of their father's wives (Gibbs, 1963: 3).

The moots run parallel with courtroom hearings and they are based on different principles. They usually take place on Sundays, at the home of the plaintiff, before an assembled group composed of kinsmen and neighbors of the litigants (Gibbs, 1963: 3). They are run by a mediator who is appointed by the complai-

---

54   "[…] *the general assembly* of the members or employees was the supreme authority in the collective and state farms, trade unions, consumers' cooperative, factories and schools" (Kideckel, 2006: 63).

nant. The mediator is both a kinsman and a person who enjoys high prestige in the society – two characteristics which enable him to indulge in mechanisms of soft governance which would make the litigants and the members of the community reach a consensus. The Kpelle moot begins with the delivery of a blessing intended to strengthen the unity of the community and the perception of this unity by the people present (Gibbs, 1963: 4). Apart from this role however, the blessing must be also seen as an element which increases the chances that the losing party will accept the consensus of the group. Following this opening ritual, there is the process of mooting, which leads to the attribution of fault by the mediator of the moot. What comes next is the admittance of fault by the parties held chiefly at blame. The losing party is expected to deliver a formal apology to the winner of the moot. Those at fault bring "gifts of apology" and local rum for the disputants and participants of the moot. Eventually, the circle of harmony is restored with the acceptance of the apologies and gifts by the winning party.

According to Gibbs, apart from being conciliatory, the Kpelle moots are also therapeutic[55]. Following the work of Parsons on the individual therapy conditions, he identifies in the development of these moots elements specific to the therapy setting. These features are:
- support and encouragement (from the therapist/group) in expressing ones feelings/complaints;
- permissiveness indicating "to the patient that every-day restrictions on making anti-social statements or acting out anti-social impulses are lessened";
- denial of reciprocity, i.e. "the therapist will not respond in kind when the patient acts in a hostile manner or with inappropriate affection";
- manipulation of rewards, i.e. the patient/the party held at blame is "coaxed to conformity by the granting of rewards. In the moot, one of the most important rewards is the group's approval which goes to the wronged person who accepts an apology and to the person who is magnanimous enough to make one" (Gibbs, 1963: 6-8).

---

55   "When successful, the moot stops the process of alienation which drives two spouses so far apart that they are immune to ordinary social-control measures such as a smile, a frown, or a pointed aside [...] A moot is not always successful, however. Both parties must have a genuine willingness to co-operate and a real concern about their discord. Each party must be willing to list his grievances, to admit his guilt, and make an open apology. The moot, like psychotherapy, is impotent without well-motivated clients" (Gibbs, 1963: 9).

According to Gibbs, the moots of the Nyoro people also function according to a therapeutic fashion. These procedures of dispute resolutions are brought about by a council of neighbors and they aim to reintegrate the defendant back into the community. Seemingly, the whole conference could be framed as an *inverted status degradation ceremony.*

> [John H. M.] Beattie correctly points out that, because the council of neighbours has no power to enforce its decision, the shared feast is *not* to be viewed primarily as a penalty, for the wrong-doer acts as a host and also shares in the food and drink. "And it is a praiseworthy thing; from a dishonourable status he is promoted to an honourable one ..." [...] and reintegrated into the community (Gibbs, 1963: 10).

What is relevant to the investigation of this study is that the party which is held to be mainly at blame is won over to conformity by the prospective of becoming again a part of the community.

Unfortunately, Gibbs' study does not point to other mechanisms of persuasion which might work to the advantage of granting the award of the groups' approval. The present study aims to fill this gap, by analyzing moots of the Ceauşescu regime. As stated, the term *moot bullying* denotes the phenomenon of bullying which occurred during all these meetings. It might consist of: criticism, pressuring, denunciation, exclusion, attempts of inducing guilt and shame, stigmatization etc. In my interpretation, the phenomenon of bullying took place irrespective of whether party moots on mass protests regarding the party cadres were followed by admittances of one's guilt/fault or not. With a closer look we will see that the same holds true also in the case of the 1987 defendants.

The term bullying also opens an opportunity for introducing the concept of humiliation in the analysis. Wedel (1986: 149) points to the role it might have played as a social-psychological experience in the communist regime: "it is day-to-day humiliation that makes socialization effective. This humiliation is based on anger and frustration from constant wounded pride". In my understanding, in addition to the above, humiliation also implies a feeling of subordination to authority. I take over a modality of distinguishing between shame and humiliati-on that drives closer to the position of Oravecz, Hárdi and Lajtai (2004: 13). Accordingly, humiliation is not an emotion – as shame is – but an "inner psychosocial effect of violence" and it is not a threat to a social bond that hitherto was positive. Did the defendants and the party activists feel humiliated? Was the drafting of discourses in terms of shame and guilt an outcome of them being humiliated? Most probably it was so. Yet, I am hesitant because of what I term as the *cognitive dissonance type of aftereffect* (a term to be introduced in the *Conclusions* of my work) these questions will be difficult to answer at the moment.

What should be stated, however, is that the bullying of the protesters was much more aggressive and radical. None of the party cadres goes as far as to ask his fellow members to be subjected to branding (degradation) ceremonies, yet this appears to be a common request as far as the so-called "guilty ones (the group of hooligans)" are concerned. Quite often these specific moots did evolve into branding (degradation) ceremonies – in other words, they developed into meetings of denunciation, expressing indignation and stigmatization. This process usually took place with respect to the so-called "acts of hooliganism"; less so with the party cadres. In fact, I was not able to find evidence of party leaders having been subject to such branding (degradation) ceremonies. Still, as it will be documented, the party leaders might have become victims/targets in similar scenarios. A distinction, however, is always maintained in the tone of denunciation as such, given that in the case of "the guilty ones (the group of hooligans)", there is expressed much more indignation and anger, a fact which leads me to conclude that the party moots on mass protests are rather ceremonies of inducing guilt, while the branding (degradation) ceremonies could be cataloged as ceremonies of inducing shame and stigmatization. As we will see, in both cases, exclusion and sanctions become imperative. A link could be established here with Elster's (2009b; see also 2007) differentiation between social and moral norms. Accordingly, the violation of social norms leads to "contempt in observer" and an action tendency to "avoid or ostracize the violator" that, in the last instance, develops "shame in violator"; while the violation of moral norms pertains to "indignation in observer" and the correlative tendency to "punish the violator" on the one hand, and feelings of "guilt in violator" on the other (Elster, 2009b: 197).

The request for the exclusion of "the guilty ones (the group of hooligans)" from the ranks of the working collective – that was voiced during the party moots on mass protests which have been held subsequent to the mass protests – resembles closely the practice of *shunning*. That is, dissociation from a person indicated by a group or an organization. This type of sanction is often linked to religious groups and closed and exclusivist organizations and communities. It usually targets whistleblowers, dissidents and persons with a deviant conduct from the established standards. The shunning usually stops when the prodigal son returns to the shunning group.

Bullying and/or Mobbing

Primarily, bullying and/or mobbing are defined as an aggressive behavior directed by one or more people against another person(s) for a sustained period of time (which is usually accounted for in terms of months). The spectrum of the activities ranges from subtitle aggressiveness, gossip and manipulation to overt and physical violence. As we saw, in the aftermath of the 1987 Braşov revolt – and to a certain degree also in the case of the 1977 strike – we are dealing only with compact episodes of bullying and/or mobbing.

There is a plethora of notions and formulas used to describe this kind of phenomena at work. In this respect, a useful instrument is Vartia-Väänänen's (2003: 9, 10) table of *Terms and Definitions for Workplace Bullying Used by Various Authors*. This contains the following notions and formulas: harassment, scapegoating, mobbing/psychological terror, workplace trauma, work harassment, bullying, abusive behavior/emotional abuse, mobbing.

With respect to bullying and mobbing, there is more of a consensus regarding a would-be distinction between the two notions than one regarding what exactly this difference stands for. Hence, one might come across analysis using the formula of "workplace bullying" (Moreno Jiménez et al., 2007; Notelaers et al., 2006) as well as that of "workplace mobbing" (Duffy and Sperry, 2007; Meseguer de Pedro et al., 2008).

An inventory of these distinctions is made by Matthiesen (2006: 25, 26). According to him, following Andrea Adams, one could distinguish between bullying studies – which focus on the *bully* or on his behavior – and the research which focuses on mobbing – which concentrates on the *victim*. Then again, Duffy and Sperry (2007: 398) deal with a distinction between bullying and mobbing according to which the former is a term used in the United States and it denotes an attack of a single individual, whereas the latter suggests a group attack on a fellow worker. Yet, Heinz Leymann regards mobbing as a phenomenon among adults which is more subtle and less aggressive than bullying (see Matthiessen, 2006: 26). Furthermore, according to some authors, the term mobbing is used in German-speaking countries, the Netherlands and some Mediterranean countries, whereas bullying gained predominance in the English-speaking world (Matthiesen, 2006: 15). The research of the phenomenon of workplace bullying proliferated in Europe; comparatively, it seems to be less researched in United States, where the field of bullying theorists is much more concerned with the occurrence of this phenomenon in schools.

Additionally, the spatial criterion of the usage of the notion seems not to have emerged in an aleatoric fashion. Presumably, it is related to differences in types of bullying and/or mobbing that could be discerned when these phenomena occur in different environments. For example, the Scandinavian usage of the term mobbing is connected to inquiries of the workplace, but it is also related to the fact that in these countries there seems to be "little power distances" between leaders and their subordinates. This should not, however, imply that bullying cannot surface between people of equal status as well (Matthiesen, 2006: 26).

The systematic research of mobbing in the workplace was pioneered by Heinz Leymann, a Swedish family therapist, in the early eighties. Peter-Paul Heinemann studied bullying – as a type of aggression among school children – in 1972[56]. According to Matthiesen a succinct definition of bullying should list the following:

> Bullying at work means harassing, offending, socially excluding someone or negatively affecting someone's work tasks. In order for the label bullying (or mobbing) to be applied to a particular activity, interaction or process it has to occur repeatedly and regularly (e.g. weekly) and over a period of time (e.g. about six months). Bullying is an escalating process in the course of which the person confronted ends up in an inferior position and becomes the target of systematic negative social acts. A conflict cannot be called bullying if the incident is an isolated event or if two parties of approximately equal "strength" are in conflict (Matthiesen, 2006: 11).

Additionally, he also identifies ten subtypes of workplace bullying, listed together with a brief clarification. The first two types are borrowed from Ståle Einarsen's work, whereas the following eight are Matthiesen's own contribution in the field.

1. *Conflict bullying* develops from interpersonal or social conflicts.
2. *Predatory bullying* is the case of the leader who tries to make a point about his authority at the expense of his subordinates. According to Vartia-Väänänen the distinction between conflict bullying and predatory bullying implies the fact that in the latter case the person experiencing bullying "has done nothing personally to provoke the negative behavior of the bully". The victim might be the representative of a group, for example (Vartia-Väänänen, 2003: 12).
3. *Scapegoat bullying* – this notion follows the work of Ingels Thylefors (Vartia-Väänänen, 2003: 8, 9, 14, 17) on scapegoating that is followed by harassment.
4. *Sexual harassment* reportedly, usually targets women.
5. *Humor-oriented bullying* – mainly, this is an asymmetrical (or at least experienced as such) "person-oriented humor [which] is directed towards someone in an out-group position".

---

56   "When bullying (in Norwegian '*mobbing*'; and '*mobbning*' in Sweden) was introduced as a concept in Scandinavia by Heinemann (1972) to characterize a specific type of aggression among school children, he had in mind the 'mob' or group attacking a specific target" (Matthiesen, 2006: 9).

6. *Work related stalking* takes place when a person impedes the work of another and sometimes even terrorizes another person.
7. *Extreme media exposure bullying* usually targets politicians and persons of higher status.
8. *Bullying of workplace newcomers,* or "rite de passage bullying".
9. *The judicial derelicts* – is perceived to come from a system, from bureaucrats and not from a person or from a group of persons as such. It is noteworthy that, according to Matthiessen, this type of bullying might occur as a result of a *secondary bullying* – a term borrowed again from Einarsen. More explicitly, bullying by the system might come subsequent to the fact that the person who feels bullied at work tries to put an end to this phenomenon by signaling it to the authorities. By way of analogy with scandal – this secondary bullying could be also termed as *second-order bullying.*
10. *Whistleblowing retaliation bullying.* A distinction should be made in this case between *whistleblowing* and *informing.* More explicitly, the latter notion denotes an action undertaken in order to promote specific career ambitions, while the former pertains to major social and ethical issues (Mathiessen, 2006: 17-22).

In addition to these notions, that of *political mobbing* – "the specific phenomenon of political pressure exerted on the constitutional justice through indirect influence" – should be also mentioned (Safjan, 2009: 3).

In the main, the behavior of the bully might resort to: slander, gossip, social isolation, criticism, assigning simple and easy tasks, threats, intimidation, pressuring, mockery, name-calling etc. The bulk of the analysis makes an inquiry into the psychological characteristics and behavior of both the bully and the victim (Harvey et al., 2006: 6-8; Ma, 2001; Parault, Davis and Pellegrini, 2007; Peterson and Ray, 2006). Except for these two characters however, the activity of bullying also engages others, such as defenders and outsiders for example (Tani et al., 2003; Salmivalli and Voeten, 2004).

Special attention was awarded also to the characteristics of the organizational setting that would encourage bullying – i.e. the so-called "environmental conditions". Duffy and Sperry (2007: 399-401) structured their analysis as to address the organizational as well as the personality dynamics alike, whereas Vartia-Väänänen (2003: 12-13) even speaks of a distinction between environmental and personality views on the antecedents of bullying.

According to Salin (2003), these factors can be classified into three groups: enabling structures and processes (such as perceived power imbalance, low perceived costs, and dissatisfaction and frustration); motivating structures and processes (internal competition, reward systems and expected benefits); and finally – precipitating processes (downsizing and restructuring, organizational changes, changes in the composition of the work group).

Harvey et al. (2006: 6) talk of four such environmental agents of bullying behavior:
1. "deficiencies in leadership behavior";
2. "deficiencies in work design";
3. "a socially exposed position of the victim";
4. "low morale standard in the department" (Harvey et al., 2006: 6).

The study of Hodson, Roscigno and Lopez (2006) tracks down bullying to relational powerlessness and organizational chaos.

Bullying and mobbing research also revealed certain gender differences regarding the prevalence of bullying and the behavior of the bully, respectively (Matthiessen, 2006: 31, 32; Kalliotis, 2000; Ma, 2001). In a study regarding the attitudes of preadolescences toward inter-group bullying, Gini (2007) argued that preadolescent boys are more inclined to approve of physical bullying than girls. The findings of Gini (2007: 85) are consonant with those of other studies which indicate a frequency of overt male bullying among male children and adolescents as compared to a prevalence of relational or social bullying among female children and adolescents.

It goes without saying that bullying and/or mobbing are both processes of shaming and of shame-induction (Duffy and Sperry, 2007: 398). These processes induce what Ehrenreich terms as "dignitary harm" (Hodson, Roscigno and Lopez, 2006: 385).

Additionally, shame can be accounted for as one of the reasons why many people are reluctant to report this abuse (Feder, 2007: 491). An interesting discussion about shame and bullying is also to be found in the study of Ahmed and Braithwaite (2004). The study adopts the framework of reintegrative shaming theory when discussing shaming (reintegration and stigmatization) by parents, children's skills (measures, ability) of shame management (e.g. "promotion of adaptive and non-adaptive strategies"), and school bullying (Ahmed and Braithwaite, 2004: 288). Briefly stated, the authors argue that – among other methods – adaptive shame management is a variable which, if promoted and encouraged, reduces considerably the prospects of the child turning into a school bully in the future.

1. Braşov 1987

In the following chapter, I will try to analyze the dynamics of moots, based on the stenographic transcripts and summary records of six meetings of the Enterprise Party Committee[57]. The documents under analysis consist of the reports/pronouncements [*referate*], the proceedings and stenographic transcripts of party meetings that were held at the level of the *Steagul Roşu* truck factory on November 15, 17, 19, 21, 23 and 25 of that same year. The bulk of the material (published in Arsene's (1997a; 1997b) collection of documents and interviews) is either hand-written or typed, amounting to approximately 180 pages. The documents are not linear; summaries are often intertwined with excerpts from dialogues or discourses. As transcripts are available mainly of party meetings on the factory level, the analysis of the scapegoating phenomenon and moot bullying will inevitably confine itself to the case of *Steagul Roşu*. This approach has obvious limitations: it does not give insight into similar processes in the police department and *Securitate* (and probably elsewhere); we will also lose sight of other measures – if any were taken – in other institutions. Cognizant of these limitations, I think that the focus on *Steagul Roşu* provides an interesting case study of scapegoating and bullying. It should be pointed out that fifty-three of the sixty-one prosecuted protesters from Braşov were employees of *Steagul Roşu*, where the demonstrations began.

As we are dealing with second-degree written documents (and often summaries, rather than transcripts), the question arises: to what extent can we talk about the dynamics which govern these speeches and interventions? It might be more appropriate to talk about the dynamics which were *perceived* and *noted down* by the persons producing the documents. There is also no guarantee that the written proceedings account for all of the speeches that were given, or that some of the plenaries had not proceeded behind closed doors. Notwithstanding such incertitude, some general conclusions emerge from the content analysis.

As the documents are not complete in that respect, I chose to concentrate the content analysis on the *topics* discussed and not the *persons* delivering the speeches. I make some annotations about the position in the party and the administrative apparatus of persons taking the floor, but these comments remain

---

57   *Steagul Roşu* was officially renamed to *Întreprinderea de Autocamioane Braşov* [Autotruck Enterprize] in 1971. In official documents, like the analyzed transcripts, the official name is often used, hence, there is often talk of an "Enterprise Party Committee" and "party cadres of the Enterprise", rather than the "*Steagul Roşu* Party Committee", or "party cadres of *Steagul Roşu*".

at a general level. In other words, the analysis cannot follow how the moot is influenced by the position of the speakers.

On the basis of the chronicle of Brudaşcu (1997) – a former party activist – I will introduce a broader scenario of the mobilization of party leaders and activists in cases of public manifestations of workers' discontent. His book, *Dosarele adevărului: Braşov (1987)* [The Dossiers of Truth. Braşov (1987)] (Brudaşcu, 1997), appeared on the background of certain animosities between the former secretary of propaganda and other local chroniclers of the 1987 revolt. For this reason, it can be also read as an endeavor to counterattack the accounts holding Brudaşcu as partly responsible for the repression that followed in the aftermath of the events (Brudaşcu, 1997: 7; Oprea and Olaru, 2002: 123). Nevertheless, the account is valuable for two reasons. Primarily, it is the first editorial initiative regarding the 1987 revolt by a former communist party member. Secondly, it minutely describes the mobilization of the party members in their attempt to mollify the citizens of Braşov in their march on the city center.

Besides Brudaşcu's testimony, the book, *Un sfert de veac de Securitate* [Quarter of a Century of *Securitate*] (2002), written by former *Securitate* officer, alias Simion Airinei, should also be mentioned. This chronicle encompasses a larger time frame, but its account of events in Braşov is of high importance, as it sheds some light on the circumstances under which, in the official framing of the events, the initial iron-guardist plot was replaced with the hooligan one[58].

Brudaşcu puts the 1987 events in the context of so called "registered dissatisfactions", which effected anxiety in the ranks of the party from Braşov. Reportedly, to all these episodes, the party reacted in a similar way: activist, party, administrative and *Securitate* delegates were sent to the spot and investigations followed. The people involved were sanctioned. On the basis of Brudaşcu's (1997: 23-27) account, one could infer that there was a certain trend of picking the guilty from the "technical, administrative and political management". Although Brudaşcu does not elaborate on this issue, it can be speculated that this type of scapegoating suits the propaganda discourse, which – in the

---

58   "The problem was that the theory [of an iron-guardist plot] was not credible, because after 2 or 3 days of interrogations, the truth was so obvious that it had to be accepted by the General [Macri] and his superiors in Bucharest. Once the fact was admitted that the revolt was the result of the workers' discontent with the poverty they were living in, it was decided that the *Securitate* would hand over the interrogation to the police and that the leaders of the demonstration would be charged with disturbing the peace and looting" (Airinei, 2002: 271) [*author's translation, author's emphasis*].

aftermath of the 1987 events – was intended to appease the discontent of the workers.

Brudaşcu mentions:
- manifestations of discontent at *Steagul Roşu* in the 1980s;
- "[d]issatisfactions registered at ICA Ghimbav, one of the newest and best performing industrial units of the county";
- "[a]nother case of revolt [...] at the beginning of October 1987 in the village of Hărman" – an incident related to the harvest of potatoes in a local agricultural production co-operative;
- regarding pay cuts and the global accord, "The biggest problems were found at *Combinatul Chimic Victoria* [The Victoria Chemical Combinate], at the one in Făgăraş, at '*6 Martie*' *Zărneşti* ['March 6' Zărneşti], *Electroprecizia Săcele* [Electricprecision Săcele], *I. Scule Râşnov* [Enterprize Tools Râşnov], *Tractorul* [The Tractor], *Metrom*, *Rulmentul* [The Bearing], *Unelte şi Scule Braşov* [Instruments and Tools Braşov], where the wages were reduced in the last months to 45-80 percent of the proper level" (Brudaşcu, 1997: 23-27) [*author's translation*].

A closer look is given to the discontents manifested by approximately 300-500 workers on November 10, 1987 at *Uzina Tractorul Braşov* [Universal Tractor Braşov]. Reportedly, they were brought about by the same factors that incited the *Steagul Roşu* workers – i.e. the equalization of wages, which meant that irrespective of section results, everybody was to receive wages in accordance with the performance of the whole enterprise (in terms of plan fulfillment). In this case, the emergency response team consisted of the first secretary of the Braşov County Party Committee and the Minister of Machine-Building Industry. According to Brudaşcu (1997: 28), the team proceeded quickly toward the implementation of technical and organizational measures.

> He [the minister] discussed tête-à-tête with the first secretary for about 30 minutes. They asked via interphone not to be bothered by anybody during this time. Even the other secretaries of the County Party Committee – who were still in the headquarters – did not dare to disturb them. Then, after several other conversations held still on the T.O. ["the famous 'short line'"] with Emil Bobu and Constantin Dăscălescu[59], they both came out of the office. The first secretary [...] and the minister [...] left towards the tractor enterprise. But, [once] they arrived there, they did not talk to the workers. They stopped at the headquarters of the Party Committee where they were

---

59   Constantin Dăscălescu (1923-2003) – member of the C.C. of the R.C.P. from July 23, 1965 until December 22, 1989; member of the Political Executive Committee of the C.C. of the R.C.P. from March 7, 1978 until December 22, 1989 (C.N.S.A.S., 2004: 202-203).

expected by the entire political-administrative management of the plant. The guests proceeded directly to technical-organizational measures. Among other things, it was about the sanctioning of section chiefs and party secretaries. That is all. After which they came back to the County Party Committee, from where they started to report again over the T.O. that it was an issue of simple disorders determined by the "incompetence and lack of revolutionary vigilance of some cadres" (Brudaşcu, 1997: 28) [*author's translation*].

Brudaşcu does not mention sanctions which were inflicted upon the workers – if there were any. Although it could be hardly stated for certain, one could speculate that his account was shaped by his own membership in the party.

The Attribution of Fault

The hypothesis that the attribution of fault governed the unfolding of the scandal over the second-order transgression follows a hypothesis advanced by Kurczewski (1993: 145). As mentioned in section II.1 – *The Dynamics of Scandal during the Ceauşescu Regime*, he pointed to the mechanism of non-acknowledgement and the lack of discourse about crises in the Soviet and Central European communist societies (at least, as far as the communist ruling class was concerned). This taboo is considered to have led to the proliferation of a debate about *who is responsible* for the problems instead. Following Gibbs (1963), I designate this process of allocation of responsibility as *attribution of fault*.

The content analysis of stenographic transcripts and summary records indicates the proliferation of the mechanism of attribution of fault under communism. It might be inferred that the allocation of responsibilities triggered some kind of a placebo effect in a system which chronically refused to discuss the causes of its crises. After all, the agenda of the 17 November 1987 plenary with the party cadres is concerned with two issues: *the attribution of fault* and *the admittance of one's guilt/fault*.

On the basis of these proceedings I was able to identify five main *fault types/levels* with an additional two subtypes:
– *fault type/level 1 for non-professionalism* belongs to mass and party organs and organizations, to the Council of Working People (C.W.P.) [*Consiliul Oamenilor Muncii, C.O.M.*];
– *fault type/level 2 for the non-enforcement of discipline* belongs to mass and party organs and organizations, trade unions and CWP organs, and organizations from the sections + *Steagul Roşu* Party Committee. It targets party cadres;
– *fault type/level 2b for the unsatisfactory carrying out of political ideological work* belongs to lower-level party cadres. It targets workers;

- *fault type/level 3 for activities inimical to the party and people* belongs to protesters. It targets the party and the people;
- *fault type/level 4a for the lack of a reaction to fault type/level 3* belongs to section chiefs, party members and functionaries. It targets protesters;
- *fault type/level 4b for the lack of a reaction to fault type/level 3* belongs to workers. It targets protesters;
- *fault type/level 5 for the adoption of an illegal procedure of remuneration* belongs to the technical manager. It targets the technical manager.

The type/level numbers 1, 2, 3, 4 and 5 follow the order of their appearance in the reports/pronouncements which were read aloud at the beginning of several plenaries. As it can be deduced, *fault type/level 3 for activities inimical to the party and people* is the actual effect of all others. I choose to regard it as a separate *fault type/level* for the reason that later on the protesters will undergo a more or less similar ritual of the admittance of one's guilt/fault as the party functionaries and party cadres. I decided to employ a dual formula of *type* and *level*, as types of responsibility are clearly distributed according to political and social stratification.

The order of the enumeration follows the individualization of the responsibility and the logic of the investigations that were carried out parallel to party meetings. In the next sub-sections I proceed to the presentation of six plenaries. We will see that each of these meetings is preoccupied with a certain fault type/level and that there is hardly a meeting which touches equally on all of them. In the final notes, I seek to estimate how the overall dynamics of the attribution of fault might have looked like.

15.11.1987 – party moot on mass protests – plenary with the aktif (body of party cadres) – 9 typed pages

19 persons took the floor, 28 interventions
comrade secretary of the C.C. of the R.C.P. – 6 interventions (the longest ones)
first secretary of the Braşov County Party Committee – 2 interventions (introductory speech)
comrade technical director – 3 interventions
Minister of Machine-Building Industry – 1 intervention
Minister of Labor – 1 intervention

For the most part, this empirical material consists of summary records (see ***, 1987a).

Altogether, the plenary reveals party cadres' anger and indignation. These are directed towards "those who inflicted material and moral damages". The meeting principally discusses *fault type/level 3 for activities inimical to the party and people* and *fault type/level 4a for the lack of a reaction to fault type/level 3* which belongs to lower-level party cadres and targets protesters. *Fault type/level 4b for the lack of a reaction to fault type/level 3* which belongs to workers and targets protesters is also signaled.

There are some talks about the Plan and the issue of remuneration. The debates, however, do not lead to any conclusions. The urge to incriminate as a strategy of self-defense notwithstanding, one should also keep in mind that, at this point in time, the investigations had barely started. Worthy of note, is the evolution of the request for punishment and exclusion of the protesters from the *working collective* [colectivul de oameni ai muncii]. Hence, according to the first two speakers, it was Ceauşescu who asked for the protesters to be punished and subjected to branding (degradation) ceremonies. Next, personal requests for the branding (degradation) ceremonies, denunciation, exclusion and punishment of the protesters are voiced. Eventually, these requests prompt the comrade secretary of the C.C. of the R.C.P. to conclude in his final remarks that, "the general secretary [Ceauşescu] will be informed that the party cadres demanded the respective people be exemplarily sanctioned". By the same token, the next possible development would be Ceauşescu asking for the punishment and exclusion of the protesters. The spiral of requests quickly turns into a closed circle.

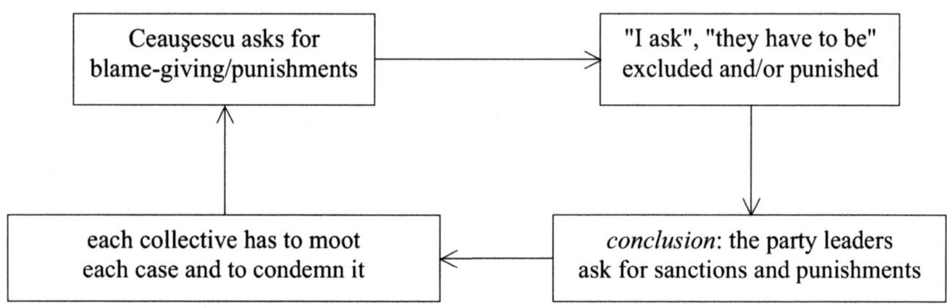

Scheme 8

Another element worthy of note for our discussion of moot bullying is that the public condemnation of the protesters was to be carried out by *the collective* [colectivul]. As a matter of fact, this collective is also to judge the cases in which the *branding (degradation)* [înfierarea]/*denunciation* has to take place. At this point, the discourse of moot bullying can be classified in terms of exclusion and punishment. The general tone is one of indignation coupled with disappointment and surprise. Similar attitudes were denoted using expressions such as: "incrimination", "we are in the situation of expressing our opprobrium", "with all due seriousness we have to manifest our disagreement" etc. It could be concluded that the act of branding (degradation) consists of expressing indignation and opprobrium and – subsequently – requesting the exclusion and severe punishment of the protesters.

A general conclusion which can be drawn from the analysis of the plenaries is: there is only one hero in the later years of communism in Romania – the working collective. At the beginning of the plenary there are some voices of half-surprise, half-disappointment with the workers' failure to appease and stop the protesters. At the same time, there seems to be a tacit understanding that the image of the collective should not be spoiled. What one is eventually left to say in the working collective's defense is that some elements of the "unhealthy background" inevitably snuck in.

In opposition to the collective, stand the protesters – along with section chiefs and some party cadres in the highest political and administrative positions who failed either to prevent, or correspondingly react to the incidents (*fault type/level 4a for lack of reaction to fault type/level 3*). By comparison, the next meetings are more and more abundant in criticism of the way in which leaders carry out their political and administrative duties. At this stage, the criticism is general; in the meetings that follow, it will become individualized. As already mentioned, this is due to the advancement of the investigations.

17.11.1987 – party moot on mass protests – plenary with the aktif (body of party cadres) – 21 typed and hand-written pages

> 15 persons took the floor, 19 interventions
> comrade secretary of the C.C. of the R.C.P. – 1 intervention (the longest one)
> first secretary of the Braşov County Party Committee – 4 interventions (introductory speech)
> comrade (technical director) – 1 intervention
> comrades' speeches of *admittance of one's guilt/fault* – 12 interventions.

The records can be structured in three parts:

> 1. the report/pronouncement of the fault types/levels for the events and of the list of sanctioned party cadres;
> 2. the admittance of one's guilt/fault by several party cadres;
> 3. the final word of the comrade secretary of the C.C. of the R.C.P.

Seemingly, the report/pronouncement of the overall responsibilities is a document which was prepared in advance and read aloud. The document is typed and coherent, whereas the admittance of one's guilt/fault and the final word are hand-written resumes of the plenary.

1. The Report/Pronouncement of the Fault Types/Levels for the Events and of the List of Sanctioned Party Cadres.

The plenary was a succession of speeches of admitting one's guilt/fault. According to hand-written proceedings, twelve men took the floor in order to acknowledge their guilt and to pledge that they will improve their behavior. These speeches take the form of apologetic responses to the report/pronouncement that was read aloud at the beginning and stipulated the basic organizations held accountable for a general unacceptable situation which degenerated into "acts of hooliganism and vandalism".

According to my reading of the proceedings, the report/pronouncement is a document dealing with the attribution of fault for the events that took place on November 15, 1987 – i.e. of the so-called "acts of hooliganism and vandalism". The report/pronouncement is two and a half pages long, and it comprises a list of 16 party cadres who were dismissed and additionally received party sanctions – vote of blame/censure, vote of blame/censure and warning, and exclusion [*vot de blam, vot de blam cu avertisment, excludere*]. It was read by the secretary of the Municipal Party Committee – a detail which might explain why, within the framework of the report/pronouncement, the Municipal Party Committee and the County Party Committee turn out to exculpate themselves eventually. Also noteworthy, is that the listing of the responsible party precedes the introduction of their crime's effect – the so-called *fault type/level 3 for activities inimical to the party and people*. Moreover, the presentation of *fault type/level 3* is dealt with in one, seven-line paragraph, whereas other types of responsibility are listed on a page and a half altogether. Another characteristic is that further down the document, the responsibility is transferred to lower and lower levels. In other words, we first hear of the party, trade unions, authorities and organizations, and eventually the section chiefs and the "inimical elements".

Firstly, the report/pronouncement discusses *fault type/level 1 for non-professionalism*. Reportedly, there is a lack of professionalism on the part of the basic party organizations, the Enterprise Party Committee, the trade unions, the Union of Communist Youth – U.C.Y. [*Uniunea Tineretului Comunist – U.T.C.*], and the Council of Working People – C.W.P. [*Consiliul Oamenilor Muncii – C.O.M*]. Hence, in spite of the benevolence of General Secretary Ceauşescu, who in the fourth semester supplemented the orders for the internal market with 2,954 trucks, the party and mass organizations failed to mobilize the workers, guarantee a proper working milieu and, thus – inevitably – to fulfill the plan. As it can be inferred from the report/pronouncement, the "leniency, tolerance and lack of revolutionary combativeness" led to the perpetuation of "a climate of disorder and indiscipline" that constituted the background for "drawbacks in the activity of production".

Thus, the transition is made to *type/level 2a for the non-enforcement of discipline* (that belongs to, and targets party cadres). This turns out to be both a background for *fault type/level 1* and a more immediate cause for *fault type/level 3*. In this respect, the main responsibility is considered to belong to the Enterprise Party Committee. In spite of having been repeatedly forewarned by the Municipal and County Party Committees, it failed to act accordingly and to "lead with firmness the whole economic and social activity of the enterprise". This – in my interpretation – is an exculpation of the Municipal and County Party Committees. The duty to "give warning", to "be firm" and to "monitor the behavior of others" is a *leitmotif* of the speeches acknowledging personal guilt. As it can be inferred from the proceedings, except acknowledging professional misgivings, the speakers also make a point that they showed too much tolerance, passivity and that they should have been more severe in respect to their fellow party cadres.

At the end of the speeches, three speakers also address what could be regarded as *fault type/level 3 for activities inimical to the party and people*. Yet, the reference to *fault type/level 3* is eclipsed by the prevalence of *fault type/level 1* and *fault type/level 2a*. Getting back to the report pronouncement, here *fault type/level 3* seems to be affected by *fault type/level 1* and *fault type/level 2a*. And, although not directly, it was also given full support from *fault type/level 4a* and *fault type/level 4b*. The definition of *fault type/level 3* lists the following:

> As a result of this state of affairs, on the day of November 15, 1987, although we were secured good conditions for fulfilling the tasks of the Plan, elements who were at loggerheads with discipline left [their] working stations, indulged in acts of en mass recruitment and instigation, [and all of this by way of] committing grave infringements which degenerated into acts of hooliganism and vandalism, [and by way of] destroying material goods in the sections of production both in the enterprise and outside (***, 1987b) [*author's translation*].

Fault type/level 4a for the lack of a reaction to type 3 belongs to section chiefs, workshop chiefs, party members, and party cadres; and it targets protesters. And *fault type/level 4b for the lack of a reaction to type 3* belongs to workers and targets protesters. According to the report/pronouncement, a combined definition of *fault type/level 4a* and of *fault type/level 4b* would list:

> The lack of an opinion and of a combative attitude of the other working people, especially of the party members and of the party cadres, starting with the team, of the workshop and of section chiefs (***, 1987b) [*author's translation*].

In the following scheme, I attempt to sketch the process of attribution of fault according to the report/pronouncement:

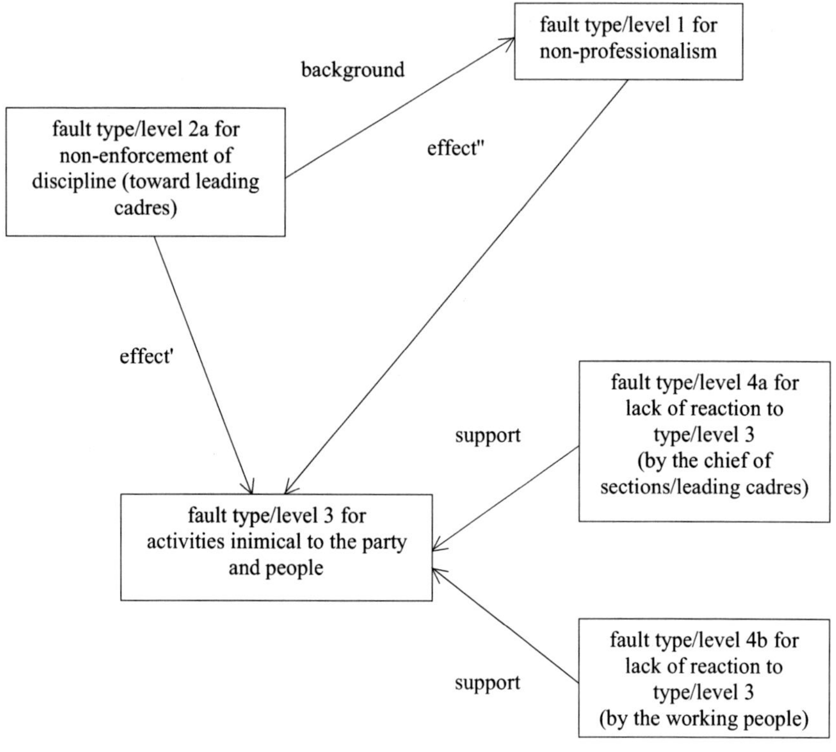

Scheme 9

2. The Admittance of One's Guilt/Fault by Several Party Cadres

The speeches of admittance of one's guilt/fault are directed toward *fault type/level 1 for non-professionalism* and toward *fault type/level 2a for the non-enforcement of discipline* (within the ranks of the party cadres)

– admittance of fault type/level 1 for non-professionalism:

> I have also practiced a defective work style which has no perspective (***, 1987b) [*author's translation*].
>
> The way I fulfilled the tasks as president of the trade union. More discipline [is needed] in preventive activity. I did not carry out appropriate political and ideological activity, create an appropriate work climate [for] the working people to have an organized milieu to manifest also [their] dissatisfactions. I will eliminate the deficiencies (***, 1987b) [*author's translation*].

I want to confess in front of the plenary that this event is the result of my inadequate activity. I did not entirely manage to engage all the party cadres in the fulfillment of the tasks of the Plan, [a fact] which brought about this dissatisfaction (***, 1987b) [*author's translation*].

– admittance of fault type/level 2a responsibility for the non-enforcement of discipline (within the ranks of the party cadres):

I showed an attitude of tolerance which was manifested within the ranks of the party cadres without taking a firm stand as this was requested by the party general secretary. Enough times I displayed a dupe attitude (***, 1987b) [*author's translation*].
Tolerant attitude regarding the management of the enterprise with the consequences which are known (***, 1987b) [*author's translation*].
I am the one at fault in the first hand [*mă fac vinovat în primul rând eu*]. I should have been more severe, more uncompromising. To have acted more severely in the field of the tasks regarding exportation (***, 1987b) [*author's translation*].

The speakers agree with the sanctions and with their subsequent transfer to another working unit:

For all these deviations I deserve the sanction which has been proposed. I assure you, comrade first secretary, that I will make all of the necessary efforts at the location to which I am sent (***, 1987b) [*author's translation*].
From the beginning it is clear that I am at fault [*mă fac vinovat*] of what has been said and that I fully deserve the measures which have been taken (***, 1987b) [*author's translation*].

The emotional tone of the speeches has strong accents of the acknowledgment of their guilt. The speakers talk about their mistakes and about the prospective of their improvement.

This is a very difficult moment in my career as a party member – to be lucid and to analyze the mistakes which I have made (***, 1987b) [*author's translation*].

Regarding the distinction between guilt and shame, some observations should be noted. The fact that the party leaders talk about their misgivings and not about their personality as such might be interpreted as a discourse in terms of guilt.

I realize that the guilt for events which took place is in large extent mine (***, 1987b) [*author's translation*].
Comrades, who would like to take the floor to address the way in which the comrades recognized their share of guilt [*parte de vină*]? (first secretary of the Braşov County Party Committee in ***, 1987b) [*author's translation*].
We are all at fault [*vinovaţi ne facem toţi*] (***, 1987b) [*author's translation*].
We are also at fault [*vinovaţi ne facem şi noi*] (***, 1987b) [*author's translation*].

The reference to the revolt is lapidary, and it is done in terms such as: "dissatisfaction", "events", and "the dissatisfaction regarding remuneration". Although this is not the main topic of the discussion, some interventions mention the connection between the changes in the remuneration policy and the so-called "events and dissatisfactions". Two speakers also signal *fault type/level 3 for activities inimical to the party and people.*

> I fully agree with the sanctions which have been proposed. I will seek in the future to work with all due firmness and to seek not to tolerate in any moment and to take immediate measures, and where inimical elements exist – trace them out (***, 1987b) [*author's translation*].

Though, a similar comment appears in the penultimate speech of the admittance of one's guilt/fault, still it is hardly elaborate. It can be inferred that *fault type/level 3* understood as *responsibility for activities inimical to the party and people* is not the main topic of the speeches of the admittance of one's guilt/fault.

3. The Final Word of the Comrade Secretary of the C.C. of the R.C.P.

The final word of the comrade secretary of the C.C. of the R.C.P. reiterates the indignation of the first meeting against the revolt by naming it: "a criminal act, by unspeakable criminals, and as an inimical act directed against the party and the people". The reaction of the party cadres was below expectations. The strong criticism of *fault type/level 4a for the lack of a reaction to type 3* lets us know that many party cadres were not on duty during the night before the events and that they failed to act accordingly. The speech also mentions unfulfilled plans for personnel reduction and continues in strong criticism with respect to *fault type/level 1 for non-professionalism.*

Conclusively, the dynamic of the meeting – as seen from the point of view of the *fault types/levels* put on the agenda – can be sketched as follows:

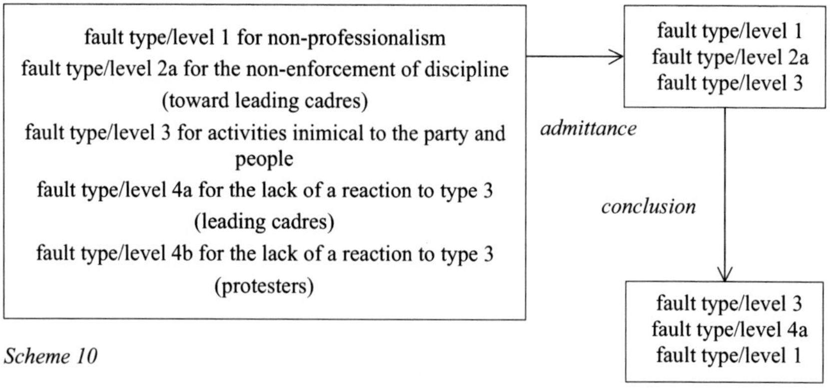

Scheme 10

19.11.1987 – party moot on mass protests – plenary with the aktif (body of party cadres) – 14 hand-written pages

> 2 persons took the floor, 2 interventions
> comrade secretary of the C.C. of the R.C.P. – 1 intervention (the longest one) secretary of the Enterprise Party Committee – 1 intervention (the final speech)

The first half of the plenary addresses mainly *fault type /level 1* and *fault type/level 2b*. And then it draws on *fault type/level 3* and *fault type/level 2b*. There is much talk about the Plan and that the data presented points to drawbacks in its fulfillment. It could be stated that this is a meeting of figures and a passionate appeal to party cadres to engage the working people in production. The conclusion of the meeting is twofold: "It is very logical – without work one cannot exist" and "[...] please, proceed seriously to talk with the working people". The first concerns the working people, while the second is addressed to the party cadres. Furthermore, the working people have to be educated. The party cadres must bring about a climate of discipline and hard work. And there is but one way in which the working people of *Steagul Roşu* can make things right: the fulfillment of the Plan.

Conclusively, this plenary introduced a turning point in the overall dynamics of the meetings: the events are finally discussed at the plenaries. In this particular meeting they are referred to as "shame", "the response of the workers from *Steagul Roşu* to the help received from the general secretary", "[this] collective is able to bring about such a shame", etc. Evidence is brought regarding the poor quality of the products. To a certain degree, the discussion about the Plan turns into a *type/level 1* form of criticism which is directed against the workers, and therefore not only against the party cadres. This meeting is the only one in which the working collective is pictured entirely in a poor light. And this is the case, even though there are distinctions being made between the collective on one hand, and the protesters – the so-called "madmen" – on the other (***, 1987c) [*author's translation*].

21.11.1987 – party moot on mass protests – plenary with the aktif (body of party cadres) – 2 hand-written pages

> 4 persons took the floor, 5 interventions
> secretary of the Enterprise Party Committee – 2 interventions (first and final speech)
> comrades' speeches of the *admittance of one's guilt/fault* – 3 interventions

The short proceedings reveal that four more party sanctions were given (see ***, 1987d).

Furthermore, a comrade who was previously dismissed and given party sanction is withdrawn the mandate of candidate and delegate to the National

Party Conference. The comrade's speeches of the admittance of one's guilt/fault are also mentioned.

23.11.1987 – party moot on mass protests – plenary with the aktif (body of party cadres) – 14 typed and hand-written pages

> 8 persons took the floor, 11 interventions
> secretary of the Enterprise Party Committee – 4 interventions (first and final speech)
> instructor of the C.C. of the R.C.P.
> secretary of the Municipal Party Committee
> secretary of the County Party Committee (the longest intervention)
> the comrades' speeches *admitting the guilt/fault of the technical manager's* + the
> speeches *admitting the guilt/fault of the party cadres – 9* interventions.

The Plenary of November 23 resembles that of November 17. There is a report/pronouncement of the fault types/levels for the events. This is followed by speeches of the admittance of one's guilt/fault. The main issue on the agenda is the exclusion from the party of the technical manager of the plant. He was already dismissed and received a vote of blame/censure [*vot de blam*] during the meeting of November 17. The technical manager of the plant had authorized the distribution of wages for October according to the fulfillment of the Plan at the level of the entire enterprise. This is considered to be an "illegal procedure" of the remuneration policy which finally instigated the workers.

The speeches of the comrades *admit the guilt/fault of the technical manager* on the one hand, and their *collective guilt/fault as party cadres* on the other. Regarding the former, this can be framed as *fault type/level 1 for non-professionalism*, while the latter is seemingly *fault type/level 2a for the non-enforcement of discipline* (with reference both to the specific technical manager and to the fellow party cadres alike). The technical manager is guilty of changing the algorithm and abuse of power, while the party cadres are at fault for letting him change the algorithm and not keeping a close eye on the activity of other, recently promoted, party cadres.

The speeches extensively use the term *guilt* regarding party leaders, and *disgrace* and *shame* when referring to the revolt. In contrast with the speeches, the formal report/pronouncement pictures the revolt as "acts of hooliganism" [*acte huliganice*].

As stated above, in a similar fashion to the November 17 plenary, the report/pronouncement was read aloud. Moreover, this report appears to be only a slightly modified version of the one from November 17. With a few exceptions – such as the table of the sixteen dismissed party cadres and the final notes – the bulk of the text of the report/pronouncement is copied from the previous one. The only new element is the part devoted to the former technical manager. Thus, a new type of responsibility is introduced: *fault type/level 5 for the adoption of an illegal procedure of remuneration.* This belongs to the technical manager solely and it was facilitated by *fault type/level 2a for the non-enforcement of discipline.*

> At the initiative of engineer [...] on the extraordinary meeting of the Executive Bureau of W.P.C. [C.O.M.], November 11, 1987, an illegal procedure of granting the remuneration of the working people was proposed and adopted for production in the month of October. We mention that, although in the discussions which were carried out, it was stated that the proposed solution is wrong, eventually a decision contrary to the legal stipulations was adopted, which generated a state of discontent of the personnel of the enterprise (***, 1987e) [*author's translation*].

Conclusively, compared to the previous plenaries, this one makes a strong step ahead in delimiting the discussion of the events from the general discussion about the Plan. Yet, the focus on the events is not as strong as it was during the first meeting of November 15, 1987. Also noteworthy, is that this is not a discussion about the events as such, but about the responsibility of the former technical manager in initiating the "illegal procedure" of remuneration.

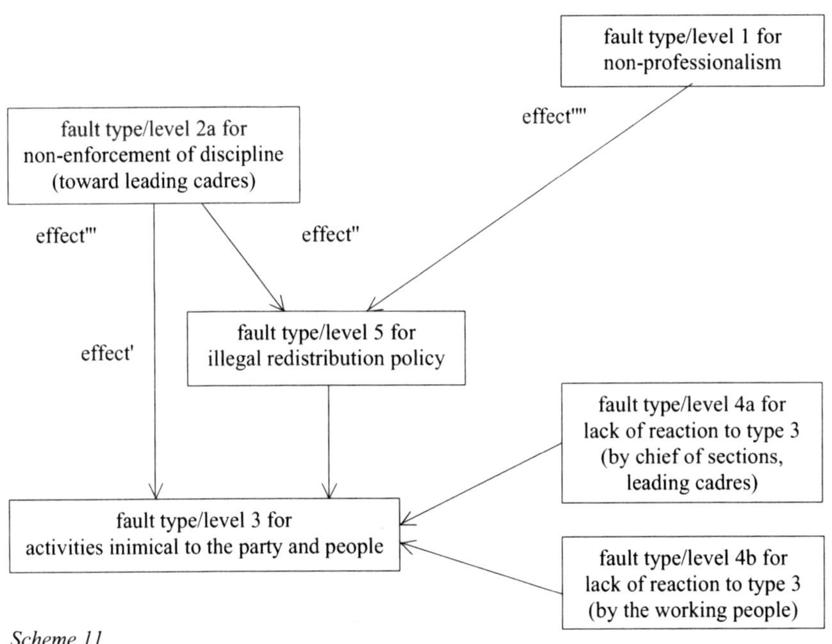

Scheme 11

25.11.1987 – party moot on mass protests – plenary with the aktif (body of party cadres) – 2 hand-written (résumés) + 37 typed pages (transcripts)

18 persons took the floor, 19 interventions
first secretary of the Braşov County Committee – 1 intervention
secretary of the Enterprise Party Committee – 2 interventions (the final speech)
comrades' speeches of *admittance of party cadres' lack of professionalism* and speeches *demanding the punishment and exclusion of the protesters* – 16 interventions

Primarily, the plenary of November 25, 1987 is concerned with three issues: fault type/level 2a for the non-enforcement of discipline, fault type level 2b for the unsatisfactory carrying out of political ideological work and fault type/level 3 for activities inimical to the party and people. The scenario of the plenary is similar to the previous ones, except for the fact that the 16 speeches do not represent the admittance of one's guilt/fault but instead the admittance of collective guilt/fault.

The comrades' speeches are anticipated first by the reading of a report regarding, "the critical analysis of the work style and methods of party organs, organizations, and the collective leadership", followed by the presentation of a "program of political-organizational and cultural-educative measures in order to increase the efficiency of the economic-social activity of the enterprise".

The addresses follow a recognizable pattern. After they express total approval of the program of measures, the speakers draw in a similar manner upon all three types of responsibility. The collective guilt belongs to the party cadres of the collectives, workshops and sections, and the protesters respectively. The delegates recognize the misgivings of the lower-level party cadres and a request is issued for severe punishment, as well as – in certain cases – exclusion from the ranks. The speakers take the floor in the name of the collective (workshop, section, basic organizations). The algorithm of guilt/disgrace is also maintained.

This is also because we, the youth organization, consider that we carry a significant amount of guilt [*apreciem că purtăm o însemnată parte din vină*] for the grave acts of certain colleagues whose behavior is a rough denial of the socialist morality and the laws of the country, [colleagues] who resorted to unaccountable "acts of hooliganism" [*acte huliganice*] [by way of] destroying material goods created by the collective of working people from our enterprise and our municipality. I would like to inform that the extraordinary plenary of the U.C.Y. Committee from the enterprise [while] debating this situation, rejected with indignation and resolution any facts of this kind, [thus] considering that they are a disgrace to the youth organization (***, 1987f) [*author's translation*].

The presentation of *fault type/level 2a* follows the lines of the previous meetings. The party cadres should be more firm, more severe and more critical toward their colleagues. In my reading, this is an encouragement of a watch-dog kind of attitude. Yet, while this is evident in regard to *fault type/level 2a*, the matter is not as obvious in connection with *fault type/level 2b*. The bulk of the speeches reproach the unsatisfactory political ideological work by the party cadres. In close connection, it is also signaled that they should pay more attention and be more involved in explaining decisions of the party to the working people. A secondary discourse calls for the imposition of more discipline at the workplace and for intransigence, when the case so requires. All in all, one might easily conclude that the discontent of the working people would not have taken the form it did if the party cadres had not lost the respect of the workers.

Fault type/level 3 is presented with indignation. As in the previous plenary, terms such as *disgrace* and *shame* are abundant. The participants destroyed the reputation of the collective of working people from *Steagul Roşu* and it will take a huge effort to undo the harm done. The participants offended and embarrassed this collective. The offense is so unpardonable that it calls for punishment and denunciation. There is an explicit demand for the participants to be tried in front of their fellow workers and be excluded by them. Several interventions signal that a ceremony of shaming (i.e. a branding (degradation) ceremony) is in store and that the working people will be given the opportunity to denunciate and condemn the "acts of hooliganism".

> As the guardian of honesty, the patriotic spirit which guides the life of every working man from our collective, I suggest the aktif [*activ*] agrees that those who ignored us and who resorted to acts of hooliganism and vandalism against quiet and peaceful people, who destroyed important material values, to be tried here in front of the workers in order to be subject not only to the rigors of the laws of the people, but also to the gaze and the attitude of contempt of the collective of lorry constructors (***, 1987f) [*author's translation*].

The General Dynamics

The general dynamics of all the six plenaries display the following fluctuation of attribution of fault:

15.11.1987
party cadres call
for *branding*
(degradation)
ceremonies
[şedinţe de înfierare]

> fault type/level 3 for activities inimical to the party and people
> fault type/level 4a for the lack of a reaction to type 3
> (by leading cadres)
> fault type/level 4a for the lack of a reaction to type 3
> (by workers)

> fault type/level 1 for non-professionalism
> fault type/level 2a for the non-enforcement of discipline
> (toward leading cadres)
> fault type/level 3 for activities inimical to the party and people

admittance
17.11.1987
conclusions

> fault type/level 3 for activities inimical to the party and people
> fault type/level 4a for the lack of a reaction to type 3
> (by leading cadres)

19.11.1987

> fault type/level 1 for non-professionalism
> fault type level 2b for the unsatisfactory carrying out of
> political ideological work
> fault type/level 3 for activities inimical to the party and people

21.11.1987

> fault type/level 1 for non-professionalism
> fault type/level 2a for the non-enforcement of discipline
> (toward leading cadres)

23.11.1987

> fault type/level 1 for non-professionalism
> fault type/level 2a for the non-enforcement of discipline
> (toward leading cadres)
> fault type/level 5 for the adoption of an illegal procedure of
> remuneration

25.11.1987
collectives call for
branding (degradation)
ceremonies
[şedinţe de înfierare]

> fault type/level 2a for the non-enforcement of discipline
> (toward party cadres)
> fault type level 2b for the unsatisfactory carrying out of
> political ideological work
> fault type/level 3 for activities inimical to the party and people

Scheme 12

2. Jiu Valley 1977

There is evidence that in the aftermath of the 1977 miners' strike, party moots on mass protests took place regarding the miners who were about to be tried for their engagement in actions of disorderly conduct during and shortly after the strike.

As compared to Braşov 1987 – which presents a compact case of "hooliganism" – Jiu Valley 1977 displays different incidents which, reportedly, unfolded independently of each other at different mines on August 2-4. In the aftermath of the 1987 revolt, "the hooligans" were condemned by the working collective of the enterprise; whereas after the 1977 strike, much smaller groups of hooligans (counting one to five members) were denunciated by their collective. Eventually in Braşov, a trial of sixty-one defendants took place. In the case of Jiu Valley, the following groups were brought to court: the Aninoasa group (1 person), the Uricani group (1 person), the Bărbăteni group (4 persons), the Lupeni group (5 persons), the Vulcan group (3 persons) and the Lonea group (1 person) (Spiridon, 2008: 242; Barbu and Boboc, 2005).

Several documents released by the Ministry of Internal Affairs – County Inspectorate Hunedoara – shed light on the place and role of party moots on mass protests and branding (degradation) ceremonies in a much broader scenario. These documents also reveal that, subsequent to the strike, a lot of energy in Jiu Valley was devoted to tracking down persons with penal antecedents, persons who did not have permanent residence in the Jiu Valley and/or who gave signs of riotous behavior at the work place. For example, *Plan de măsuri. Întocmit cu prilejul evenimentelor din 2-3 august 1977* [Plan of Measures. Drawn up on the Occasion of the Events of 2-3 August 1977] (Ministry of Internal Affairs – County Inspectorate Hunedoara, 1977a) stipulates thirty specific duties which are to be carried out, the persons responsible and the time-frame at their disposal.

> 12. Identification, getting to know and research of the elements [*Identificarea, cunoaşterea şi cercetarea elementelor*] who resorted to acts of violence and disorder on 2.08 of the current year, [and this] with the intention of holding them accountable from the administrative and criminal [penal] point of view [*în scopul tragerii lor la răspundere administrativă şi penală*].
> Deadline: 20.09.1977
> 13. Identification, getting to know and informative framing [*Identificarea, cunoaşterea şi încadrarea informativă*] of all the elements who have been exponents of actions of disorder on the days of 3.08.1977 [and this] with the intention of undertaking some [intelligence] operative measures [*în scopul luării unor măsuri operative*].
> Accountable: [...]
> Task: permanent

14. Mooting by the working collectives [*Punerea în discuţia colectivelor de muncă*] of all the persons who were administered evidence of guilt for having committed offences before sending the files to the prosecutor's office.
Responsibility: [...]
Deadline: 15.9.1977
[...]
16. On the basis of the indications given by the C.C. brigade of the R.C.P., measures are to be taken taken toward the removal from the Jiu Valley of the elements with penal antecedents, who display inadequate behaviour in the workplace and in society, and [who] do not have a permanent place of residence in the jurisdiction of the municipality; and toward sending these [individuals] to [their] place of residence.
Accountable: [...]
Deadline: 30.08.1977
17. With the intention of establishing and getting to know all the elements with penal antecedents [*În scopul stabilirii şi cunoaşterii tuturor elementelor cu antecedente penale*], all the employees of enterprises and units belonging to C.S. Petroşani are going to be researched in the operative files [*evidenţa operativă*] [Coal Station Petroşani – *Centrala Cărbunelui Petroşani*].
Accountable: [...]
Deadline: 30.08.1977
18. In collaboration with the management of C.S. Petroşani, measures are to be taken to research in the operative files [*evidenţa operativă*] all the persons who present themselves for employment in the mining enterprises, and [as a result] to refuse employment to those with penal antecedents.
Accountable: [...]
Deadline: 11.09. 1977
[...]
20. Measures of warning and attention drawing on the level of the *Securitate*, and [measures] of police warnings will be applied [*Se vor aplica măsuri de avertizare şi atenţionări pe linie de securitate şi avertismente miliţieneşti*] to all the persons known for tendentious and *turbulent* behaviours, [and this] with the intention of prevention, after which all these persons will be taken under informative framing [*vor fi încadrate informativ*].
Accountable: [...]
Task: permanent
(Ministry of Internal Affairs – County Inspectorate Hunedoara, 1977a in Boboc and Barbu, 2007: 576-577) [*author's translation, author's emphasis*].

All these tasks point to a phobia of penal antecedents which eventually materialized in *en masse* verifications and exclusions. *Notă–Raport. Cuprinzând principalele activităţi desfăşurate de către organele noastre în Municipiul Petroşani* [Note–Report. Containing the Main Activities Unfolded by Our Organs in the Municipality of Petroşani] (Ministry of Internal Affairs – County Inspectorate Hunedoara, 1977b) indicates the following results:

- on the basis of more than "1,500 [notes of] information" which were received by the Police and *Securitate* organs, "350 more active and instigator elements" were selected. The majority of these have been "neutralized by way of intelligence operative measures [*neutralizate prin măsuri operative*] and by way of sending to court those who committed acts of disorder and offense against good morals" (Ministry of Internal Affairs – County Inspectorate Hunedoara, 1977b: 625);
- "16 elements who committed acts of violence" were "mooted" by the working collectives, and 15 of these were eventually sent to court (Ministry of Internal Affairs – County Inspectorate Hunedoara, 1977b: 626);
- regarding the leader of the miners, "it was acted in a combinative way" upon him [*s-a acţionat combinativ asupra lui*], in order to force the leader to leave Jiu Valley (Ministry of Internal Affairs – County Inspectorate Hunedoara, 1977b: 629);
- it was discovered that from the total of 22,637 employees of the Mining Enterprises belonging to the Mining Combinate, as much as 1,883 persons had penal antecedents (Ministry of Internal Affairs – County Inspectorate Hunedoara, 1977b: 629);
- it was established that 197 employees with former convictions for acts of violence also displayed inadequate behavior in the work place. As they also did not have a stable residence in the Valley, their contract was terminated and they were subsequently relocated. By the same token, another 50 persons "who could not justify their presence within the jurisdiction" were also sent to their residences (Ministry of Internal Affairs – County Inspectorate Hunedoara, 1977b: 629-630);
- out of 1,384 persons who applied for employment, a total of 155 were found to have penal antecedents and had their application rejected (Ministry of Internal Affairs – County Inspectorate Hunedoara, 1977b: 630);
- the *Securitate* organs gave warnings to 96 persons, and notifications to 403 others for engaging in "hostile manifestations and tendentious activity", whereas the police gave out 460 such warnings (Ministry of Internal Affairs – County Inspectorate Hunedoara, 1977b: 630) [*author's translation, author's emphasis*].

In the above citations, I gave excerpts from the Plan of Measures and I summarized some of its accomplishments in order to provide a context for framing the branding (degradation) ceremonies which were held in the aftermath of the 1977 Jiu Valley strike. In the following section, I will briefly present some of their features.

Hence, from *Referat privind punerea în dezbatere a faptelor comise de N[...]C[...], S[...]C[...] şi P[...]P[...] – angajaţi ai I.M. Vulcan* [Report Regarding the Mooting of the Actions Committed by N[...]C[...], S[...]C[...] and P[...]P[...] – Employees of M.E. Vulcan] (***, 1977b), we find that the mooting was held on September 3, 1977. From a total of 200 miners present, 16 took the floor. The report summarizes these interventions. Reportedly, the speeches express indignation. Although there is one speech which requires the three persons to be tried in front of the collective, the mainstream attitude is to simply demand conviction. Their actions are denounced, and the speakers call for punishment and exclusion. As in the case of Braşov, the speakers employ formulas such as: "hooligan acts" and "disgrace". Also noteworthy – an element which did not make itself conspicuous in the case of Braşov – is that the delegates point to the existence of "parasite elements" [*elemente parazitare*] in the city and "demand" that the local organs take the necessary corrective measures. It might be inferred that, to a certain degree, there is a correspondence between the measures which were taken by the powers-that-be and the demands issued by the speakers. In other words, the dynamics of the meetings are molded upon the course of measures. And at this point, it might be speculated that the branding (degradation) ceremonies might have held the function of a belated legitimization.

Referat privind punerea în dezbatere a faptelor săvârşite de către un grup de huligani la data de 2 august 1977, la I.M. Lupeni [Report Regarding the Mooting of the Actions Committed by a Group of Hooligans on August 2, 1977, at M.E. Lupeni] (***, 1977d) does not summarize the meeting as such, but it reproduces the report/pronouncement which most probably was read at the beginning of the mooting. The "acts of hooliganism" of the five miners are presented in terms of scandal – in the sense of "making/producing scandal". In sum, the report calls for branding (degradation) and for justice.

Also noteworthy, is *Referat privind punerea în dezbatere a faptelor comise de către un grup de huligani în data de 4.08.1977 la I.M. Bărbăteni* [Report Regarding the Mooting of the Actions Committed by a Group of Hooligans on 4.08.1977 at M.E. Bărbăteni] (***, 1977c). The interventions of the speakers are interesting, as they portray the inadequate and riotous behavior of each of the four persons mooted at the meeting. Their absences without leave were most commonly given as evidence of inadequate behavior. Eventually, the collective asks for their exclusion and for holding them responsible for actions they committed.

After the same token, there is also *Referat privind punerea în dezbatere a faptelor comise la data de 4 august a.c., de către I[...]C[...] angajat la I.M. Uricani* [Report Regarding the Mooting of the Actions Committed on August 4, Current Year, by I[...]C[...], Employee at M.E. Uricani] (***, 1977a). The main difference being that in this case the energy of the working people is directed towards one person solely.

Conclusions

The main purpose of the chapter was to introduce the notion of moot bullying and to identify mechanisms of guilting and shaming in this type of bullying. I sought to substantiate that the general process of scapegoating which took place in the aftermath of the 1977 strike and the 1987 revolt ware based on mechanisms of bullying and the admittance of one's guilt/fault. Analyzing scheme (12) – the general dynamics of attributing fault in the aftermath of the 1987 events – one cannot escape noticing that the mechanisms of bullying have been there from the very beginning – there is, however, an evolution of the bullies. With the advancement of the investigations, the attribution of fault is more and more individualized. In parallel, the bully evolves from individual party cadres to the working collective.

Furthermore, I tried to show that mechanisms of moot bullying are present in the aftermath of both Jiu Valley 1977 and Braşov 1987. An important difference is, however, the existence in the case of Jiu Valley 1977 of speeches pointing to the existence of "parasite elements" [*elemente parazitare*] in the city and the "demand" for the local organs to take the necessary measures against these.

PART V
SCRIPTS OF OTHER CASES OF CONVERGENCE IN REPLY TO SCANDALS OVER MASS PROTESTS

The present chapter continues the discussion on scandals over mass protests during the Ceauşescu regime. It seeks to show that, in the case of the December 1989 events in Timişoara, Ceauşescu initially came up with a convergence between hooliganism and a *coup d'état* of foreign powers. This was shortly thereafter replaced with an ideological convergence between hooliganism and an *anti-socialist coup d'état* of foreign powers. Eventually, on December 20 the Romanian TV delivered a story of the ideological convergence between hooliganism – fascism – terrorism and an *anti-national coup d'état* of foreign powers. In the case of the 1990 University Square demonstration in Bucharest (a 52 day-long marathon protest against the former communists in power) – President Iliescu advanced a convergence between hooliganism – political idealists – students and *a plot of "historical parties" and other organizations – plus "an outside force"* aiming to overturn the democratically instated post-revolutionary regime.

In the previous chapters I also attempted to show that this specific mechanism of the official framing of mass protests cannot be properly understood as the workings of one man. There is always a collective engine awarding legitimacy to the endeavor. In part IV – *The Ritualization of Party Moots during the Ceauşescu Regime*, I pointed to the admittance of one's guilt/fault and moot bullying as mechanisms which guarantee the engagement and the approval of a larger collective. The following sub-chapters deal with similar inquiries into the cases of the 1989 Timişoara events and the 1990 miners' marches on Bucharest.

1. The Timişoara Events of 15-21 December 1989

This section concentrates on two issues. The first part introduces the December 1989 events in Timişoara and the reaction of the communist regime. This presentation is grounded in the findings of the Supreme Court of Justice, Military Section [*Curtea Supremă de Justiţie, Secţia Militară*], Court File no. 24/1991 regarding *Procesul celor 25 (Ion Coman, Radu Bălan, Ilie Matei, Filip Teodorescu, ş.a.* [Trial of the 25 (Ion Coman, Radu Bălan, Ilie Matei, Filip Teodorescu etc.)] (Mioc, 2004) – a trial of former communist officials and secret police operatives; and the findings of the Supreme Court of Justice, Criminal Section [*Curtea Supremă de Justiţie, Secţia Penală*], Court File no. 2955/1998 regarding *Procesul Chiţac–Stănculescu* [Trial of Chiţac–Stănculescu] – a trial of the reserve generals, Victor Atanasie Stănculescu and of Mihai Chiţac (Mioc, 2004).

The second part is devoted to the content analysis of the stenographic transcripts of the party meeting with the Political Executive Committee (***, 2006a; ***, 2006b; ***, 2007) and of the teleconference with communist officials (Romanian Communist Party, Braşov County [Party] Committee, 1989) which were both held on December 17, 1989. Furthermore, I will also discuss the televised speech delivered by Ceauşescu on December 20, 1989 (Ceauşescu's Address to the Nation – December 20, 1989; Mioc, 2002).

Before opening the discussion, I would like to clarify the applied time frame of December 15-21. The date of December 15, 1989 indicates the start of the demonstrations in the city of Timişoara. This is the point when parishioners started gathering in support for the Hungarian Reformed pastor Tőkés László, who faced eviction from his house (Siani-Davies, 2005: 56-63). Reportedly, under pressure from communist authorities, László Papp, the bishop of Oradea, decided to move Tőkés to Mineu, a village in Northern Transylvania (Mioc, ***a).

Tőkés refused to obey the eviction decree and claimed that his destitution was not carried out in accordance with the clerical law of the Reformed Church (Mioc, ***a). The bishop counter-attacked by suspending Tőkés' salary, and filing a suit against him on the grounds of an illegal occupation of a church-owned flat. The Judge gave Tőkés a deadline of December 15 to abandon the apartment. And on the final day, a protest of parishioners started, which soon evolved into an anti-communist demonstration which engaged the whole city.

The decision of relocating Tőkés was made after the pastor had criticized the regime in international media. This was not the first time he had problems with the authorities. While a priest in the town of Dej, he took part in the publishing of the Hungarian *samizdat* magazine *Ellenpontok*, for which he was dismissed in 1983. In 1986, he was appointed as secondary priest in the Timişoara parish (Mioc, ***a). In 1988, Tőkés was involved in the organization of a cultural manifestation which included the public reading of poetry by Hungarian authors highly disagreeable in the eyes of the communist regime. It was quite a sensation that he did not restrain his activities after the warnings were issued. As a result, members of the amateur theater group *Thalia* – who took part in the cultural manifestations organized by the Reformed Church – were forbidden to perform. Tőkés sent a letter of protest to the Reformed bishop of Oradea. When it was broadcast by Radio Budapest in May 1989, his name started to gain notoriety in Hungary, and hence also in Transylvania. Besides the issue of the theater group, Tőkés also criticized the plan of rural systematization. Shortly afterward, he gave other interviews to Hungarian TV and Radio Free Europe (Mioc, ***a).

According to Romanian authorities, more than displaying a fervent anti-communist attitude, Tőkés was rather inciting ethnic hatred. Some members of the communist State Security Department considered Tőkés a Hungarian spy, but the powers-that-be deemed it risky to openly act on this assumption fearing that the popularity he enjoyed in the Hungarian media might result in a real international scandal. Measures against Tőkés were primarily taken on two fronts. First, there was the decision of moving him to Mineu. In parallel, a process "of harassment through profession" also unfolded, targeting not only the pastor, but also his close friends (Mioc, ***a; Siani-Davies, 2005: 57).

The date of December 21 signals the beginning of the anti-communist Romanian revolution of 1989 in Bucharest. In my interpretation, this is a moment when the protest in Timişoara ceases to be the main point of concern for the communist powers, as protests spread throughout the whole country. While the demonstrations in Timişoara went on after December 21, they received a new meaning. From this point on they can be considered part of the Romanian anti-communist revolution.

On December 22, 1989 Ceauşescu and his wife, along with Emil Bobu and Manea Mănescu[60], fled the capital by helicopter (see Cartianu 2011; Mioc, ***b; Mioc, ***c). Eventually, on December 25, 1989 – after being sentenced to death by a military court – Ceauşescu and his wife were executed by a firing squad in Târgovişte.

The December 17, 1989 Meeting of the Political Executive Committee

The purpose of the meeting was to give a critical review of the failure of the army, police and State Security Department to suppress the demonstrations in Timişoara. Three ministers were harshly reproached by Ceauşescu for their lack of resolution (Siani-Davies, 2005: 66). At Ceauşescu's request the meeting mooted the dismissal of the Minister of National Defense (General Colonel Vasile Milea), the Minister of Internal Affairs (Tudor Postelnicu) and the Head of the State Security Department (Colonel General Iulian Vlad). Although this is not reflected in the stenographic transcript (which, however, is incomplete), several testimonies recall an outburst of the general secretary, who reportedly urged the members of the Political Executive Committee to look for a better replacement instead of him (Mioc, 2004).

---

60   Manea Mănescu (1916-2009) – member of the Permanent Bureau of the C.C. of the R.C.P. from November 24, 1989 until December 22, 1989 (C.N.S.A.S., 2004: 387-388).

The meeting resulted in a decision to use lethal force in an attempt to silence the demonstration in Timişoara. The decision was communicated via teleconference to the officials sent to Timişoara by Ceauşescu. Hence, for many, the significance of the December 17, 1989 meeting of the Political Executive Committee resides in the fact that if the high ranking communist officials had been brave enough to confront the general secretary, the meeting could have had a totally different outcome (Mioc, 2004). Opinions regarding the stenographic transcript are divided. In the main, for those who took part, it constitutes proof of the fact that Ceauşescu had already made his decision (Mioc, 2004). For others, Ceauşescu's resolve notwithstanding, the members of the Political Executive Committee are guilty at least on the grounds of their tacit approval of Ceauşescu's decision. In the following section, I will try to show that the stenographic transcript (incomplete, as it is) allows the identification of mechanisms traceable in the moots analyzed in connection with the 1987 Braşov revolt. My analysis, nonetheless, does not attempt to contribute to the contentious discussion regarding to what degree the members of the Political Executive Committee share the guilt for the unfolding of the reprisal. Regarding this issue, the content of the stenographic transcript was under close scrutiny in *The Trial of the Members of the Political Executive Committee* (September 17, 1990 – April 20, 1992) [Procesul mebrilor CPEx, Lotul membrilor CPEx, Loturile "CPEx"], in *Procesul celor 25 (Ion Coman, Radu Bălan, Ilie Matei, Filip Teodorescu etc.)* [The Trial of the 25 (Ion Coman, Radu Bălan, Ilie Matei, Filip Teodorescu etc.)] (Mioc 2004) and in *Procesul Chiţac–Stănculescu* [The Trial of Chiţac–Stănculescu] (Mioc, 2004).

The following content analysis is much indebted to the interpretation given to these events within the framework of the dissenting opinion of Judge M.E. with respect to the sentences which were passed in *Procesul celor 25 (Ion Coman, Radu Bălan, Ilie Matei, Filip Teodorescu etc.)* [The Trial of the 25 (Ion Coman, Radu Bălan, Ilie Matei, Filip Teodorescu etc.)] (Mioc 2004). For the most part, the arguments advanced by Judge M.E. ran counter to the decision of the court to drop the original charges of genocide and complicity to commit genocide [*infracţiunea de genocid, complicitate la infracţiunea de genocid*] in favor of the lesser charges of first-degree murder, attempt to commit first-degree murder, complicity to commit first degree-murder and complicity to attempt to commit first-degree murder [*infracţiunea de omor deosebit de grav, tentativă la omor deosebit de grav, complicitate la infracţiunea de omor deosebit de grav, complicitate la tentativa la infracţiunea de omor deosebit de grav*] (Mioc, 2004). Judge M.E.'s analysis of the stenographic transcripts, testimonies and the relevant evidence brought him to the conclusion that indeed it was this meeting which led to the official recognition of the decision to resort to firearms and sharp ammunition.

The meeting reveals the following facts: during the night of December 16/17, the leadership of the Ministry of National Defense, the Ministry of Internal Affairs and the State Security Department did not comply with the orders they received from Ceauşescu requesting the harshening of the repression against the demonstrators. This lack of resolution allowed the demonstrators to occupy the headquarters of the County Party Committee in Timişoara the following afternoon. According to Judge M.E., given this state of affairs, the meeting also served Ceauşescu's purpose of overpowering the leadership of the three ministries (Mioc, 2004). In his reading, there are "three categories of protagonists": Nicolae and Elena Ceauşescu, the three ministers whose dismissal was mooted and the other participants, respectively. Furthermore, the outburst of Ceauşescu – i.e. the moment when he presented his resignation – was supposedly effected by the opposition of some communist officials to the destitution of the three ministers. According to Judge M.E., this is an element pointing to a breach in the authority of the general secretary. The meeting ultimately ended in a compromise – Ceauşescu had to try to work things out with the three ministers; they on the other hand, pressured by other members of the Committee, had to accept the rules of the repression established by the general secretary. With respect to the main point of his argumentation – that is, to substantiate his claim that the 1989 events in Timişoara constitute a case of genocide and complicity in genocide – the Judge considered that the analysis of the meeting was quite conclusive in documenting that, if the Ceauşescus – as initiators of the measure – and other military leaders – as its first-rate executors – can be qualified as masterminds behind the offense of genocide, other members of the Political Executive Committee who participated in the respective meeting can be juridically qualified as instigators of genocide (Judge M[...]E[...] in Mioc, 2004).

The Moots

By and large, the December 17, 1989 meeting of the Political Executive Committee constitutes a moot. Yet, even though it comprises elements of the party moots on mass protests we had the chance to discuss in the previous chapters, this moot actually belongs to a different genre. As elements of differentiation between the two, I would first of all point to the fact that the December 17, 1989 meeting is held concurrently with the demonstration in Timişoara, while the analyzed November 1987 moots took place after the mass protest. In the case of Timişoara, we are dealing with several days of demonstrations, whereas in the case of Braşov the turbulences unfolded within several hours. Furthermore, the December 17, 1989 meeting discusses the lack of resolution of the police, army and state security units; whereas the 1987 Braşov moots allocate responsibility to "the guilty ones (the group of hooligans)" and the party cadres. The differences boil down to the fact that except for the attribution of fault, the December 17 meeting has to bring up an important decision with respect to the measures to be taken against the demonstrators. As Judge M.E. (in Mioc, 2004) indicated, the purpose of the discussion was to go over the heads of the three ministers and to guarantee that the orders of Ceauşescu would be followed.

In the main, two things were mooted at the meeting of the Political Executive Committee (***, 2006a; ***, 2006b; ***, 2007). What I designate as *moot 1* discusses the measures which should be taken – if any – against the three ministers. The moot starts with a strong criticism of their performance. The last part of the stenographic transcript reveals that a so-called "misunderstanding" led to the determination of the ministers not to order the use of firearms. In my interpretation – though I acknowledge its uncertainty – this can be also viewed as a discursive maneuver which allows Ceauşescu and the three ministers to close the meeting on good terms. This misunderstanding offers ground for reconciliation. Ceauşescu assumes part of the guilt for *not expressing himself more clearly*, and the ministers for *not having asked for clarification*.

Moot 1 makes its debut with a strong criticism of the lack of resolution on the part of the heads of the three ministries, which is strangely combined with acknowledgment of the fact that some sort of a misunderstanding might have actually taken place. Ceauşescu also makes insinuations regarding the lack of honesty of the three ministers (***, 2006a; ***, 2006b; ***, 2007).

In parallel, *moot 2* discusses the necessity of employing firm measures against the demonstrators in Timişoara. The two moots complement each other in an interesting way. The main common element is: *state of emergency* [stare de necesitate]. *Moot 1* reveals that the ministers did not comprehend that there was a state of emergency. Once the misunderstanding was brought into the open and the ministers got a clear picture of the gravity of the situation and of what was expected of them, there was room for reconciliation with Ceauşescu. Simultaneously, *moot 2* persuades the ones who were not already convinced that there is indeed a state of emergency. In *moot 1*, it is the duty of the ministers to argue in front of Ceauşescu that they had fallen victim to a misunderstanding. Whereas in *moot 2* it is Ceauşescu who has to convince them that there is a state of emergency. Both moots are comprised of mechanisms of *persuasion, attribution of fault* and *admittance of one's guilt/fault*. Persuasion is necessary, and as in *moot 1*, the ministers reply to Ceauşescu's criticism by formulating excuses in a defensive manner. Only later do they engage in the admittance of one's guilt/fault. Besides the three ministers, Ceauşescu also delivers an admittance of one's guilt/fault, though in an indirect manner.

> Com. N.C.: Why didn't you ask[?]
> Com. I.V.: This is a fundamental mistake [on our part].
> Com. N.C.: I told [you] to shoot a warning, if they do not withdraw to shoot in the legs. I did not think [I did not mean] that you [would] shoot with maneuver bullets [blanks – *gloanţe de manevră*]. Fiddlesticks[!] The people who entered the headquarters of the County Party Committee were not supposed to get out of there anymore, they were supposed to be down, to be down on the ground (***, 2007) [*author's translation*].

As can be deduced from the stenographic transcript, the majority of the speeches are quite concise. As a matter of fact, besides the speeches of self-criticism, the interventions of the ministers limit themselves to a few words only:

> Com. M.V.: I executed the reshuffle of forces from the East to the West (***, 2006a) [*author's translation*].
> Com. T.P.: I report, comrade general secretary, the police are armed (***, 2006a) [*author's translation*].
> Com. I.V.: I know, comrade general secretary, I gave the order (***, 2006b) [*author's translation*].
> Com. M.M.: We agree with you and with all the measures which have been taken (***, 2006b) [*author's translation*].
> Com. V.M.: I am guilty. I thought it would not take such proportions (***, 2006b) [*author's translation*].

I try in the following scheme to give a brief presentation of the meeting and to illustrate its dynamics. As stated already, the stenographic transcript is incomplete. On the basis of the nine pages of proceedings which survived, I was able to identify the following:

1'.
moot 1 – Nicolae Ceauşescu, Elena Ceauşescu:
 description of the situation
 criticism of the lack of resolution
 question: Which units have been armed and which have not?
 question: Why were some units unarmed?
 question: Why were shots not fired?

1"
moot 1 – two of the three ministers:
 answers: Which units have been armed and which have not

2'.
moot 2 – Nicolae Ceauşescu:
    description of the situation
    call for mooting: necessity of taking "firm measures"
2''.
moot 2 – one party official in the name of all communist officials:
    approval of the firm measures
2'''.
moot 2 – Elena Ceauşescu, Nicolae Ceauşescu:
    arguments in favor of strong measures

3'.
moot 1 – Nicolae Ceauşescu, Elena Ceauşescu:
    criticism of the lack of resolution
    call for mooting: dismissal of the three ministers
    question: Why were some units unarmed?

3''.
moot 1 – two of the three ministers:
    defense: They did not expect the manifestations to take such proportions
    defense: They did not know that the units had to be armed
    admittance of one's guilt/fault
    full acceptance of the sanctions
3'''.
moot 1 – Elena Ceauşescu, Nicolae Ceauşescu:
    criticism of the lack of resolution

4'
moot 1 – Elena Ceauşescu, Nicolae Ceauşescu:
    question: Why did they not ask?
    question: Which units are usually armed and which are not?
    question: Why did they not use the units which are usually armed?
4''.
moot 1 – the three ministers:
    defense: They did not expect the manifestations to take such proportions
    defense: They did not know that the units had to be armed
    admittance of one's guilt/ fault (for not having asked)
4'''.
moot 1 – Nicolae Ceauşescu:
    (indirect) admittance of one's guilt/fault (for not having thought that they
    were going to use maneuver bullets (blanks [*gloanţe de manevră*]))

5'.
moot 1 – one of the three ministers:
            attempt to criticize subordinates
5".
moot 1 – Nicolae Ceauşescu:
            rejection of the critique
5'''.
moot 1 – two of the three ministers:
            admittance of one's guilt/fault
            full acceptance of the sanctions

6'.
moot 1 – Nicolae Ceauşescu:
            call for mooting: dismissal of the three ministers
6".
moot 1 – the communist officials, the three ministers:
            arguments against the dismissal: bad timing
            arguments against the dismissal: misunderstanding
6'''
moot 1 – Nicolae Ceauşescu:
            criticism of the lack of resolution
6''''
moot 1 – the three ministers:
            pledge
            excuses, misunderstanding

7'.
moot 1 – Nicolae Ceauşescu:
            call for mooting: *no* dismissal of the three ministers
7".
moot 1 – all the comrades:
            approval of *no* dismissal

8.
moot 2 – Nicolae Ceauşescu:
            definition of the situation
            description of the firm measures
moot 1 – Nicolae Ceauşescu:
            misunderstanding
8".
moot 2 – all the comrades:
            approval of the measures.

Scheme 13

Ideological Convergence:

Hooliganism – Coup D'état of Foreign Powers from the East and from the West

In my reading, the foregoing sketch indicates that the *moot of the measures of reprimand* (i.e. *moot 2*) was less intense in comparison with the *moot of the dismissal of the three ministers* (i.e. *moot 1*). It also shows that the two moots complement each other. After the meeting, Ceauşescu held a teleconference with county party heads and senior officials (Siani-Davies, 2005: 64). The secretary of the Central Committee, who was responsible for military and security affairs, had just arrived in Timişoara and was appointed general commander for the city. Another official taking part was the first secretary of the Timişoara County Party Committee. The teleconference communicates two issues.

First, it gives a description of "some very grave events which took place yesterday and today in Timişoara", and the reason why "order was not yet reestablished" (Romanian Communist Party, Braşov County [Party] Committee, 1989). The former pertains to *moot 2*, whereas the latter, to *moot 1*. The official definition of the protests depicts them as an anti-Romanian and anti-socialist plot of foreign powers which began as a protest against the eviction of Tőkés. Ceauşescu is more vigorous in his conviction that everything which took place recently in Central and Eastern Europe is part of a broader *anti-socialist coup d'état*. He also clearly makes a point at the end of the Political Executive Committee meeting – these "*coup d'états* have been organized also with the support of the chaff of society" [*cu sprijinul plevei societăţii*] (***, 2007).

> Everybody has to know that we are in a state of war. Everything which has happened and is happening currently in Germany, Czechoslovakia and Bulgaria, and in the past in Poland and Hungary are things organized by the Soviet Union with American support and [with the support] of the West. This thing has to be very clear. And what has happened in the last three countries – German DR., Czechoslovakia and Bulgaria were *coup d'états* organized also with the support of the chaff of society, the chaff of society with foreign support. In this way things have to be understood. They cannot be judged in a different way (***, 2007) [*author's translation*].

Besides Soviet and American interests – at the very beginning and later in connection to the actions of "the so-called Reformed bishop" – Ceauşescu also mentions Budapest, more explicitly, "the involvement of foreign intelligence circles, starting with Budapest" (***, 2006a). Another point which is worthy of note, is that Ceauşescu also mistakenly refers to Tőkés several times, as "bishop".

There is a state of emergency and the general secretary calls for harsh measures of reprimand. Other measures include closing the borders for tourists and the interruption of frontier traffic (Romanian Communist Party, Braşov County [Party] Committee, 1989).

The Patriotic Guards

The second issue on the agenda is the mobilization of the Patriotic Guards. If the case so requires, they have to be armed and prepared to intervene. The measures which are taken concern not only the police and army, but the whole society as such. They all have to be involved and report any "element which tries to provoke disorder" (Romanian Communist Party, Braşov County [Party] Committee, 1989). The mobilization of the Patriotic Guards has a broader goal than just reinforcement – they provide legitimization. This strategy has roots in Ceauşescu's reaction to the Warsaw Pact invasion of Czechoslovakia in 1968, which I discussed above as a reaction to first-order transgressions in the Communist Bloc. As stated, the then formed paramilitary Patriotic Guards, were to be engaged in a counterstrike in the case of a would-be Soviet led attack against Romania.

In the December 17 meeting of the Political Executive Committee, Ceauşescu associates the 1989 *anti-socialist coup d'état* with the danger of a Soviet-led invasion which was facing the country in 1968. According to him, if it were not for the mobilization of the people and the arming of the Patriotic Guards, the country would have been invaded as well. Ceauşescu even gives names – "the Soviets as well as the Bulgarians were at the border" (2006b).

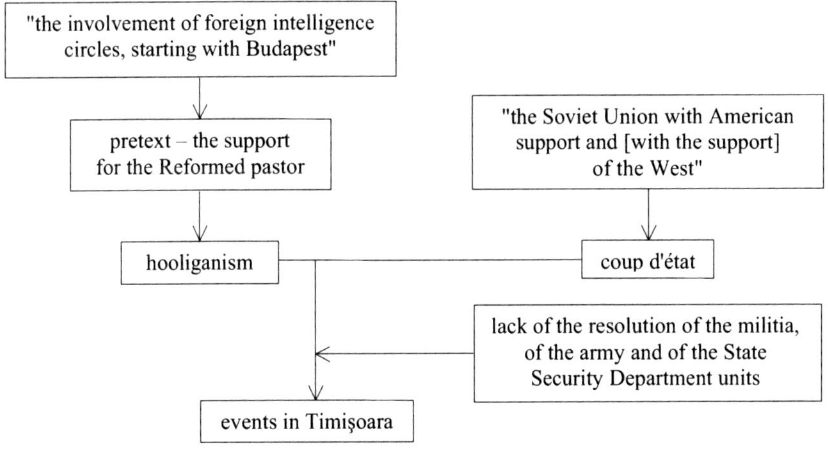

Scheme 14   Meeting of the Political Executive Committee – December 17, 1989

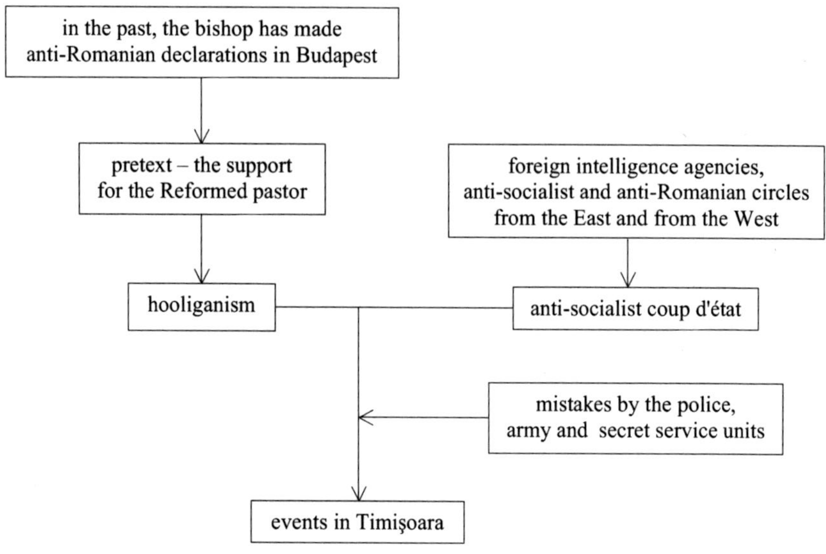

Scheme 15   Teleconference: Ceauşescu with two Communist Officials in Timişoara December 17, 1989

Ideological Convergence:

Hooliganism – Larger Plan against the Independence and Sovereignty of Nations

On the evening of December 20, just after returning from his visit to Iran, Ceauşescu delivers a speech broadcast by the national radio and television stations (Siani-Davies, 2005: 65). This is the first official recognition of the fact that some protests against the policy of the party were taking place in Timişoara. It is also a sign that Ceauşescu had already given up any diplomatic scruples. New noteworthy elements of the discourse include: "fascist-type actions", "terrorist acts", "anti-national actions" and the explicit mentioning of Budapest – this time, however, not in relationship with the particular initiatives of the Reformed pastor, but in connection with broader anti-national activities.

> The purpose of those anti-national actions was to cause disorder, to destabilize the political and economic situation, to create the conditions for the territorial dismant-ling of Romania, the destruction of the independence and sovereignty of our socia-list country. Not accidentally, the radio stations from Budapest and from other coun-

tries started a shameless campaign of lies against our country even during those anti-national and terrorist acts (Ceauşescu's Address to the Nation – December 20, 1989) [*author's translation*].

In comparison with the December 17 meeting of the Political Executive Council and with that day's teleconference with Timişoara, the Soviet Union is not directly mentioned in the televised speech. Seemingly, this is a case of the following ideological convergence: *hooliganism – the larger plan against the independence and sovereignty of nations*. Two mentions of attempts to stop the socialist development of the country notwithstanding, it is evident that the hypothesis of the *anti-socialist coup d'état of foreign powers* has been dropped. The speech also makes an appeal to the population of Timişoara: "to do everything for the peace and order of their city and to contribute to the peace and order in the whole country" (Ceauşescu's Address to the Nation – December 20, 1989) [*author's translation*]. It is noteworthy that no reference is made to the previous lack of resolution in the police and army forces. Quite on the contrary, Ceauşescu says that the army "responded only when attacked by the terrorist groups and when the fundamental institutions [and] the order in the county had been put in danger" (Ceauşescu's Address to the Nation – December 20, 1989) [*author's translation*].

This type of ideological convergence is much closer to that presented during the framework of the Political Executive Committee meeting. As elements of dissonance, I would mention that the emphasis on the anti-national character of the protests is stronger. Notions such as "fascists" and "terrorist actions" appeared. At the beginning of the December 17 meeting, Ceauşescu recognizes that there are, "certain expectations of changes in Romania". In the end, he even makes direct reference to Germany, Czechoslovakia and Bulgaria. In the ideological convergence of the first meeting, the *coup d'état* is presented not as anti-national, but as aimed toward changing the political regime. As documented, the content of the stenographic transcript develops the hypothesis of an anti-socialist plot, however there is no mention of individual cases. Eventually, the TV speech advances the ideological convergence between hooliganism and a "larger plan against the independence and sovereignty of nations". Except for the direct mention of Budapest, other references are more blurred. In my interpretation, the usage of formulas such as: "terrorist", "fascist" and "anti-national" is meant to repudiate the obvious fact that the purpose of the demonstrations is to effect political change. Furthermore, soldiers leaving for Timişoara were told that they should be expecting to encounter resistance from Hungarian insurgents (Siani-Davies, 2005: 65).

The following scheme tries to illustrate the changes in the ideological convergence with which the communist leadership was operating subsequent to Ceauşescu's December 20 address to the nation.

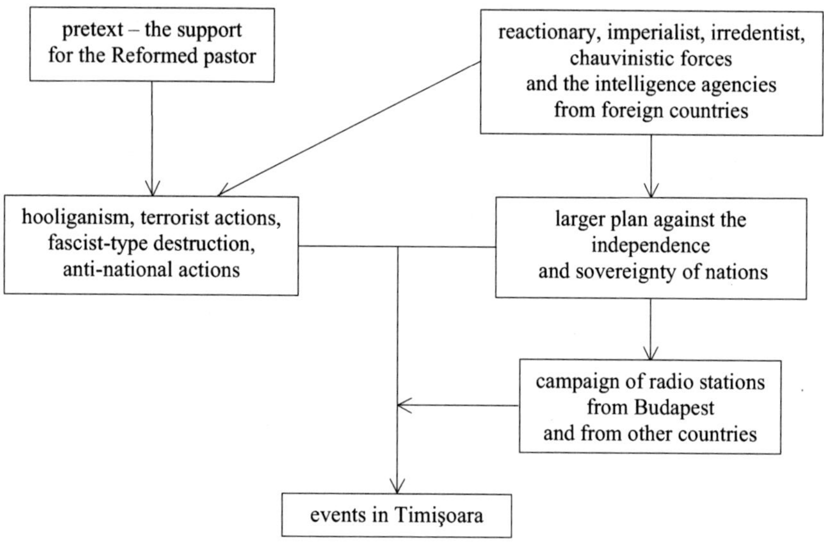

Scheme 16   Ceauşescu's Address to the Nation – December 20, 1989

The State of Emergency

The declaration of a state of emergency in Timiş County was signed by Ceauşescu only on December 20 and the authorities did not manage to publish it in the Official Bulletin of the Socialist Republic of Romania. It was read aloud in Timişoara in the morning from the balcony of the County Party Committee and published in the newspapers. On December 22, Ceauşescu extended the state of emergency to the whole country. Again, this was done without publishing the decree in the Official Bulletin (Mioc, 2004). Hence, the unfolding of the reprimand in Timişoara on the days of December 17, 18 and 19 preceded the proclamation of the state of emergency for the county of Timiş. By the same token, the December 22 proclamation of the state of emergency for the whole country came after victims were already registered on December 21 (Mioc, 2004).

2. The June 1990 Miners' March on Bucharest

The following chapter focuses on the *1990 University Square phenomenon* and on the June 14-15, 1990 miners' march on Bucharest. The former designates a 52-day long protest, held in the University Square in Bucharest, against the neo-communist government instated after the 1989 revolution. The latter is commonly referred to as the *third mineriad* [a treia mineriadă]. Two previous miners' marches – of much smaller proportions – took place on January 29 and February 18. Following the line of inquiry established in the previous chapters, I am interested in the types of ideological convergence employed in the authorities' definition of the demonstrations and the legitimization given to the miners on June 14. My obvious hypothesis is that the reaction of President Iliescu to the clashes between the demonstrators and the law enforcement on June 13 should resemble the discourse of Ceauşescu in 1989 with respect to the protests in Timişoara. If so, key common elements would be: stressing the fact that there is a state of emergency and the designation of the events as being of a fascist-type.

Some clarifications are due before I proceed. I will only deal indirectly with the reaction of the government to the University Square demonstrations. My analysis focuses on the reaction to the very riots of June 13 and on Iliescu's welcome of the miners in the capital. Second, I am not so much concerned with the extent to which the three 1990 miners' marches were planned in advance and received logistical support from the authorities, although, I am fully aware of the topic and take it into account. There are several hypotheses regarding the arrival of the miners in the capital. After presenting them, I would like to show how these events can also be viewed in close connection with the regime's reaction to the 1977 strike in the Jiu Valley, the 1987 revolt in Braşov and the beginning of the 1989 revolution in Timişoara.

The 1990 mineriads [mineriadele din 1990]

The six *mineriads* [mineriade] took place in 1990, in 1991, and finally in 1999 (Flonta, 1999; Rus, 2003; Rus, 2007). The term refers to several violent clashes in Bucharest. On all three occasions, after the initial outbreak of disorder, miners (hence the popular name mineriad) arrived in Bucharest as an extra-legal force in charge of reinstating order. Each of the three marches of 1990 was preceded by large, public manifestations of protest against the neo-communist character of the provisional government (the Front) and President Iliescu. In response, large masses of workers from several factories from Bucharest and its vicinity (firmly in support of the interim leadership and the incumbent President), were mobilized. Out of the total of six miners' marches to Bucharest (three more were to follow in 1991 and 1999), the June 1990 march is considered to have been symptomatic of the contentious relationship developed in the communist period between Romanian workers and intellectuals, and of the anti-intellectual character of the newly instated power which was thought to be of a neo-communist orientation.

The January 1990 Mineriad [mineriada din ianuarie 1990]

On January 29, 1990 – the *first mineriad* [prima mineriadă] – instigated by the National Salvation Front [*Frontul Salvării Naţionale – FSN*], the miners devastated the headquarters of the "historical parties". The National Christian Democratic Peasants' Party [*Partidul Naţional Tărănesc Creştin şi Democrat – PNŢCD*], the National Liberal Party *[Partidul Naţional Liberal – PNL]* and other small parties held a big demonstration the previous day against the National Salvation Front taking part in the elections (Pavel, 2003). This episode witnessed the first appearance of the slogan, "We are working, not thinking!" [*Noi muncim, nu gândim!*] (Pavel, 2003: 35) [*author's translation*], thought to be symptomatic of the perspective toward intellectuals held by the majority of workers following the 1989 Revolution.

The February 1990 Mineriad [mineriada din februarie 1990]

The *second mineriad* [a doua mineriadă] generally followed the same pattern, except for the fact that even some of the demonstrators turned aggressive. On February 18 the Government building was besieged by demonstrators. The next morning, about 4,000 miners flooded the capital. Yet, as the police and army had already reinstated order, there was not much left to be done by the miners.

The June 1990 mineriad [mineriada din iunie 1990]

The *third mineriad* [a treia mineriadă] is thought to have left the most indelible scars, and its overtly anti-intellectual character primarily determines this fact (Cristea, 2007; Berindei, Combes and Planche, 2010). The official data indicates six deaths in the riots of June 13, 1990; however, the Association of the Victims of the Mineriad and several articles published in 1991 give a higher number. A rather controversial issue exists regarding the mass grave discovered at Strǎuleş-ti Cemetery (near Bucharest) by *România Liberă* journalist, Petre Mihai Băcanu (Rus, 2007: 163-170). It is believed that 128 unidentified bodies – which, according to witnesses, were buried by soldiers in 1990 – belong to victims of the June riots in the capital (Rus, 2007: 165-167).

Miners from Jiu-Valley came to Bucharest in order to put an end to the civic organizations' demonstration which lasted for "52 days and nights" (Pavel, 2003: 61) in the University Square. They attacked not only the protesters, but also the headquarters of opposition parties, the university, the Institute of Architecture and the offices of some anti-government newspapers and NGOs.

In the imagery of the democratic intellectuals, the three bitter confrontations are recalled as the "proletarian assault" on the educated stratum of the society. In this respect, Pavel's (2003: 61) description and analyses of the third mineriad is quite relevatory, painting it in terms of "paramilitary proletarian detachments, some sort of 'black shirts' of the new regime, who – in their 'march' on Bucharest – wanted to teach a lesson to the forces who were opposing those who had already won the elections" [*author's translation*]. Following Gledhill (2005: 84), this perspective could be regarded as illustrative of the tendency among Romanian analysts to initially interpret the 1990 events as having been effected by a "social schism". According to the author, this indicates that Marxist thought in the early 1990s was quite influential in Romanian academic circles.

Besides the anti-intellectual profile of the riot, it should be stated that the miners also devastated the headquarters of the historical parties and burst into Roma neighborhoods (Rus, 2007: 137-139). The attack on party offices took the form of a mock police search – groups of miners revealed large sums of money and vast stashes of medicine, drugs etc. Reportedly, all of this was to substantiate the hypothesis that the historical parties were illicitly supporting and manipulating the anti-communist demonstration in the University Square. Furthermore, as an objective, they also sought to evidence that the University Square phenomenon was more than a mere political demonstration, but rather a second-rate and delayed Romanian version of the Woodstock festival.

The 1991 Mineriad [mineriada din 1991]

The *fourth mineriad* [a patra mineriadă] (September 24-27, 1991) started with labor union demands and finally led to the resignation of Prime Minister Petre Roman (Dobrescu and Rughiniş, ***: 470).

A common denominator of the first three mineriads is that they were clearly supporting the powers that be. In comparison, the *September 1991 mineriad* [mineriada din septembrie 1991] turned against the government, and to a certain degree also against President Iliescu. This fourth mineriad effected a change in the profile of the miners' marches, in the sense that they started to be governed by economic demands. According to the mainstream interpretation, the fourth mineriad turned against the measures taken by the reformist minister, Petre Roman. The miners also went to the Chamber of Deputies where they requested

Iliescu's resignation. They also clashed with special units of the municipal police in Victory Square. Iliescu managed to channel the mutiny of the miners to force the resignation of Petre Roman, in whom he had lost trust.

A contentious issue regarding this miners' march – of which the Romanian civil society does not like to be reminded – is that the September 1991 mineriad received the approval (applause even) of some members of the historical parties – i.e. the same which were targeted during the June 1990 mineriad. The approbation of the fourth mineriad by several segments of civil society came as a result of the fact that the miners asked for the resignation of the government and Iliescu. According to Rus (2007), the anachronism did not go unnoticed by the miners themselves. Hence, an article in a local newspaper entitled, *Do you love us now ma'am?* [Acum ne iubiți, doamnă?], indicates the unexpected change of attitude – as far as the Jiu Valley miners are concerned – of one former opponent of the communist regime.

The January 1999 Mineriad [mineriada din ianuarie 1999] *and the February 1999 Mineriad* [mineriada din februarie 1999]

Two final mineriads came on the background of what – following the studies of Gamal Ibrahim and Galt Vaughn – Friedman (2007b: 426) refers to as, "delayed shock therapy", for the mining industry. The shock therapy effected mass layoffs, skyrocketing unemployment and the closure of non-profitable mines. The fifth and the sixth miners' marches (January 18-22 and February 16-17, 1999) posed a serious threat to state order, and eventually army intervention was needed (Pavel, 2003). In January, miners managed to cross a barricade installed in the town of Costești and overpower *gendarmerie* units near the city of Râmnicu Vâlcea, where they sequestered the prefect of Vâlcea County together with his daughter and neighbor (Rus, 2007: 395-398). The negotiations with the miners were led by Prime Minister Radu Vasile. A final agreement was signed with the miners' leader, Miron Cozma, at the nearby monastery of Cozia [*pacea de la Cozia*].

The *sixth mineriad* [a şasea mineriadă] was a reaction to a ruling which sentenced Miron Cozma to 18 years in prison for the 1991 mineriad. The miners were dissipated by police units at Stoenești Olt and Cozma himself was arrested and sent to the Rahova prison.

Theoretical Expositions

Several interpretations were given for the 1990 miners' marches on Bucharest. Generally speaking, those theories which disavow the hypothesis of a voluntary initiative of the miners trace the phenomena of the mineriads back to the aftermath of the strike in Jiu Valley in 1977. From the 1980s onward, and especially after the miners' marches, Jiu Valley was predominantly portrayed as *little Siberia*. This perspective is considered to offer an explanation as to why the miners were called in to help quell the University Square phenomenon in 1990[61].

Even though the hypothesis linking the ease of the miners' mobilization in 1990 to policies of attracting the labor force to the Valley after 1977 is disputable, there is clear evidence that 1977 was a turning point in the social history of the region, as well as its *image* outside its borders. Kideckel (2008: 42-43, 172-173) indicates several changes which were effected as a result of the 1977 strike – the alienation of the mining population from other regional groups and the deepening of gender segregation are cases in point[62]. As documented, the production was militarized after the strike. In parallel, a large number of workers of Moldavian origin were imported. According to Kideckel (2008: 42), this was intended to weaken the political power of the miners and to ensure stable coal production in the region. The migratory input of mainly unskilled workers effected a local attitude which, rephrasing Edward Said's term – *orientalism* – could be regarded as "a type of Moldavian 'Orientalism'" (Kideckel, 2008: 124). In terms of social stratification, a distinction was felt between the "'pre-1977' non-mining Jiu Valley population" on the one hand, and the "post-1977 population" on the other. Where, the former holds the latter culpable for "the decline of Jiu Valley culture and the *minerit*" [mining activity] (Kideckel, 2001: 6-8). The practical result of this suspicion was the precarious absence of the "post-1977 population" from the ranks of the organs of government, education, media and healthcare.

---

61   For the relations between the demographic and control policies in the Valley after 1977 and the stormy marches of 1990 see Vasi (2004).

62   "Social change in mining was even greater than that in production. Prior to 1977 the region's miners were well integrated into regional social and political networks. However, the strike separated the mining population from other regional groups, depriving the miners of political support other than that of their own union leaders. Social rifts developed between the new miners and the non-mining population, who blame the decline in Jiu Valley life on the low-brow culture of these immigrants. Unlike earlier Valley immigrants, those who arrived after 1977 came with their families. Male and female roles became more sharply separated after the strike, as new apartment complexes were built whose male residents nearly all worked in the mines and whose wives nearly all remained at home [...]. In the 'golden period' of the Jiu Valley mining industry, i.e., from before socialism until the strike of 1977, there was an unwritten rule that miners did not speak of sex and women in the mine. The 'old-timers' say that doing so diverted attention from the dangerous work at hand. With changes in mining after 1977 and especially with the new work force, sexual banter became ubiquitous and a chief way of relating in the underground" (Kideckel, 2008: 42-43, 172-173).

> One significant effect of the bimodal Jiu Valley population is felt in civic life. Because
> of the disdain in which they are held, and their mutual suspicion in return, there is next
> to no Moldavian or immigrant presence in Jiu Valley organs of government, educati-
> on, media, and healthcare. In fact, the representatives of civil society level the most
> stringent critique at the post-1977 population (Kideckel, 2001: 7).

In comparison with Jiu Valley, the city of Braşov hosts more pleasant urban legends. One of the most telling moments was the organization of an inter-class meeting at Braşov – September 7-8, 1990 – under the name of "Romanian resistance". This was intended as a post-communist Romanian replica of the Polish inter-class coalition between workers and intellectuals and it ended with a final symbolic conciliatory gesture[63].

> Although it began in animosity, and though it certainly did not obliterate all diffe-
> rences, the meeting ended with an embrace between Marian Munteanu, the Students'
> League leader who had almost been killed by the miners in June, and Miron Cozma,
> the leader of the Jiu Valley miners' trade union (HU OSA, 300-8-32, Box 2, De-
> cember 14, 1990: 17) [*author's translation*].

Other explanations were also given regarding the main causes of the miners' marches of 1990. One of the most original interpretations was made by Alexe (2006), who depicts the episode of the mineriads as being subsequent to "anthropological and psychological experiences of a Nazi type which lasted for more than twenty-five years". According to the author, the experiment – which was in part initiated by Iliescu[64] – started off in two mining regions in Muscel (Berevoieşti and Câmpulung) and it documented, "the differentiated access to material goods", and the "rumor" as being the main factors for inciting the miners (Vasi, 2004).

An alternative and quite novel approach to the mineriads is presented by Gledhill (2005). To a certain degree, it could be claimed that his is the first study

---

63   In her discourse, Ana Blandiana – the future president of the Civic Alliance – made the
     point that the model for the opposition to the neo-communist regime was to be found in
     the Civic Forum and the Polish *Solidarity* organization.
     "Actually, the alliance should have existed 10 years before. The alliance must [now]
     replace what existed in Czechoslovakia and in other [communist] countries 10 years
     ago. It is late, but not too late. I hope that the extraordinary speed [of events] will help
     us make up for this delay, for which we are responsible" (Ana Blandiana in HU OSA,
     300-8-32, Box 2, December 14, 1990: 21) [*author's translation*].
64   "Starting in 1967, the Central Committee of the UWY [Union of Working Youth]
     became deeply involved in the Nazi experiment and was headed by its first secretary –
     comrade Ion Iliescu – and the Ministry of Youth Problems which was 'shepherded' by
     the same Ion Iliescu, 'engineer of souls' [who was] educated in the USSR, during Sta-
     lin's time" (Alexe, 2006) [*author's translation*].

which puts into scientific perspective the standpoint of Iliescu on the first three mineriads. Regarding the so-called *dossier of the June 1990 mineriad* [dosarul mineriadei din iunie 1990] (***, 2008), in the last years Iliescu appeared to be quite often subjected to what could be regarded as *extreme media exposure bullying* (Matthiesen, 2006). The formula pertains to cases in which the mechanism of bullying targets politicians and persons of higher status, and can be applied to developments subsequent to Iliescu's signing of a pardon lifting the prison sentence of Miron Cozma – the leader of the third and later mineriads. The President was criticized both for having granting the pardon, as well as revoking it shortly after in reaction to civil society's protests. It is also noteworthy that, in his turn, Iliescu seems quite determined to substantiate his stand on the miners' marches. The episodes of the 1990 and of the 1991 mineriads were presented in the book, *Revoluţie şi reformă* [Revolution and Reform] (Iliescu, 1994). The former President also devoted a separate book to the subject: *Viaţa politică, între violenţă şi dialog* [Political Life between Violence and Dialog] (published in 2005) (see Iliescu, ***). Furthermore, articles (Drăgotescu, 2003) and documents relating to the episode are often published on his blog (Iliescu, ***), where he also announced his decision not to run for a parliamentary seat.

As could be expected, Iliescu's books on the Romanian revolution and transition received a cold welcome amongst the so-called Romanian democratic intellectuals. In this regard, Tismăneanu's (2004) long interview, *Marele şoc din finalul unui secol scurt: Ion Iliescu în dialog cu Vladimir Tismăneanu despre comunism, postcomunism, democraţie* [The Great Shock at the End of a Short Century: Ion Iliescu in Dialog with Vladimir Tismăneanu on Communism, Post-Communism, and Democracy], proved especially contentious. The much-awaited book effected disappointment, due to the obvious reluctance of the interviewer to corner Iliescu on the issues of the Romanian anti-communist revolution and the orchestration of the 1990 miners' marches. Allegations were made that, "Tismăneanu was 'bought off' by Iliescu, the ex-apparatchik who was the President of Romania for eleven years after Ceauşescu's demise" (Stoica, 2006a: 181). Clearly, the antipathy and the distrust toward the former President is an inevitable sequel to the "contentious politics" of early post-communist Romania. The last notion brings us back to Gledhill's (2005) study of the third mineriad. Following the model of "contentious politics" introduced by Doug McAdam, Sidney Tarrow and Charles Tilly, Gledhill's (2005: 78) point is that the mineriads of 1990 represent sequences of organized political power, "enacted outside the realm of official state institutions". He argues that the state's engagement in extrainstitutional politics appeared in the context of a contentious opposition to a weakly legitimized government[65].

As stated earlier, this argumentation agrees on many points with those advanced by Iliescu (1994) himself. In his turn, the President also pointed to the weakness of the institutions in the aftermath of the Revolution of 1989. Still, the two perspectives inevitably collide when it comes to the degree of state involvement in generating and coordinating acts of violence in 1990. Iliescu (Drăgotescu, 2003) promotes the thesis of the miners' voluntary initiative, whereas Gledhill (2005: 76) talks openly about "state-led political violence in Post-Socialist Romania".

A valuable contribution to the analysis of the *mineriad* social phenomena is put forward by Vasi (2004). The author introduces several theoretical foundations which viewed together illuminate the social, political and historical dimensions of the miners' marches. In my interpretation, the article has two key strong points. Firstly, it discusses the mineriads from the point of view of theories of social movement and collective action, urban ecology, political opportunity structures etc. Secondly, it attempts to compare the Romanian case with the 1991 Russian and Ukrainian miners' movement. Vasi (2004) also seeks to explain the difference in the political ethos of the Russian and Ukrainian miners' movement on the one hand, and the Jiu Valley miners on the other.

Out of Rus' vast work on Jiu Valley, his last book, *Mineriadele. Între manipulare politică şi solidaritate muncitorească* [The *Mineriads* – between Political Manipulation and Workers' Solidarity] (2007), deserves special mention. Rus manages to give a local perspective on the phenomena. His interviews reveal, for example, that one of the mechanisms of persuading the miners to take part in the 1990, 1991 and 1999 marches was also subjecting them to bullying by unionists and colleagues. Furthermore, he also marks out changes in the perceptions of the mineriads by the inhabitants of the Valley. An interesting

---

65   "By June 1990, the FSN had gained formal legitimacy through a resounding electoral victory, but a contentious opposition persisted and was perceived by the nascent government as an extrainstitutional threat to the FSN's grip on power. Faced with this informal challenge, the Front felt impelled to avail of the opportunities presented by a weak institutional structure by engaging in extrainstitutional politics. In so doing, the Front was able to overcome the threat presented by a 'contentious' opposition [...]. By recurring in an intermittent fashion, the miners' actions partially satisfy the definition of contentious political behaviour put forward by McAdam, Tarrow, and Tilly, for whom contentious politics are 'episodic, public, collective interactions among makers of claims', enacted outside the realm of formal politics and against the central state authority" (Gledhill, 2005: 79).

chapter is devoted to the evolution of unionist Miron Cozma from being a thorough miner to an imposing, flamboyant and feared local leader.

> This metamorphosis of the former trade union leader also talks about [points to] changes in the Romanian civil society over the period of 16 years. If in 1990 a model of the worker who is "[as] poor as anybody else" but [who] is determined, rightful and honest had the highest chances to be appreciated, after 2005 an elegant dandy getting out from a luxury car surrounded by beautiful women might enjoy greater success in the eyes of the public (Rus, 2007: 433) [*author's translation*].

The Golaniad

The term *golaniad* [golaniada], derived from Romanian *golan* [rascal, hoodlum] is used to designate the University Square protest phenomenon. The word is meant to ridicule the ideological convergence which was employed by Iliescu when he referred to the demonstrators in University Square as hoodlums or iron-guardists (Cristea, 2007: 29-31). Also noteworthy, is the use of the word *golan*, rather than *hooligan*. Seemingly, Iliescu's presidency brought about a major refashioning of the vocabulary employed in the labeling of mass protests. Still, not unlike his predecessor, Iliescu also resorted to notions such as "iron-guardist" and "fascist".

Besides ridiculing, the word *golan* [hoodlum] was also displaying an attitude of the high moral authority of the opposition to the former communists still in power after the 1989 revolution. The demonstrators quickly seized the moment and accepted the invective as their name. *Golan* was featured on badges and played an important role in the hymn of the protesters.

The Content Analysis

In the present chapter, I focus on the *Report – Parliamentary Committee of Enquiry into the Events that Took Place from 13-15 June 1990*, drafted in January 1991 (Romanian Parliament, 1991; see also The Chamber of Deputies of Romania, 1990).

In fact we are dealing with two separate reports presented to the Council of Europe (Helsinki Watch, 1991: 13-22). The first one is the would-be *majority report* of politicians from the National Salvation Front, the Agrarian Democratic Party of Romania, the Romanian National Unity Party and the Parliamentary Group of National Non-Magyar Minorities. The second, the would-be *minority report,* was issued by representatives from the opposition parties: the National Liberal Party, the Magyar Democratic Union of Romania, the National Christian

Democratic Peasants' Party and the Ecologist and Social Democratic Parliamentary Group (Romanian Parliament, 1991: 6-7).

In the following, I seek to analyze the content of two types of materials. The first type consists of the reports of the two groups – i.e. the so-called "Group A" and "Group B" (Romanian Parliament, 1991: 8-17). The second empirical material consists of the chapters dealing with the episode of the third mineriad from Iliescu's book: *Revoluţie şi reformă* [Revolution and Reform] (1994). The analysis is similar to that which I utilized in the previous chapter.

Preliminary Conclusions of Group A (the Majority Report)

The report is five pages long and the conclusions are structured in 17 points. Several of these points also list the dissenting opinion of Sorin Botnaru, a member of parliament from the National Salvation Front. There are two additional paragraphs regarding the conduct of the police and the Minister of the Interior.

The conclusions of Group A are in concordance with the account given by former President Iliescu. There are, however, some vital dissenting elements. The most important distinction concerns the involvement of the Ministry of the Interior. The preliminary conclusions of Group A find the police – and specifically the Minister of the Interior – directly responsible for the escalation of violence and the en-mass illegal arrests during the riot. Furthermore, as we will see, the former President is more meticulous in describing the conditions and the general context which led to the events of June 13-15. He also refers to an atmosphere of panic and to the potential involvement of "outside forces" in support of the University Square protest.

The preliminary conclusion of Group A presents the following sequence of events. On June 13 and 14, the capital witnessed a violent clash between civilians and the forces of the Ministry of the Interior and of the Ministry of Defense. A general context of the violent outburst is provided, along with some specific causes. For example, the former pertains to "major upheaval and social unrest" in Romania and other former communist countries following the 1989 anti-communist revolution. The provisional nature of the government is also referenced. On a more specific level, the "deep-seated cause of the violence was the fact that certain groups which wanted to gain power by undemocratic means were contesting the outcome of the elections on 20 May, without any grounds for doing so" (Romanian Parliament, 1991: 9).

It can be inferred from the report, that the development of the University Square manifestation and the subsequent "climate of tension" took place in close connection with attempts to politically destabilize the country. It is argued therefore that the decision to have the University Square cleared by the police is legitimate. Also noteworthy is that the report of the *majority group* does not make reference to the circumstances in which this conclusion was reached. In comparison, the report of the *minority group* documents that the decision to clear the Square was made on June 11, at a meeting chaired by the President and the Prime Minister (Romanian Parliament, 1991: 13). Moreover, according to the second report, it was also then established that the police would receive a back-up of some 5,000 civilians.

The report of the *majority group*, further argues that the riots started "on the pretext of clearing the demonstrators from University Square on the morning of 13 June" (Romanian Parliament, 1991: 8); and that, seemingly, "certain political parties and groups were involved" in agitating the spirits that day. From the dissenting opinions of several members of parliament, we find that the above formula refers actually to the "historic political parties". The next development in the evolution of the events was that, subsequent to the state of emergency which was effected by the violent clashes, the President and the provisional government "appealed to the public to help put a stop to the violence" (Romanian Parliament, 1991: 10). After the miners' arrival, "the groups that were supposed to keep order, formed on an ad hoc basis from miners and other people" quickly appeared (Romanian Parliament, 1991: 10). Furthermore, it is stated that the escalation of violence was inevitable, because these ad hoc groups were not trained to enforce the laws of the country.

> 11. By their very nature, the groups that were supposed to keep order, formed on an ad hoc basis from miners and other people, were not in a position to observe the rules that specifically applied to the police. These groups used violence against the public, wrought havoc in the headquarters of certain political parties and institutions, causing serious damage to property, and intimidated the managers of several newspapers and many politicians (Romanian Parliament, 1991: 10).

All of these effected a "general state of confusion". Reportedly, the police and army units also engaged in the game of the groups, having "formed on an ad hoc basis from miners and other people", and they started taking into custody persons who were thought to have participated in the assault on state institutions. Reportedly, their number amounted to 1,021. Still, the police and the army targeted only the demonstrators, and failed to keep a close eye on "the groups" as well. This fact is interpreted as a sign that these institutions did not implement the necessary break with the practices of the former totalitarian regime. Hence, this is the second time that the police and the Minister of the Interior are allocated major responsibility for the escalation of violence. More explicitly, previously a point was made about the inappropriate manner in which they conducted the clearing of the University Square on the morning of June 13. The Minister of the Interior and the Chief

Inspector of the Bucharest Police were eventually dismissed. And at the end of the report, the police forces are held accountable for the way in which the containment of the riot was conducted following the input received from the miners.

> 6. [...] The implementation of the decision on the morning of 13 June was justifiable, given the need to create the climate necessary for the start of parliamentary proceedings and the investiture of the elected President. The police measures were badly organized, however, and the Minister of the Interior and the Chief Inspector of the Bucharest Police were dismissed on this account. [...]
>
> 12. In the general state of confusion resulting from the intervention of groups of citizens that had formed on an ad hoc basis, the police and army took into custody people suspected of having committed acts of violence against the state institutions. Some of their actions were unjustified, as is borne out by the fact that the 1,021 people held, including some adolescents, were released within a few hours. [...]
>
> 13. The police did not, however, immediately take into custody and prosecute the members of the ad hoc groups of miners or others that had formed on an ad hoc basis to maintain law and order and had acted unduly violently or been guilty of other infringements of the law, as would have been normal.
>
> 14. The activities of the Minister of the Interior and the police reflected mentalities specific to the totalitarian regime and a tendency to use methods and practices peculiar to that regime: excessive violence during arrests, inhuman treatment in prisons, inadequate medical care for prisoners, arbitrary procedures, illegal criminal investigation methods, and the refusal to allow contact with a lawyer, among other things (Romanian Parliament, 1991: 9-11).

Additionally, there were dissenting opinions which invoked arguments recalling Iliescu's thesis of the lack of legitimate instruments for reinstating public order and of the institutional weakness of the police following the December Revolution. They pointed to the absence of straightforward legal provisions at that time (Romanian Parliament, 1991: 11).

The *majority report* contains one element which is absent from the conclusions of the *minority group* – the occurrence of actions of "manifestly anti-Romanian intent" in the city of Miercurea Ciuc, where several police headquarters were attacked.

Altogether, it could be argued that the report of the *majority group* directed a clean escape for the political powers-that-be from the scene of the June 13-15, 1990 events. The main burden of responsibility is allocated to the Minister of the Interior (never mentioned by his name in the report), the Chief Inspector of the Bucharest Police and the police department itself. Moreover, the image of the miners emerging from the document is neutral. Once they arrived in the capital, their actions become actions of "groups that were supposed to keep order, formed on an ad hoc basis from miners and other people", centrifuged by the spiral of violence witnessed those days. A lapidary mention of a combination of civic and psycho-sociological motives serves as explanation for their presence in Bucharest. There is also talk of a general panic which started to overcome the population – including the miners – after the interruption of Romanian television broadcasts. While we recognize the fact that their arrival was *partly planned*, the paragraph elaborating on this subject focuses on the local authorities and institutions which organized their departure to Bucharest.

> 10. [...] The organization took place at local level, by means of machinery that varied from case to case. In some places it was the trade unions which mobilized the miners, while in others it was the formal local authorities – the provisional Councils of National Unity, to which the local political party representatives belonged. There were also cases where the instigation for the transport of the miners came from company managers (Romanian Parliament, 1991: 10).

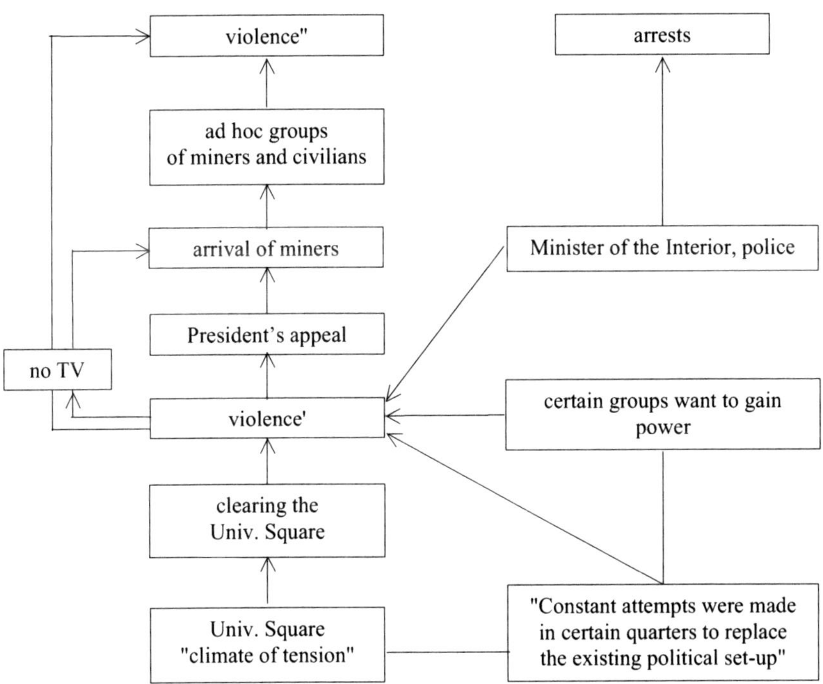

Scheme 17

Preliminary Conclusions of Group B (the Minority Report)

The *minority report* lists 14 conclusions. At the end of each paragraph it also indicates the institutions and the persons which should be held responsible for the acts of violence on June 13-15, 1990. For instance:

> 6. The selective way in which the public was informed by television on 13, 14 and 15 June, the unjustified television blackout on the evening of 13 June and the instigatory intervention of the television managers on the evening in question did much to cause the situation to escalate, involve civilians in aggressive activities and incite them to take action against the Romany community.
>
> Responsibility rests, to varying degrees, with the Romanian television managers and the Ministry of Telecommunications. [...]
>
> 8. Although the army had restored order in the capital by dawn on 14 June, the President of Romania gave a speech to the miners who had come to Bucharest, urging them to reoccupy University Square. The speech contained untruths and was also an incitement to aggression.
>
> Responsibility lies solely with the President of Romania.
>
> (Romanian Parliament, 1991: 15).

The *minority report* maintains the convergence between the University Square protest and a general state of discontent which "was the result of concern that the country was moving towards a new communist dictatorship". This convergence is, however, maintained at a rather general level. The report talks about "a sizeable section of the population", and not about "historical" and other political parties and organizations which were manifesting their opposition vis-à-vis Iliescu, the National Front of Salvation and the provisional government. Two decisive moments are seen as having led to the outburst of violence on the afternoon of June 13. First, there is the June 11 decision to clear the University Square. The fact that it was predetermined that they would resort to utilizing civilians seems to have a long term effect, as it anticipates at least the President's appeal to the population. According to the first report, the President's speech facilitated the arrival of the miners in the capital. The second element is the violent actions of the police. Hence, in comparison with the *majority report* – where the police units are presented as being initially disorganized and defensive and become highly aggressive only after the arrival of the miners – in the *minority report* they are said to had been aggressive from the very beginning. According to the report, this fact unleashed a similar answer on behalf of the demonstrators. At this moment, the report stipulates that the responsibility falls both on the demonstrators who attacked state institutions and on the police forces who failed to defend them.

3. The violence perpetrated in response to the actions of the police by the demonstrators, who reoccupied the square and attacked state institutions (the Bucharest Police Headquarters, the Ministry of the Interior, the Romanian Information Service and the television headquarters) was a serious, criminal violation of the law.

Responsibility rests with the accused, whose trial is under way. The extent of their responsibility must be proved according to the offences with which they are charged.

4. The fact that the police abandoned their task of guarding and defending the targets that were attacked and withdrew at a time when the capital needed their presence and needed them to intervene revealed a serious lack of military discipline on the part of those in command.

Responsibility for the situation rests with the Prime Minister, who failed to control and supervise those in charge of the Ministry of the Interior, and with the Minister of the Interior and his senior deputy, who themselves directed the police operations of 13 June.

(Romanian Parliament, 1991: 14).

The President's appeal to the population is seen as unnecessary and disproportionate. This is a contentious issue which also surfaces in Iliescu's (1994) book. According to the former President, in spite of the fact that the June 13 clash between the demonstrators and the police did not represent a serious political threat, it did, however, lead to a thorough panic in the population. And, it is further argued, considering this state of affairs, the President's actions were both necessary and justified (Iliescu, 1994).

The notion of escalating panic in the population is also presented in the *majority report* (Romanian Parliament, 1991: 13-17). Hence, it is therein stated that the arrival of the miners in the capital "is a direct consequence of the effects of the violent events of 13 June and the interruption of Romanian television broadcasts" (Romanian Parliament, 1991: 10). In his turn, Iliescu also argues that the attack on the television network "incited panic within the population" (Iliescu, 1994: 133).

Returning to the *minority report,* we see that it gives a detailed account of state-led violence in which the miners indulged. It also indicates that the groups of miners "were taken to Romany districts" (Romanian Parliament, 1991: 16). Furthermore, the detention of more than 1,000 people is mentioned. In comparison with the *majority report,* the *minority* one considers that "Responsibility rests with the prosecuting authorities and the criminal investigation authorities" (Romanian Parliament, 1991: 16).

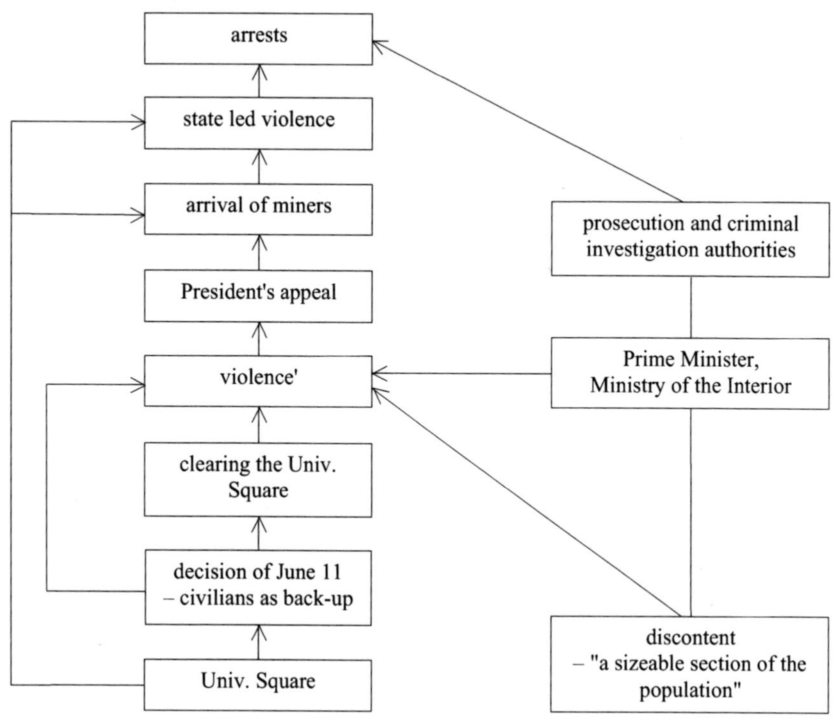

Scheme 18

The Account of President Iliescu

The account of the former President of Romania comes quite close to the preliminary conclusions of the *majority report*. There are however some dissenting elements. First of all, the Minister or the Ministry of the Interior is no longer singled out as the main scapegoat. A thesis is put forward claiming there was a *lack of legitimate instruments for maintaining public order* following the December 1989 Revolution (Iliescu, 1994: 134). A point is made that on the morning of June 13 the police were forbidden from using firearms and that the protesters took advantage of this fact. The decision to resort to extra-institutional politics does not appear to be voluntary. Quite to the contrary, it is presented as a "necessary evil" called for by the eruption of panic in the population. Iliescu portrays the arrival of the miners in Bucharest as voluntary. Accordingly, the population of Bucharest welcomed them as thorough guardians of the tranquility of the capital (Iliescu, 1994: 137). In a similar fashion to the "violent crowd" [*mulțime violentă*] which tried to "overturn by force the legitimate power", the miners are depicted as "defenders who are as bitter [as the violent crowd] and over whom [the legitimate power] does not exert any control" (Iliescu, 1994: 137) [*author's translation*].

The *majority report* operates with the thesis that *violence leads to violence*. The hypothesis of the *state-led violence* as documented in the *minority report* is replaced in Iliescu's account with that of the *inevitable and unfortunate escalation of violence*. From this point of view, the final speech of Iliescu – the one in which he thanked the miners for their support – is presented as having been aimed at putting an end to their activity in the capital and, thus, preventing the further escalation of violence.

Talking about the University Square phenomenon, Iliescu maintains the convergence with the historical parties and other organizations (the Group for Social Dialogue, the League of the Students, the newspaper *România Liberă*, the National Liberal Party and the National Christian Democrat Peasants' Party). Their activity however is linked to so-called "outside forces" which reportedly were also involved in the development of more or less similar manifestations in Belgrade, Sofia and other capitals of the former communist countries in Central and Eastern Europe. The purpose of these actions would be "to stop the democratic evolution of certain countries of the East" (Iliescu, 1994: 123-124). It could be observed, that this discursive pattern closely resembles Ceaușescu's hypothesis of an "anti-socialist plot".

In comparison with the *majority report* (Romanian Parliament, 1991: 13-17), Iliescu's (1994: 124-127) account also presents a diagram of the social and anthropological types of participants of the University Square protest: the "marginal element" (the so-called *golani* – hoodlums), "political idealists" such as "the radicals", "Jacobins", "the pure" (considered to be potential victims of a fascist-type movement); students with strong anti-communist convictions and who "expressed the most unrelenting intransigence with respect to the generation of their parents"; intellectuals who tried to make good on the fact that they did not protest during communism; "professional protesters" [*manifestanții de profesie*] and persons who were easily manipulated.

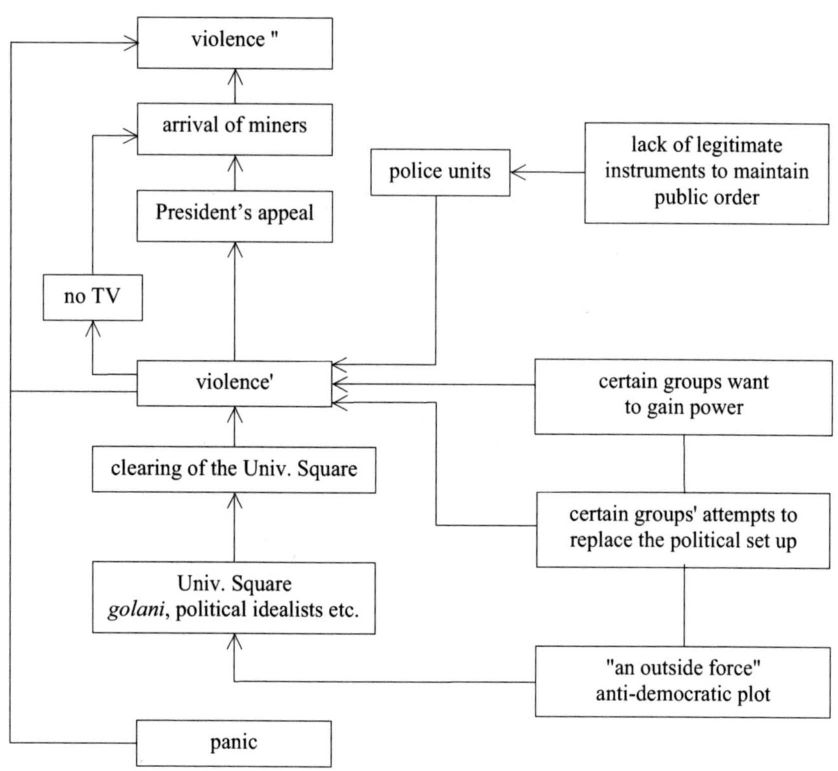

Scheme 19

Conclusions

This chapter has sought to illustrate that President Iliescu's framing of the June 13, 1990 street fights in Bucharest recalls Ceauşescu's official interpretation of the Timişoara events. And at this point, I mainly have in mind the invocation of the so-called *state of emergency* and the appeal to the population for support, which can be regarded as analogous to Ceauşescu's resorting to the Patriotic Guards in 1989. The current political, historical, sociological, anthropological and journalistic fields advance several hypotheses for explaining and contextualizing the 1990 miners' marches on Bucharest. While none of them has complete explanatory power, each helps in grasping the broad picture. To a certain degree the same holds true for the present study. I aimed to show that the practice of convergence between *hooliganism and delinquency and recidivism* (the case of Jiu Valley 1977), between *hooliganism and a lack of discipline* (the case of Braşov 1987) and between *hooliganism and a subterfuge of foreign powers* (the case of Timişoara 1989) paved the way for the eventuality of *resorting to the miners' assistance* in 1990.

CONCLUSIONS

This book is an attempt to investigate the mechanisms governing the dynamics of scandals over mass protests in communist Romania. It could also be framed as a study of the social-psychology of regime preservation. The main inquiry presented herein deals with the manner in which Romanian communist authorities framed acts of mass protest. It also looks into the evolution revealed in the transition from the first- to second-order transgressions within the dynamics of the scandal.

In order to answer the above subject, I first had to explore the degree to which a discussion about scandals in communism could withstand the test of empirical reality. I applied theoretical findings and presented case studies in support of my hypothesis. What paved the way for my argumentation was Adut's definition of scandal in terms of the "publicization of an apparent transgression to a norm audience" – i.e. a disruptive publicization. Thereupon, in searching for parallels, I tried to analyze different scandals and other developments that were governed by the form of scandal in communist Romania.

Not surprisingly, all analyzed episodes involved some form of external participation. Furthermore, using Adut's notions of *norm audience* and *norm offender*, Nałkowski's *scandal as a factor of evolution* (further developed by Kurczewski), and the one of *kibitzer audience* (developed in reference to Lang and Lang, and Thompson), I tried to come up with an incipient typology of *first-* and *second-order transgressions*. For this purpose, I relied on *scandals over mass protests* (e.g. the 1977 Jiu Valley Strike, the 1987 Braşov revolt); *scandals over the defection of sportsmen* (the 1981 defection of Marcel Răducanu, the 1984 defection of Béla and Márta (Martha) Károlyi and Géza Pozsár, the 1989 defection of Nadia Comăneci etc.); *scandals over the reaction to first-order transgressions in the Communist Bloc* (the reaction of Ceauşescu to the Warsaw Pact invasion of Czechoslovakia in 1968); *scandals over the reaction to second-order transgressions in the Communist Bloc* (the sports scandal in Los Angeles, 1984) etc. I also attempted to anatomize the unfolding of processes such as: contamination, provocation and convergence. The first two notions I borrowed from Adut's work on scandal, whereas the latter is specific to the area of research dealing with moral panic (Cohen; Hall and Jefferson; Hall et al.).

The cases under review outlined several assumptions. Thus, the phenomenon of ideological convergence became more conspicuous when the norm offender was an internal actor, and when the norm audience was played by the Romanian communist authorities. This notwithstanding, there is also a rather preeminent category of scandals in which the norm offender was represented by the Romanian powers, while the Soviet leaders could be regarded as having been the norm audience. By and large, these cases have the profiles of a genuine scandal and until the late 1970s they had usually effected an increase of the popularity of Ceauşescu's reign.

The second finding is related to the exposure of contamination in cases of scandals over mass protests – i.e. in cases where the so-called *ideological convergence* reaches its peak. More explicitly, in the case of the 1977 strike in Jiu Valley and the 1987 revolt in Braşov, the investigations which followed the first-order transgression – that of the protesters – revealed deficiencies within the local party community. And hence, the outcome of the contamination was a second-order transgression, where the norm offenders were party members and functionaries, not the protesters. In my opinion, the possibility of observing the dynamics of contamination represents one of the main arguments in favor of applying a scandal perspective in the study of mass protests during the Ceauşescu regime. Conclusively, the signification of the mass protests by the communist authorities was not a dead-end process. Contrary to what might be expected, the scandal dynamics (i.e. the processes of contamination and provocation) proceeded to the next levels.

Furthermore, the case studies of the dynamics of scandal revealed that the Ceauşescu regime was as equally easily scandalized by internal offenders, as it was easily scandalizing norm audiences outside the country. In the former case the communist authorities usually played the role of a norm audience (in the first-order transgressions), while in the latter they often took on the role of a first-order kibitzer audience which subsequently developed from a norm offender into an external actor (in second-order transgressions).

The formula kibitzer audience points to the fact that the communist authorities did not directly participate in the first-order transgression (either as norm offender or as norm audience), rather they witnessed and commented upon the events. However, the lack of an active role for the Romanian regime in the launching of the scandal proved less important than how its position vis-à-vis the events further effected their development and – through it – the attitude of the Romanian society. The kibitzer audience might be viewed as an audience of the development of the whole scandal which involved the performance of both the offender and the norm audience. In contrast, the norm audience was a player in the first-order transgression.

The distinction between the two notions proved particularly relevant in designing a typology of scandals in communist Romania, as it pointed to moments when Ceauşescu enjoyed high popularity with several kibitzer audiences (both inside and outside the country). In this respect, my approach might offer a complementary explanation for the much delayed emergence of overt opposition to the communist regime in Romania.

The fact that, during the Ceauşescu reign, the regime was quite prone to being scandalized by cases of strikes and revolts has also influenced the perception of these events after the 1989 Revolution. The scandalization they provoked at that time was taken as further evidence of the extremely repressive character of Ceauşescu's rule in the 1970s and 1980s. After 1989, what worked in favor of this interpretation was also the lack of comparative studies between Romania and other former socialist countries – an absence which is strongly felt even today.

The empirical material regarding the 1977 strike in Jiu Valley and the 1987 revolt in Braşov indicates that, as far as the party members and leaders are concerned, contamination and convergence were the main mechanisms governing the dynamics of scandal over mass protests in communist Romania. Furthermore, the authorities resorted to two different dispute settlement procedures: the *party moots on mass protests* (for party members and leaders who were held at fault for the outburst of mass protests) and *trials* (primarily for the direct participants of mass protest). Although, the "scene" of the trial has also been presented (for the 1977 Jiu Valley strike), this book focuses predominantly on the *party moots* held following the scandals over the mass protests. These party meetings fulfilled both *investigative* and *conciliatory* roles. The investigative portion revealed those guilty of the scandal, whereas the conciliatory aspect reintegrated them into the community. The findings indicate that in the case of the 1987 Braşov revolt, these party moots concord to a *reintegrative shaming* logic (as far as both the party members and the protesters are concerned), while in the case of the Jiu Valley strike the dimension of *stigmatizing shaming* (regarding at least the protestors) was more predominant. Thus, the empirical data gives theoretical legitimacy to the incorporation of Braithwaite's reintegrative shaming framework within scandal theory.

As noted, the party moots on mass protests recall elements of the *Kpelle moots,* identified by Gibbs – i.e. the *attribution of fault* and the *admittance of one's fault*. However, when presenting Gibbs' study on the Kpelle moots as a therapeutic model for the informal settlement of dispute, I have pointed out that the manipulation of rewards (the prospect of being restored as a part of the community) is unlikely to constitute in itself an explanation of how the person who is held to blame is won over to conformity. To that end, for the Ceauşescu regime, such an additional mechanism of persuasion could be represented by *moot bullying* for example. Ideally, moot bullying should be viewed as a subtype of *scapegoat bullying.*

As stated, the party moots on mass protests fulfilled both an investigative and a reconciliatory role. In comparison, the court hearings were mainly of a reconciliatory nature. However, the reconciliatory goal was only achieved after days of diatribes attributing fault and shame, not to mention the fact that quite often the party moots on mass protests transformed into *branding (degradation) ceremonies.*

The above considerations brought me to the sociology of emotions, and more explicitly to the distinction between *guilt* and *shame*, which revealed further nuances between the self-criticism of party cadres (carried out in terms of *guilt*) and the criticism of the protesters (drawing on *disgrace* and *shame*). In my opinion, the guilt–shame equation remains an irreplaceable tool for any researcher of branding (degradation) ceremonies.

As matters currently stand, there is a *cognitive dissonance type of aftereffect* that inhibits the research of these kinds of phenomena in Romania. By indicating a cognitive dissonance type of aftereffect, I point to a phenomenon by which one's former (active or not) participation in such meetings is today often represented as an "effect of forced compliance" (i.e. "public compliance without private acceptance" (Festinger) or as a collective enterprise of "preference falsification" (i.e. the public presentation of preferences which are not held in private) (Kuran). Reportedly, these ceremonies were not only staged – it was also common knowledge that this was the case. Hence, the book puts forward an inquiry into what Elster designates as the "misrepresentation and transmutation of one's motivation" (in this case: both before and after 1989) to participate in these meetings of symbolic blame-giving and shaming.

The 1989 events in Timişoara are all the more valuable for analysis given that they present a case study of a scandal over mass protests and of moots unfolding simultaneously. In actuality, the moots, and the contamination (on behalf of party leaders) that they generated developed concurrently with the provocation effected by the scandals. In this case, the reviewed documents allowed the identification of the mechanisms of ideological convergence and attempts of contamination. Additionally, mechanisms such as: the attribution of fault, the admittance of one's guilt/fault and also – to a certain extent – moot bullying were revealed.

Finally, the book analyses one more case study: the June 1990 miners' march on Bucharest. The episode was chosen because of its chronological proximity to the events in Timişoara and because it allowed the identification of mechanisms of convergence. The case of the third mineriad, however, is rather autonomous. To a certain degree, it could be stated that the findings of the study develop a background for the framing of this episode, not the other way around. By the same token, the chapter also seems to go beyond the actual purpose of the book. This notwithstanding, the 1990 protests against ex-communists in the Romanian government and the subsequent miners' marches on Bucharest, when framed from the scandal perspective, bear such a resemblance to the previously analyzed events of the Ceauşescu regime that a presentation of the latter should necessarily touch upon the early post-communist revolutions.

References

***. 1979. "Un raport al lui Amnesty International relevă că cei doi conducători ai grevei minerilor din 1977 au fost asasinaţi" [*A Report of Amnesty International Reveals That the Two Leaders of the 1977 Miners' Strike Were Murdered*], *B.I.R.E.*, no. 702, September 16, p. 2

***. 1981. "Arestări – Deportări – Muncă forţată – Asasinate şi internări în aziluri psihiatrice în România roşie comunistă" [*Arrests – Deportations – Forced Labor – Assasinations and Internments in Psychiatric Asylums in Red Communist Romania*], *B.I.R.E*, no. 732, March 1, p. 7

***. 2004. "The Perfect Ten," *The Observer*, July 4

***. 2008. "Dosarul mineriadei din iunie 1990 ajunge, din nou, la procurorii militari" [*The Dossier of the June 1990 Mineriad Found Itself Again on the Table of the Military Prosecutors*], *Mediafax*, June 24

Administrator. 2007. "Raportul Tismăneanu este bun de maculatură" [*The Tismăneanu Report is Good for Pulp Literature*], *Civic Media Association*, April 16, accessed December 22, 2011
http://civicmedia.ro/acm/index.php?option=com_content&task=view&id=434&Itemid=1

Admin. 2007. "Cele trei variante ale cameleonicului raport Tismăneanu" [*The Three Versions of the Chameleonic Tismăneanu Report*], *Civic Media Association*, February 14, accessed December 22, 2011
http://civicmedia.ro/acm/index.php?option=com_content&task=view&id=219&Itemid=49

Adut, A. 2004. "Scandal as Norm Entrepreneurship Strategy: Corruption and the French Investigating Magistrates," *Theory and Society*, vol. 33, no. 5, pp. 529-578

Adut, A. 2005. "A Theory of Scandal: Victorians, Homosexuality, and the Fall of Oscar Wilde," *AJS*, vol. 111, no. 1, pp. 213-248

Adut, A. 2008. *On Scandal. Moral Disturbances in Society, Politics, and Art.* Cambridge: Cambridge University Press

Ahmed, E. and Braithwaite, V. 2004. "'What, Me Ashamed?' Shame Management and School Bullying," *Journal of Research in Crime and Delinquency*, vol. 41, no. 3, pp. 269-294

Airinei, S. 2002. *Un sfert de veac de Securitate* [Quarter of a Century of Securitate]. Braşov: Transilvania Expres

Aldescu, I. 2001. *Armata Română în Valea Jiului. Repere istorice. 1916-1999* [The Romanian Army in the Jiu Valley. Historical Landmarks. 1916-1999]. Bucureşti: Editura Militară

Alexe, V. 2006 "Nazistul Iliescu" [*The Nazist Iliescu*], *Ziua*, January 31

Arsene, M. 1997a. *Un tablou uriaş arde* [A Huge Painting is Burning]. Braşov: Erasmen

Arsene, M. 1997b. *Dosar: Braşov, 15 noiembrie, 1987* [Dossier: Braşov, November 15, 1987]. Braşov: Erasmen

Aquecheek, A. 2006. "Moot (thing)," *Everything2*, March 26, accessed December 22, 2011
http://everything2.com/title/moot

Bachman, R. D. (ed.). 1989. *Romania: A Country Study*. Washington: GPO for the Library of Congress, accessed December 22, 2011
http://countrystudies.us/romania/

Barbu, M. and Chirvasă, G. 1997. *După 20 de ani sau Lupeni '77 – Lupeni '97* [After 20 Years or Lupeni '77 – Lupeni '97]. Petroşani: Cotidianul Matinal and Editura Cameleonul

Barbu, M. and Boboc, M. 2005. *Lupeni '77: Sfânta Varvara versus Tanti Varvara* [Lupeni '77. Saint Varvara versus Auntie Varvara]. Cluj: Editura Fundaţiei pentru Studii Europene

Badea, D. 2006. "Măgureanu mi-a cerut să-l asasinez pe generalul Macri" [*Măgureanu Asked Me to Assassinate General Macri*], *Gardianul*, May 18

Baron, M. 1998. *Cărbune şi societate in Valea Jiului. Perioada interbelică* [Coal and Society in Jiu Valley. The Interwar Period]. Petroşani: Editura Universitas.

Baron, M. 1999. *Istoria mineritului în România – Curs* [The History of Mining in Romania – Course]. Petroşani

Bell, E. 2006. "Social Dramas and Cultural Performances: All the President's Women," *Liminalities*, vol. 2, no. 1, accessed December 22, 2011
http://liminalities.net/2-1/issue.htm

Berindei, M., Combes, A. and Planche, A. 2010. *Mineriada 13-15 iunie 1990. Realitatea unei puteri comuniste* [The 13-15 June 1990 Mineriad. The Reality of a Communist Power]. Bucureşti: Humanitas

Betea, L. 2001a. *Maurer şi lumea de ieri. Mărturii despre stalinizarea României* [Maurer and Yesterday's World. Testimonies on the Stalinization of Romania]. Cluj: Dacia

Betea, L. 2001b. *Convorbiri neterminate. Corneliu Mănescu în dialog cu Lavinia Betea* [Unfinished Conversations. Corneliu Mănescu in Dialogue with Lavinia Betea]. Iaşi: Polirom

Betea, L. 2006. *Lucreţiu Pătrăşcanu – Moartea unui lider comunist* [Lucreţiu Pătrăşcanu – Death of a Communist Leader]. Bucureşti: Curtea Veche

Berberova, N. 2005. *Afacerea Kravcenko* [The Kravcenko Affair]. Bucureşti: Humanitas

Boboc, M. and Barbu, M. 2007. *Strict Secret. Lupeni 1977. Filajul continuă!* [Highly Confidential. Lupeni 1977. The Survaillence Continues!]. Craiova: Autograf MJM

Botchkovar, E. and Tittle, C. R. 2008. "Delineating the Scope of Reintegrative Shaming Theory: An Explanation of Contingencies Using Russian Data," *Social Science Research*, vol. 37, no. 3, pp. 703-720

Braithwaite, J. 1992. *Crime, Shame and Reintegration.* Cambridge: Cambridge University Press

Brudaşcu, D. 1997. *Dosarele adevărului: Braşov (1987)* [The Dossiers of Truth: Braşov (1987)]. Cluj-Napoca: Sedan

Bruha, J., Ionaşcu, D. and Jeong, B. 2003. *Organized Labor and Restructuring: Coal Mines in the Czech Republic and Romania,* Working paper, December, accessed December 22, 2011
http://www.cerge.cuni.cz/pdf/events/papers/031208_t.pdf

Callon, M. 1986. *Some Elements of Sociology of Translation: Domestication of the Scallops and the Fishermen of St Brieuc Bay.* pp. 1-29, accessed December 22, 2011
http://www.vub.ac.be/SOCO/tesa/RENCOM/Callon%20(1986)%20Some%20elements%20of%20a%20sociology%20of%20translation.pdf

Capelos, T. and Wurzer, J. 2009. "United Front: Blame Management and Scandal Response Tactics of the United Nations," *Journal of Contingencies and Crisis Management*, vol. 17, no. 2, pp. 75-94

Cartianu, G. 2011. *Cartea Revoluţiei* [The Book of Revolution]. Bucureşti: Adevărul Holding

Cătănuş, A.-M. 2008. "Disidenţă şi represiune în epoca Nicolae Ceauşescu. O analiză comparativă: Paul Goma–Vlad Georgescu" [Dissidence and Repression in the Nicolae Ceauşescu Epoque. A Comparative Analysis: Paul Goma–Vlad Georgescu], in: C. Budeancă and F. Olteanu (eds.), *Forme de represiune în regimurile comuniste* [Forms of Repression in Communist Regimes]. Iaşi: Polirom, pp. 256-265

Câmpeanu, P. 2002. *Ceauşescu: anii numărătorii inverse* [Ceauşescu: The Years of the Reversed Counting]. Iaşi: Polirom

CBC Sports. 2008. "The Los Angeles Games: The Boycotts Continue," *CBC*, May 28

Cesereanu, R. 2004. "Greva minerilor din Valea Jiului, 1977" [The Strike of the Jiu Valley Miners, 1977], *22*, August 3-11

Cesereanu, R. 2008. "The Final Report on the Holocaust and the Final Report on the Communist Dictatorship in Romania," *East European Politics and Societies*, vol. 22, no. 2, pp. 270-281

Chen, X. 2002. "Social Control in China: Applications of the Labeling Theory and the Reintegrative Shaming Theory," *International Journal of Offender Therapy and Comparative Criminology*, vol. 46, no. 1, pp. 45-63

Cimpoiaşu, G. 2006. "Hagi nu m-a vrut!" [*Hagi Did Not Want Me!*], *Libertatea*, February 13

C.N.S.A.S. 2004. *Membrii C. C. ai P. C. R. (1945-1989). Dicţionar* [C.C. Members of the R.C.P. (1945-1989). Dictionary]. Bucureşti: Editura Enciclopedică

Cohen, S. 1993. *Folk Devils and Moral Panics: The Creation of the Mods and Rockers*. Oxford: Blackwell

Comaroff, J. and Comaroff, J. L. 1999. "Occult Economies and the Violence of Abstraction: Notes from the South African Postcolony," *American Ethnologist*, vol. 26, no. 2, pp. 279-303

Comşa, A. and Saiu, F. 2007. "'Am fugit din ţară din cauza lui Valentin Ceauşescu'" ["I Defected because of Valentin Ceauşescu"], *Libertatea*, May 7

Cornwell, B. and Linders, A. 2002. "The Myth of 'Moral Panic': An Alternative Account of LSD Prohibition," *Deviant Behavior: An Interdisciplinary Journal*, vol. 23, no. 4, pp. 307-330

Cristea, R. 2007. *Piaţa Universităţii 1990* [University Square 1990]. Ploieşti: Editura Filocalia-FOC and Editura româno-engleză KARTA-GRAPHIC

Day, A. J. et al. 1991. *Political Scandals and Causes Célèbres since 1945: An International Reference Compendium*. Harlow (U.K.): Longman Current Affairs

Deletant, D. 2004. *Romania within the Warsaw Pact – Ambivalence & Ambiguities. 1955-1981, Collection*, accessed June 28, 2009
http://www.ispaim.ro/warsaw/fore.htm

Deletant, D., Ionescu, M. E. and Locher, A. 2004. *Romania and the Warsaw Pact: Documents Highlighting Romania's Gradual Emancipation from the Warsaw Pact, 1956-1989*, Parallel History Project on Cooperative Security (PHP), accessed December 22, 2011
http://www.php.isn.ethz.ch/collections/colltopic.cfm?lng=en&id=15342

Dobre, F. (coord.), Neagoe-Pleşa, E. and Pleşa L. 2006. *Securitatea. Structuri – cadre, obiective şi metode. Vol. II (1967-1989)* [The *Securitate* – Staff, Objectives and Methods. Vol. II (1967-1989)]. Bucureşti: Ed. Enciclopedică

Dobrescu, A. and Rughiniş, C. ***. "Managing Labor Crises. A Case Study of the Jiu Valley, Romania," ***, pp. 465-484

Douglas, M. 1992. *Purity and Danger. An Analysis of the Concepts of Pollution and Taboo*. London and New York: Routledge.

Drăgotescu, C. 2003. "Interviu Corina Drăgotescu *2003 [cu Ion Iliescu]" [*Interview Corina Drăgotescu *2003 (with Ion Iliescu)*], published on the *political blog of Ion Iliescu*, accessed December 22, 2011
http://ioniliescu.wordpress.com/media/interviu-corina-dragotescu/

Duffy, M. and Sperry, L. 2007. "Workplace Mobbing: Individual and Family Health Consequences," *The Family Journal*, vol. 15, no. 4, pp. 398-404

Ekström, M. and Johansson, B. 2006. "Talk Scandals," submitted to ICA'S Annual Conference in San Francisco, May 24-28

Elias, N. 1994. *The Civilizing Process*. Oxford: Blackwell Publishers LTD

Elster, J. 1999. *Alchemies of the Mind: Rationality and the Emotions*. Cambridge: Cambridge University Press

Elster, J. 2007. *Explaining Social Behavior: More Nuts and Bolts for the Social Sciences*. Cambridge: Cambridge University Press.

Elster, J. 2009a. "Emotions," in: P. Hedström and P. Bearman (eds.), *The Oxford Handbook of Analytical Sociology*. Oxford: Oxford University Press, pp. 51-71

Elster, J. 2009b. "Norms," in: P. Hedström and P. Bearman (eds.), *The Oxford Handbook of Analytical Sociology*. Oxford: Oxford University Press, pp. 195-217

Esser, F. and Hartung, U. 2004. "Nazis, Pollution, and No Sex: Political Scandals as a Reflection of Political Culture in Germany," *American Behavioral Scientist*, vol. 47, no. 8, pp. 1040-1071

Feder, L. 2007. "Editorial: Bullying as a Public Health Issue," *International Journal of Offender Therapy and Comparative Criminology*, vol. 51, no. 5, pp. 491-494

Festinger, L. 1957. *A Theory of Cognitive Dissonance*. Evanston (Illinois) and White Plains (New York): Row, Peterson and Company

Flonta, V. 1999. "Valea Jiului – Un caz atipic în economia românească" [*Jiu Valley – an Atypical Case for the Romanian Economy*], *Sfera politicii*, no. 67, accessed December 22, 2011
http://www.dntb.ro/sfera/67/mineriade-4.html

Fogel, J. F. and Rosenthal, B. 1999. *Sfârșit de secol la Havana* [Fin de Siglo en La Habana]. București: RAO

Friedman, J. 2007a. "Shame and the Experience of Ambivalence on the Margins of the Global: Pathologizing the Past and Present in Romania's Industrial Wastelands," *ETHOS*, vol. 35, issue 2, pp. 235-264

Friedman, J. 2007b. "Shock and Subjectivity in the Age of Globalization. Marginalization, Exclusion, and the Problem of Resistance," *Anthropological Theory*, vol. 7, no. 4, pp. 421-448

Florin, M. 2007. "Dobre a fost declarat mort de Tismăneanu" [*Dobre Declared Dead by Tismăneanu*], *Jurnalul național*, April 20

Garfinkel, H. 1956. "Conditions of Successful Degradation Ceremonies," *The American Journal of Sociology*, vol. 61, no. 5, pp. 420-424

Gavrielides, T. 2008. "Restorative Justice – the Perplexing Concept: Conceptual Fault-Lines and Power Battles within the Restorative Justice Movement," *Criminology and Criminal Justice*, vol. 8, no. 2, pp. 165-183

Gibbs, J. L. Jr. 1963. "The Kpelle Moot: A Therapeutic Model for the Informal Settlement of Disputes," *Africa: Journal of the International African Institute*, vol. 33, no. 1, pp. 1-11

Gini, G. 2007. "Who Is Blameworthy? Social Identity and Inter-Group Bullying," *School Psychology International*, vol. 28. no. 1, pp. 77-89

Girard, R. 1988. *The Scapegoat*. London: The Athlone Press

Gledhill, J. 2005. "States of Contention: State-Led Political Violence in Post-Socialist Romania," *East European Politics and Societies*, vol. 19, no.1, pp. 76-104

Gluckman, M. 1963. "Papers in Honor of Melville J. Herskovits: Gossip and Scandal," *Current Anthropology*, vol. 4, no. 3, pp. 307-316

Goffman, E. 1982. *Interaction Ritual – Essays of Face-to-Face Behaviour*. New York: Pantheon Books

Goffman, E. 1990. *The Presentation of Self in Everyday Life*. Harmondsworth: Penguin

Goode, E. and Ben-Yehuda, N. 1994. *Moral Panics: The Social Construction of Deviance*. Oxford: Blackwell

Goma, P. 1999. "Vin minerii! (I)" [*The Miners are Coming! (I)*], January 20, accessed March 26, 2009
http://old.ournet.md/~ob/goma/scrisuri35.html

Gomoescu, D. and Corbeanu, M. 2006. "Daciada de partid" [*The Party Daciada*], *Jurnalul Naţional*, May 5

Grosescu, R. and Ursachi, R. 2009. *Justiţia penală de tranziţie. De la Nürnberg la postcomunismul românesc* [Transitional Criminal Justice from Nuremberg to Post-Communist Romania]. Iaşi: Polirom

Hall, S. and Jefferson, T. 1991. *Resistance through Rituals: Youth Subcultures in Post-War Britain*. London: Harper Collins.

Hall, S., Critcher, C., Jefferson, T., Clarke, J., and Roberts, B. 1994. *Policing the Crises. Mugging, the State, and Law and Order*. London: Macmillan

Harris, N., Walgrave, L. and Braithwaite, J. 2004. "Emotional Dynamics in Restorative Conferences," *Theoretical Criminology*, vol. 8, no. 2, pp. 191-210

Harvey, M. G., Heames, J. T., Richey, R. G., and Leonard, N. 2006. "Bullying: From the Playground to the Boardroom," *Journal of Leadership and Organizational Studies*, vol. 12, no. 4, pp. 1-11

Herdt, G. (ed.). 2009. *Moral Panics, Sex Panics: Fear and the Fight over Sexual Rights*. New York and London: New York University Press

Hier, S. P. 2002. "Conceptualizing Moral Panic through a Moral Economy of Harm," *Critical Sociology*, vol. 28, issue 3, pp. 311-334

Hodson, R., Roscigno, V. J. and Lopez, S. H. 2006. "Chaos and the Abuse of Power: Workplace Bullying in Organizational and Interactional Context," *Work and Occupations*, vol. 33, no. 4, pp. 382-416

Hosser, D., Windzio, M. and Greve, W. 2008. "Guilt and Shame as Predictors of Recidivism: A Longitudinal Study with Young Prisoners," *Criminal Justice and Behavior*, vol. 35, no. 1, pp. 138-152

Iliescu, I. ***. *Political Blog*, accessed December 22, 2011
http://ioniliescu.wordpress.com/

Iliescu, I. 1994. *Revoluţie şi reformă* [Revolution and Reform]. Bucureşti: Editura Enciclopedică

Istrati, P. 1969. *Pentru a fi iubit pământul* [For Having Loved the Fatherland]. Bucureşti: Ed. Tineretului

Jela, D., Strat, C. and Albu, M. 2004. *Afacerea Meditaţia Transcendentală* [The Transcendental Meditation Affair]. Bucureşti: Humanitas

Jiménez, F. 2004. "The Politics of Scandal in Spain: Morality Plays, Social Trust, and the Battle for Public Opinion," *American Behavioral Scientist*, vol. 47, no. 8, pp. 1099-1121

Johansson, T. 2000. "Moral Panics Revisited," *Young*, vol. 8, no. 1, pp. 22-35

Jowitt, K. 1970. "The Romanian Communist Party and the World Socialist System: A Redefinition of Unity," *World Politics*, vol. 23, no. 1, pp. 38-60

Kalliotis, P. 2000. "Bullying as a Special Case of Aggression: Procedures for Cross-Cultural Assessment," *School Psychology International*, vol. 21, no. 1, pp. 47-64

Kamiński, A. 1992. *An Institutional Theory of Communist Regimes: Design, Function, and Breakdown*. San Francisco (California): ICS Press

Kaufman, G. S. 1955. "The Great Kibitzers' Strike," in: A. A. Ostrow (ed.), *The Bridge Players Bedside Companion*. Englewood Cliffs (New Jersey): Prentice Hall, Inc (book contributor: Universal Digital Library), pp. 103-106, accessed December 22, 2011
http://www.archive.org/details/bridgeplayersbed002174mbp

Kideckel, D. A. 2001. "Labor and Society in the Jiu Valley and Fagaras Regions of Romania, Part I: Variations in Response to the Crises," *NCEEER (The National Council for Eurasian and East European Research*. Washington (District of Columbia), accessed December 22, 2011
http://www.ucis.pitt.edu/nceeer/2001-815-18g-Kideckel.pdf

Kideckel, D. A. 2006. *Colectivism şi singurătate în satele româneşti. Ţara Oltului în perioada comunistă şi în primii ani după revoluţie* [The Solitude of Collectivism: Romanian Villagers to the Revolution and Beyond]. Iaşi: Polirom

Kideckel, D. A. 2008. *Getting By in Postsocialist Romania. Labor, the Body, and Working-Class Culture*. Bloomington (Indiana): University Press

King, A. 1981. "Religion and Rights: A Dissenting Minority as a Social Movement in Romania," *Social Compass*, vol. 28, no.1, pp. 113-119

Király, B. K. (ed.) 1994. *The Hungarian Minority's Situation in Ceauşescu's Romania*. Atlantic Studies on Society in Change, no. 68. New York: Columbia University Press

Kligman, G. 2000. *Politica duplicităţii. Controlul reproducerii în România lui Ceauşescu* [The Politics of Duplicity. Controlling Reproduction in Ceauşescu's Romania]. Bucureşti: Humanitas

Kulick, D. 1996. "Causing a Commotion: Public Scandal as Resistance among Brazilian Transgendered Prostitutes," *Anthropology Today*, vol. 12, no. 6, pp. 3-7

Kulick, D. 2009. "Sex, Soccer and Scandal in Brazil," *Anthropology Now*, vol. 1, no. 3, pp. 32-42

Kulick, D. and Klein, C. 2009. "Scandalous Acts: The Politics of Shame among Brazilian Travesti Prostitutes," in: D. Halperin and V. Traub (eds.), *Gay Shame*. Chicago: University of Chicago Press, pp. 312-338

Kuran, T. 1997. *Private Truths, Public Lies: The Social Consequences of Preference Falsification*. Cambridge (Massachusetts) and London: Harvard University Press

Kurczewski, J. 1993. *The Resurrection of Rights in Poland*. Oxford: Clarendon Press

Kurczewski, J. 1995. "The Politics of Human Rights in Post-Communist Poland," in: I. Pogany (ed.), *Human Rights in Eastern Europe*. Aldershot: Edward Elgar, pp. 111-134

Kurczewski, J. 2003. "Is a Sociology of Corruption Possible?" in: G. Skąpska, A. Orla-Bukowska and K. Kowalski (eds.), *The Moral Fabric in Contemporary Societies*. Leiden: Brill, pp. 157-164

Kurczewski, J. (ed.). 2004. *Umowa o kartki* [The Contract about Coupons]. Warszawa: Trio

Kurczewski, J. 2009a. "Bronisław Malinowski Misunderstood – or How Leon Petrażycki's Concept of Law Is Unwittingly Applied in Anthropology of Law," *Societas/Communitas* vol. 1, no. 7, pp. 47-62

Kurczewski, J. 2009b. "The Spoiled Drama of Emancipation: Conflicting Narratives," *Polish Sociological Review*, vol. 4, no. 168, pp. 539-554

Levant, C. 2007. "Reţeaua Caraman, glonţ pe ţeavă între NATO şi KGB" [*The Caraman Network – Bullet down a Pipe between NATO and KGB*], *Adevărul*, November 3

Lu, H., Zhang, L. and Miethe, T. D. 2002. "Interdependency, Communitarianism and Reintegrative Shaming in China," *The Social Science Journal*, vol. 39, no.2, pp. 189-201

Lupu, M. 2007. "Funcţionarea Academiei 'Ştefan Gheorghiu' sau ce putem recupera în folosul mobilităţii elitelor actuale din România" [*The Functioning of the Academy 'Ştefan Gheorghiu' or What Could Be Recovered to the Advantage of the Mobility of the Present Elites in Romania*], in: *Anuarul Institutului de Investigare a Crimelor Comunismului în România, II – Elite comuniste înainte şi după 1989* [Yearbook of the Institute for the Investigation of Communist Crimes in Romania, II – Communist Elites before and after 1989]. Iaşi: Polirom, pp. 265-277

Łoś, M. 1988. *Communist Ideology, Law and Crime: A Comparative View of the USSR and Poland*. London: MacMillan Press

Lyndon, P. 1994. "The Leader and the Scapegoat: A Dependency Group Study," *Group Analysis*, vol. 27, pp. 95-104

Ma, X. 2001. "Bullying and Being Bullied: To What Extent Are Bullies Also Victims?" *American Educational Research Journal*, vol. 38, no. 2, pp. 351-370

Maha, R. 2006. "Secretele Nadiei" [*The Secrets of Nadia*], *Cotidianul*, March 21

Maha, R. 2007. "Fuga soţilor Karoly în SUA de sub umbrela securistului" [*The Escape of the Karolys from the Umbrela of the Securitate-Man*], *Cotidianul*, August 18

Malinowski, B. 1989. *Crime and Custom in Savage Society*. New Jersey: Rowman & Littlefield Publishers, Inc.

Malinowski, B. 2002. *The Sexual Life of Savages in North-Western Melanesia*. London: Routledge.

Matthiesen, S. B. 2006. *Bullying at Work. Antecedents and Outcomes*, PhD thesis, University of Bergen, Norway

McGraw, K. M. 1990. "Avoiding Blame: An Experimental Investigation of Political Excuses and Justifications," *British Journal of Political Science*, vol. 20, no. 1, pp. 119-131

McGraw, K. M. 1991. "Managing Blame: An Experimental Test of the Effects of Political Accounts," *The American Political Science Review*, vol. 85, no. 4, pp. 1133-1157

McRobbie, A. and Thornton, S. L. 1995. "Rethinking 'Moral Panic' for Multi-Mediated Social Worlds," *The British Journal of Sociology*, vol. 46, no. 4, pp. 559-574

Merriam – Webster Online. ***
http://www.merriam-webster.com/

Merton, R. 1968. *Social Theory and Social Structure*. New York: The Free Press; London: Collier Macmillan Publishers.

Meseguer de Pedro, M., Soler Sánchez, M. I., Sáez Navarro, M. C. and Izquierdo, M. G. 2008. "Workplace Mobbing and Effects on Workers' Health," *The Spanish Journal of Psychology*, vol. 11, no. 1, pp. 219-227

Mica, A. 2008a. "Discussion on the 1977 Jiu Valley Strike as Scandal in Romania," *Sfera politicii*, vol. 16, no. 129-130, pp. 31-42

Mica, A. 2008b. "Would-be 'European Norms' of Decommunization in Romania," in: J. Niżnik (ed.), *Normative Environment of European Integration. Social, Political and Cultural Obstacles to Compliance to European Norms*. Warsaw: IFIS Publishers, pp. 141-163

Mica, A. 2009a. "Coal Miners from Jiu Valley – from Moral Panic to Moral Anxiety. Discussion of Jack R. Friedman and David A. Kideckel," *Societas/Communitas*, vol. 1, no. 7, pp. 281-285

Mica, A. 2009b. "Reply to Disclosure Scandals in Romania. Political Parties and the Romanian Orthodox Church," *Polish Sociological Review*, vol. 1, no. 165, pp. 41-56

Mica, A. 2010. "Moral Panic, Risk or Hazard Society – the Relevance of a Theoretical Model and Framings of *Maidan* Dogs in Chişinău and Bucharest," *Polish Sociological Review*, vol. 1, no. 169, pp. 39-61

Mica, A. 2011a. "Janine R. Wedel, Shadow Elite: How the World's New Power Brokers Undermine Democracy, Government, and the Free Market, New York: Basik Books, 2009," *Polish Sociological Review*, vol. 2, no. 174, pp. 263-266

Mica, A. 2011b. "Skandal i panika moralna" [*Scandal and Moral Panic*], *Tematy z Szewskiej*, vol. 2, no. 6, pp. 33-41

Mig. G. 2006. "Kibitz Me Not," *chessninja.com*, May 19, accessed December 22, 2011
http://www.chessninja.com/dailydirt/2006/05/kibitz-me-not.htm

Mihu, L. 2007a. "'77, versiunile Dobre şi Cozma" ['*77 – The Versions of Dobre and Cozma*], *Evenimentul zilei*, August 3

Mihu, L. 2007b. "Dobre, nume de cod 'Dodu'" [*Dobre, Code Name 'Dodu'*], *Evenimentul zilei*, August 6

Mioc, M. ***a. *Revoluţia fără mistere. Începutul revoluţiei române: cazul László Tőkés* [A Revolution without Mysteries. The Beginning of the Romanian Revolution: The Case of László Tőkés], Document, accessed December 22, 2011

http://www.procesulcomunismului.com/marturii/fonduri/mmioc/revmistere/
default.asp.htm

Mioc, M. ***b. *Revoluția din 1989 și minciunile Jurnalului Național. Mitul agenturilor străine. Mitul Securității atotputernice, care l-a dat jos pe Ceaușescu* [The 1989 Revolution and the Lies of *Jurnalul Național*. The Myth of the Foreign Intelligence Agencies. The Myth of the Over-Powerful *Securitate* Which Overthrew Ceaușescu], Document, accessed December 22, 2011
http://www.procesulcomunismului.com/marturii/fonduri/mmioc/revjurnat/de
fault.asp.htm

Mioc, M. ***c. *Blogul lui Marius Mioc despre revoluția din 1989 și ceea ce a urmat după ea* [Marius Mioc's Blog about the 1989 Revolution and What Followed Afterwards], accessed December 22, 2011
http://mariusmioc.wordpress.com/

Moreno Jiménez, B., Muñoz, A. R., Martínez Gamarra, M. and Gálvez Herrer, M. 2007. "Assessing Workplace Bullying: Spanish Validation of a Reduced Version of the Negative Acts Questionnaire," *The Spanish Journal of Psychology*, vol. 10, no. 2, pp. 449-457

Nałkowski, W. 1952. "Skandale jako czynnik ewolucji" [*Scandal as a Factor of Evolution*], in: Stefan Kałuski (ed.). *Wybór pism*, Wrocław: Wydaw. Zakł. Narod. im. Ossolińskich, pp. 19-25

Notelaers, G., Einarsen, S., de Witte, H. and Vermunt, J. K. 2006. "Measuring Exposure to Bullying at Work: The Validity and Advantages of the Latent Class Cluster Approach," *Work & Stress*, vol. 20, no. 4, pp. 288-301

Olaru, S. 2003. *Cei cinci care au speriat estul. Atacul asupra legației RPR de la Berna* [The Five Who Scared the East. The Attack on the Legation of the PRR in Berna]. Iași: Polirom

Olaru, S. and Herbstritt, G. 2005. *Stasi și Securitatea.* [Stasi and the *Securitate*]. București: Humanitas

Olteanu, C., Duțu, A. and Constantin, A. 2005. *România și tratatul de la Varșovia. Istoric. Mărturii. Documente. Cronologie.* [Romania and the Warsaw Pact. Historical Account. Testimonies. Documents. Chronology]. București: Ed. Pro Historia

Oprea, M. 2002. *Banalitatea răului. O istorie a Securității in documente* [The Commonness of Evil. A History of the *Securitate* based on Documents. 1949-1989]. Iași: Polirom

Oprea, M. 2004. *Moștenitorii Securității* [The Successors of the *Securitate*]. București: Humanitas

Oprea, M. and Olaru, S. 2002. *Ziua care nu se uită. 15 noiembrie, 1987, Brașov* [The Day We Won't Forget. November 15, 1987, Brașov]. Iași: Polirom

Oprea, M. 2005. "Armaghedonul spionilor: 'Reţeaua Caraman'" [*The Armageddon of the Spies: "the Caraman Network"*], *Ziua*, February 7

Oravecz, R., Hárdi, L. and Lajtai, L. 2004. "Social Transition, Exclusion, Shame and Humiliation," *Torture*, vol 14, no. 1, pp. 3-15.

Pacepa, I. M. 1988. *Orizonturi roşii* [Red Horizons]. New York: The publishing house of the newspaper Universul

Paraschiv, V. 2005. *Lupta mea pentru sindicate libere în România. Terorismul politic organizat de statul comunist* [My Fight for Free Trade Unions in Romania. Political Terrorism Organized by the Communist State]. Iaşi: Polirom

Parault, S. J. and Davis, H. A and Pellegrini, A. D. 2007. "The Social Contexts of Bullying and Victimization," *The Journal of Early Adolescence*, vol. 27, no. 2, pp. 145-174

Patrichi, V. 2001. *Ochii şi urechile poporului. Convorbiri cu generalul Nicolae Pleşiţă* [The Eyes and Ears of the People. Conversations with General Nicolae Pleşiţă]. Bucureşti: Ed. Ianus Inf

Pavel, D. 2003. *Nu putem reuşi decât împreună: o istorie analitică a Convenţiei Democratice, 1989-2000* [The Only Way We Could Succeed Is Together: An Analytical History of the Democratic Convention, 1989-2000]. Iaşi: Polirom

Pawlik, W. 2004. "Kultura bez wstydu i winy" [*Culture without Shame and Guilt*], in: M. Kempny, K. Kiciński and E. Zakrzewska (eds.): *Od kontestacji do konsumpcji. Szkice o przeobrażeniach współczesnej kultury* [From Contestation to Consumption. Sketches of the Transformations of Contemporary Culture]. Warszawa: ISNS UW, pp. 29-42.

Pelin, M. 2007. *Operaţiunile Meliţa şi Eterul. Istoria Europei Libere prin documente de Securitate* [*Meliţa* and *Eterul* Intelligence Operations. History of Free Europe based on *Securitate* Documents]. Bucureşti: Compania

Peterson, J. S. and Ray, K. E. 2006. "Bullying and the Gifted: Victims, Perpetrators, Prevalence, and Effects," *Gifted Child Quarterly*, vol. 50, no. 2, pp. 148-168

Pospíšil, L. 1971. *Anthropology of Law: A Comparative Theory*. New York, Evanston, San Francisco and London: Harper & Law Publishers.

Pozsar's Gymnastics. ***. "Geza Pozsar" http://www.pozsarsgymnastics.com/coaches.geza.htm

Roseti, R. 2007. "7,2 grade Richter" [*The Grade 7,2 Richter Scale*], *Jurnalul Naţional*, March 3

Rus, A. 2003. *Valea Jiului, o capcana istorică* [Valea Jiului – a Historical Trap]. Petroşani: Ed. Realitatea Românească

Rus, A. 2007. *Mineriadele. Între manipulare politică şi solidaritate muncitorească* [The *Mineriads* – between Political Manipulation and Workers' Solidarity]. Bucureşti: Curtea Veche

Russell, S. 1998. "Reintegrative Shaming and the 'Frozen Antithesis': Braithwaite and Elias," *Journal of Sociology*, vol. 34, no. 3, pp. 303-313

Rychard, A. 1993. *Reforms, Adaptation and Breakthrough*. Warsaw: IFIS Publishers

Safjan, M. 2009. "Politics – and Constitutional Courts (Judges Personal Perspective)," *Polish Sociological Review*, vol. 1, no. 165, pp. 3-25

Salin, D. 2003. "Ways of Explaining Workplace Bullying: A Review of Enabling, Motivating and Precipitating Structures and Processes in the Work Environment," *Human Relations*, vol. 56, no. 10, pp. 1213-1232

Salmivalli, C. and Voeten, M. 2004. "Connections between Attitudes, Group Norms, and Behaviour in Bullying Situations," *International Journal of Behavioral Development*, vol. 28, no. 3, pp. 246-258

Scurtu, I. ***. *Nicolae Ceauşescu şi evenimentele din Polonia (1981, 1989)* [Nicolae Ceauşescu and the Events in Poland (1981, 1989)], in: *www.ioanscurtu.ro*, accessed February 3, 2009
http://www.ioanscurtu.ro/content/view/95/1/

Sherman, L. W. 1978. *Scandal and Reform. Controlling Police Corruption*. Berkeley, Los Angeles and London: University of California Press

Siani-Davies, P. 2005. *The Romanian Revolution of December 1989*. Ithaca: Cornell University Press

Sims, R. 2009. "Toward a Better Understanding of Organizational Efforts to Rebuild Reputation Following an Ethical Scandal," *Journal of Business Ethics*, vol. 90, no. 4, pp. 453-472

Spiridon, R. N. 2003. *August '77: Ceauşescu în 'vulcanul' grevei din Valea Jiului* [August '77: Ceauşescu in the 'Vulcano' of the Jiu Valley Strike], *Dosarele istoriei*, no. 11, p. 63

Spiridon, R. N. 2008. "Reprimarea mişcărilor muncitoreşti de protest în perioada 1977-1987: evenimentele din Valea Jiului (1-3 august 1977) şi revolta de la Braşov (15 noiembrie 1987)" [*The Putting down of the Workers' Opposition Movements in the Interval 1977-1987: The Events of Jiu Valley (1-3 August, 1977) and the Revolt in Braşov (15 November, 1987)*], in: C. Budeancă and F. Olteanu (eds.), *Forme de represiune în regimurile comuniste* [Forms of Repression in Communist Regimes]. Iaşi: Polirom, pp. 229-247

Stan, L. 2002a. "Access to Securitate Files: The Trials and Tribulations of a Romanian Law," *East European Politics and Society*, vol. 16, no. 1, pp. 55-90

Stan, L. 2002b. "Moral Cleansing Romanian Style," *Problems of Post-Communism*, vol. 49, no. 4, pp. 52-62

Stan, L. 2004. "Spies, Files and Lies: Explaining the Failure of Access to Securitate Files," *Communist and Post-Communist Studies*, vol. 37, no. 3, pp. 341-359

Stan, L. 2007. "Comisia Tismăneanu – Repere internaţionale" [*Tismăneanu Committee – International Landmarks*], *Sfera politicii*, no. 126-127, pp. 7-13

Stan, L. 2009. "Truth Commissions in Post-Communism: The Overlooked Solution?" *Open Political Science Journal*, vol. 2, pp. 1-13

Stan, L. 2010. *Prezentul trecutului recent: lustraţie şi decomunizare în postcomunism* [Transitional Justice in Eastern Europe and the former Soviet Union]. Bucureşti: Curtea Veche

Stan, L. and Turcescu, L. 2005. "The Devil's Confessors: Priests, Communists, Spies and Informers," *East European Politics and Societies*, vol. 19, no. 4, pp. 655-685

Stoica, C. A. 2005. "Once upon a Time There Was a Big Party: The Social Bases of the Romanian Communist Party (Part I)," *East European Politics and Societies*, vol. 19, no. 4, pp. 686-716

Stoica, C. A. 2006a. "A Tale of Two Books," *East European Politics and Societies*, vol. 20, no. 1, pp. 180-198

Stoica, C. A. 2006b. "Once upon a Time There Was a Big Party: The Social Bases of the Romanian Communist Party (Part II)," *East European Politics and Societies*, vol. 20, no. 3, pp. 447-482

Tangney, J. P. 1995. "Recent Advances in the Empirical Study of Shame and Guilt," *American Behavioral Scientist*, vol. 38, no. 8, pp. 1132-1145

Tani, F., Greenman, P. S., Schneider, B. H. and Fregoso, M. 2003. "Bullying and the Big Five. A Study of Childhood Personality and Participant Roles in Bullying Incidents," *School Psychology International*, vol. 24, no. 2, pp. 131-146

The Explicative Dictionary of the Romanian Language. ***, accessed December 22, 2011
http://dexonline.ro/

Tracy, M. 2010. "The Mutability of Melamine: A Transductive Account of a Scandalby Megan Tracy," *Anthropology Today*, vol. 26, no. 6, pp. 4-8

Thompson, J. B. 2008. "Natura Skandalu Politycznego" [*The Nature of Political Scandal*], in: P. Sztompka and M. Bogunia-Borowska (eds.), *Socjologia codzienności*, Kraków: Wydawnictwo Znak, pp. 562-591

Thompson, J. B. 2010. *Skandal polityczny. Władza i jawność w epoce medialnej* [Political Scandal]. Warszawa: Wydawnictwo Naukowe PWN.

Tismăneanu, V. 2003. *Stalinism for All Seasons: A Political History of Romanian Communism*. Berkeley (California): University of California Press

Tismăneanu, V. 2004. *Marele Şoc din finalul unui secol scurt: Ion Iliescu în dialog cu Vladimir Tismăneanu* [The Great Shock at the End of a Short Century: Ion Iliescu in Dialogue with Vladimir Tismăneanu on Communism, Post-Communism, and Democracy]. Bucureşti: Editura Enciclopedică

Trevaskes, S. 2004. "Propaganda Work in Chinese Courts. Public Trials and Sentencing Rallies as Sites of Expressive Punishment and Public Education in the People's Republic of China," *Punishment & Society*, vol. 6, no. 1, pp. 5-21

Turner, Victor. 1975. *Dramas, Fields and Metaphors. Symbolic Action in Human Society*. Ithaca (New York): Cornell University Press

Ţiu, I. 2008. "Cutremurul din '77 şi Securitatea" [*The '77 Earthquake and the Securitate*], *Jurnalul naţional*, May 18

van Stokkom, B. 2002. "Moral Emotions in Restorative Justice Conferences: Managing Shame, Designing Empathy," *Theoretical Criminology*, vol. 6, no. 3, pp. 339-360

Vartia-Väänänen, M. 2003. *Workplace Bullying – a Study on the Work Environment, Well-Being and Health*, Academic dissertation, University of Helsinki Department of Psychology, accessed February 3, 2009
http://ethesis.helsinki.fi/julkaisut/hum/psyko/vk/vartia-vaananen/workplac.pdf

Vasi, I. B. 2004. "The Fist of the Working Class: The Social Movements of Jiu Valley Miners in Post-Socialist Romania," *East European Politics and Societies*, vol. 18, nr. 1, pp. 132-157

Velica, I. and Schreter, C. 1993. *Călătorie prin vârstele Văii Jiului* [Journey through the Ages of Jiu Valley]. Deva: Ed. Destin

Velica, I. and Velica, D. Ş. 2002. *Lupeni 77. Laboratorul puterii* [Lupeni 77. The Laboratory of Power]. Deva: Edit. Polidava

Waisbord, S. R. 2004. "Scandals, Media, and Citizenship in Contemporary Argentina," *American Behavioral Scientist*, vol. 47, no. 8; pp. 1072-1098

Warren, D. 2007. "Corporate Scandals and Spoiled Identities: How Organizations Shift Stigma to Employees," *Business Ethics Quarterly*, vol. 17, no. 3, pp. 477-496

Welch, M., Price., E. A. and Yankey, N. 2002. "Moral Panic over Youth Violence: Wilding and the Manufacture of Menace in the Media," *Youth & Society*, vol. 34, no. 1, pp. 3-30

Wedel, J. R. 1986. *The Private Poland: An Anthropologist's Look at Everyday Life*. New York: Facts on File

Wedel, J. R. 2009. *Shadow Elite. How the World's New Power Brokers Undermine Democracy, Government, and the Free Market*. New York: Basic Books.

Empirical material

1977

***. 1977a. "Referat privind punerea în dezbatere a faptelor comise la data de 4 august a.c., de către I[…]C[…] angajat la I.M. Uricani" [*Report Regarding the Mooting of the Actions Committed on August 4, Current Year, by I[…]C[…], Employee at M.E. Uricani*], September 2, in: M. Boboc and M. Barbu. 2007. *Strict secret. Lupeni 1977. Filajul continuă!* [Highly Confidential. Lupeni 1977. The Surveillance Continues]. Craiova: Autograf MJM, pp. 552-555

***. 1977b. "Referat privind punerea în dezbatere a faptelor comise de N[…]C[…], S[…]C[…] şi P[…]P[…] – angajaţi ai IM. Vulcan" [*Report Regarding the Mooting of the Actions Committed by N.C., S.C. and P.P. – Employees of M.E. Vulcan*], September 3, in: M. Boboc and M. Barbu. 2007. *Strict secret. Lupeni 1977. Filajul continuă!* [Highly Confidential. Lupeni 1977. The Surveillance Continues]. Craiova: Autograf MJM, pp. 155-161

***. 1977c. "Referat privind punerea în dezbatere a faptelor comise de către un grup de huligani în data de 4.08.1977 la I.M. Bărbăteni" [*Report Regarding the Mooting of the Actions Committed by a Group of Hooligans on 4.08.1977 at M.E. Bărbăteni*], September 6, in: M. Boboc and M. Barbu. 2007. *Strict secret. Lupeni 1977. Filajul continuă!* [Highly Confidential. Lupeni 1977. The Surveillance Continues]. Craiova: Autograf MJM, pp. 486-493

***. 1977d. "Referat privind punerea în dezbatere a faptelor săvârşite de către un grup de huligani la data de 2 august 1977, la I.M. Lupeni" [*Report Regarding the Mooting of the Actions Committed by a Group of Hooligans on August 2, 1977, at M.E. Lupeni*], September 8, in: M. Boboc and M. Barbu. 2007. *Strict secret. Lupeni 1977. Filajul continuă!* [Highly Confidential. Lupeni 1977. The Surveillance Continues]. Craiova: Autograf MJM, pp. 411-422

Ministry of Internal Affairs – County Inspectorate Hunedoara. 1977a. "Plan de măsuri. Întocmit cu prilejul evenimentelor din 2-3 august 1977" [*Plan of Measures. Drawn up on the Occasion of the Events of 2-3 August 1977*], August 3, in: M. Boboc and M. Barbu. 2007. *Strict secret. Lupeni 1977. Filajul continuă!* [Highly Confidential. Lupeni 1977. The Surveillance Continues]. Craiova: Autograf MJM, pp. 572-580

Ministry of Internal Affairs – County Inspectorate Hunedoara. 1977b. "Notă–Raport. Cuprinzând principalele activităţi desfăşurate de către organele noastre în Municipiul Petroşani" [*Note–Report. Containing the Main Acti-*

vities Unfolded by our Organs in the Municipality of Petroşani], October 1, in: M. Boboc and M. Barbu. 2007. *Strict secret. Lupeni 1977. Filajul continuă!* [Highly Confidential. Lupeni 1977. The Surveillance Continues]. Craiova: Autograf MJM, pp. 622-635

1987

***. 1987a. "Plenara cu activul din 15.11.1987 – proces-verbal" [*Meeting with the Aktif from 15.11.1987 – Proceedings*], November 15

***. 1987b. "Plenara Comitetului P.C.R. din 17.11.1987 – stenogramă şi referat" [*The Meeting of the R.C.P. Committee from 17.11.1987 – Stenographic Transcript and Referat*], November 17

***. 1987c. "Plenara cu activul din 19.11.1987 – tabel nominal şi stenogramă" [*Meeting with the Aktif from 19.11.1987 – Nominal Table and Stenographic Transcript*], November 19

***. 1987d. "Plenara Comitetului de partid din 21.11.1987 – proces-verbal" [*Meeting with the Party Committee from 21.11.1987 – Proceedings*], November 21

***. 1987e. "Plenara Comitetului PCR din 23.11.1987 – referat, stenogramă, proces-verbal" [*Meeting with the RCP Committee from 23.11.1987 – Report, Stenographic Transcript, Proceedings*], November 23

***. 1987f. "Plenara Comitetului de Partid cu activul din 25.11.1987 – proces-verbal" [*Meeting of the Party Committee with the Aktif from 25.11.1987 – Proceedings*], November 25

1989

***. 2006a. "Stenograma Şedinţei CPEx al CC al PCR, 17 decembrie 1989 – Partea I" [*Stenographic Transcript of the Meeting of the Political Executive Committee of the Central Committee of the Romanian Communist Party, December 17, 1989 – Part I*], *Monitorul drepturilor omului*, no. 10, accessed December 22, 2011
http://www.oado.ro/index.php?unde=rev&id=101&art=674&PHPSESSID =3df49d2381682895f7d0ee08bbe275b5

***. 2006b. "Stenograma Şedinţei CPEx al CC al PCR, 17 decembrie 1989 – Partea II" [*Stenographic Transcript of the Meeting of the Political Executive Committee of the Central Committee of the Romanian Communist Party, 17 December 1989 – Part II*], *Monitorul drepturilor omului*, no. 11, accessed December 22, 2011
http://www.oado.ro/index.php?unde=rev&id=102&art=694&PHPSESSID =3df49d2381682895f7d0ee08bbe275b5

***. 2007. "Stenograma Şedinţei CPEx al CC al PCR, 17 decembrie 1989 – Partea III" [*Stenographic Transcript of the Meeting of the Political Executive Committee of the Central Committee of the Romanian Communist Party, 17 December 1989 – Part III*], *Monitorul drepturilor omului*, no. 1, accessed December 22, 2011
http://www.oado.ro/index.php?unde=rev&id=106&art=730&PHPSESSID=3df49d2381682895f7d0ee08bbe275b5

Ceauşescu's Address to the Nation – December 20, 1989

Mioc, M. 2002. *The Romanian Anticommunist Revolution of 1989*. Timişoara: Marineasa, accessed December 22, 2011
http://www.procesulcomunismului.com/marturii/fonduri/mmioc/anticomrev/default.asp.htm

Mioc, M. 2004. *Curtea Supremă de Justiţie – Procesele revoluţiei din Timişoara (1989), adunate şi comentate de Marius Mioc* [The Supreme Court of Justice – The Trials Concerning the Revolution in Timişoara (1989), Collected and Commented by Marius Mioc]. Timişoara: Editura Artpress, accessed December 22, 2011
http://www.procesulcomunismului.com/marturii/fonduri/mmioc/curteasup/default.asp.htm

Romanian Communist Party, Braşov County [Party] Committee. 1989. "Stenograma teleconferinţei din ziua de 17 decembrie 1989, cu tovarăşul Secretar general Nicolae Ceauşescu" [*The Stenographic Transcript of the Teleconference with Comrade General Secretary Nicolae Ceauşescu from the Day of 17 November, 1987*], in: *Portalul Revoluţiei Române* [The Portal of the Romanian Revolution]. ***, accessed December 22, 2011
http://www.portalulrevolutiei.ro/index.php?menu=3

1990

The Chamber of Deputies of Romania. 1990. "Hotărâre nr. 11 din 19 iunie 1990 pentru desemnarea reprezentanţilor Adunării Deputaţilor într-o comisie parlamentară de anchetă" [*Decison No. 11 of June 19th, 1990 on the Appointment of the Representatives of the Chamber of Deputies in the Parliamentary Committee of Inquiry*], published in *Monitorul Oficial al României*, No. 85-86, June 20, 1990, accessed December 22, 2011
http://www.cdep.ro/pls/legis/legis_pck.htp_act_text?idt=11328

Helsinki Watch. 1991. "Romania: Aftermath [of] the June Violence in Bucharest," *News from Helsinki Watch*, May 1

HU OSA [The Open Society Archives at Central European University], 300-8-32, Box 2, December 14, 1990, p. 17

Romanian Parliament. 1991. "Report – Parliamentary Committee of Enquiry into the Events that Took Place from 13-15 June 1990", *Report*

Legislative Acts

Decretul nr. 253/1955 privind înlesnirea repatrierii unor cetăţeni şi foşti cetăţeni români şi amnistierea celor repatriaţi [Decree no. 253/1955 concerning the facilitation of the repatriation of some Romanian citizens and former Romanian citizens and of the amnesty of the repatriated ones], published in *Buletinul Oficial,* June 30, 1955

Decretul nr. 313 din 17 octombrie 1981 privind unele măsuri referitoare la întărirea autoconducerii şi autoaprovizionării teritoriale, precum şi la asigurarea autoaprovizionării în bune condiţii a populaţiei cu pâine, făină şi mălai [Decree no. 313 from October 17, 1981 concerning some measures regarding the strengthening of territorial auto-management and auto-provision, as well as the assurance of auto-provision in proper conditions of population with bread, flour and maize]

Lege nr. 3 din 30 iunie 1977 privind pensiile de asigurări sociale de stat şi asistenţă socială [Law no. 3 from June 30, 1977 regarding state social insurance and social assistance pensions], published in *Buletinul Oficial*, no. 82, August 6, 1977.